GOOD HOUSEKEEPING
Complete Book of
HOME
BAKING

GOOD HOUSEKEEPING

Complete Book of

HOME
BAKING

EBURY PRESS
LONDON

Published by Ebury Press
an imprint of Century Hutchinson Ltd.
Brookmount House
62–65 Chandos Place
Covent Garden
London WC2N 4NW

First impression 1989
Copyright © 1989 Century Hutchinson Ltd. and
The National Magazine Company Ltd.

Editors: Heather Rocklin and Sarah Bailey
Art Director: Frank Phillips
Designer: Grahame Dudley Associates
Home Economists: Janet Smith, Emma-Lee Gow, Helen Casey
Stylist: Cathy Sinker
Cover photograph: Alan Newnham
Photographs on pages 32, 53, 56, 61, 68, 69, 72, 84, 108, 120, 125, 128,
137, 141, 144, 172, 188, 193, 200, 212 by James Murphy
Other photographs by Jan Baldwin, Laurie Evans, Melvin Grey,
Paul Kemp, Peter Myers, Grant Symon

British Library Cataloguing in Publication Data
Good housekeeping complete book of home baking.
1. Baking—Recipes
641.7'1

ISBN 0-85223-748-0

Filmset by Advanced Filmsetters (Glasgow) Ltd
Printed and bound in Italy by New Interlitho S.p.a., Milan

CONTENTS

COOKERY NOTES

1 Follow either metric or imperial measures for the recipes in this book as they are not interchangeable.

2 The metric equivalent for 4 oz is 100 g or 125 g, depending on the recipes.

3 All spoon measures are level unless otherwise stated.

4 Sets of measuring spoons are available in both metric and imperial size to give accurate measurement of small quantities.

5 When measuring milk the exact conversion of 568 ml (1 pint) has been used.

6 Size 2 eggs should be used except where otherwise stated.

7 Where margarine is stated use either block or soft tub margarine. Otherwise use as specified in the recipes.

8 Raw eggs are used in some recipes. We believe that at the time of going to press the proven risk for healthy people using fresh eggs is minimal. However, the elderly, pregnant women, the sick and very young should not eat raw eggs.

9 Where reference is made to microwave cooking, the wattage of the cooker used is 650. HIGH refers to 100% full power output, MEDIUM refers to 60% of full power, and LOW is 35% of full power.

OVEN TEMPERATURE SCALES

°Celsius Scale	Electric Scale °F	Gas Oven Marks
110°C	225°F	¼
130	250	½
140	275	1
150	300	2
170	325	3
180	350	4
190	375	5
200	400	6
220	425	7
230	450	8
240	475	9

INTRODUCTION

Who can resist a freshly baked cake or a warm crusty loaf? Nothing is as tempting as the smell of home baking filling every corner of the kitchen. (They say if you want to sell your house, have a baking session before the prospective buyers arrive!) You will find lots of recipes and photographs to inspire you and the results are not only delicious to eat but also marvellously satisfying to make and serve.

To remain healthy, our bodies need proteins, carbohydrates, fats, fibre, minerals and vitamins, from a variety of foods. The major ingredients used in baking like butter, flour and sugar provide some of these essential nutrients and should be enjoyed as part of your sensibly balanced diet. Variety is the spice of life!

INGREDIENTS

·

FLOUR

Wheat is one of the most commonly used grains in the Western world. The whole wheat grain is made up of the bran, the endosperm (or starch and protein store), and the germ, which is the most nutritious part.

Wheat is important in baking because it has the ability to form an elastic dough which can be raised by carbon dioxide or air to form light, spongy cakes and bread.

Wheat can be classified as either hard or soft, depending on its gluten content.

Strong flour When hard wheat is milled it provides a strong flour rich in protein, containing a sticky, rubber-like substance called gluten. In bread making, the gluten stretches like elastic and, as it is heated, it expands and traps in the dough the carbon dioxide, released by the yeast. The gluten then sets and forms the 'frame' of the bread. It is the gluten content in a strong flour that gives volume and an open texture to bread.

Soft flour When soft wheats are milled they produce a soft flour with different gluten properties to those of hard wheat. This ordinary soft flour can be used for bread making, but the results will be disappointing: it will give a small rise, a close, crumbly texture and a pale, hard crust. Soft flour is either plain or self-raising (self-raising is plain flour with added raising agents) and is more suitable for making cakes and pastries, where a smaller rise and a closer, finer texture are required. Self-raising flour can be used successfully in recipes for quick breads.

Wholemeal (or wholewheat) flour contains 100 per cent of the wheat (i.e. the entire grain is milled). Bread, pastry and cakes made with this type of flour are coarse-textured, have a nutty taste, and are brown in colour. Strong, plain and self-raising types of wholemeal flour are available. When making cakes or teabreads, it is worth sifting wholemeal flour as any air that can be incorporated will give a better result. Sift the flour, then tip the bran from the sieve back into the bowl. Stir well.

Brown (wheatmeal) flour contains 80–90 per cent of the wheat (i.e. some of the bran is removed). It is more absorbent than white flour and produces bread with a denser texture than that made with white flour, but less coarse than that made from wholemeal flour. Brown flour is available in strong, plain and self-raising forms.

Stoneground flour takes its name from the specific process of grinding which heats the flour and gives it a slightly roasted, nutty flavour. Both wholemeal and brown flours can be stoneground.

Granary flour is strong brown flour with added malted wheat flakes, which give a nutty flavour.

White flour contains 72–74 per cent of the wheat. The bran and wheatgerm which give wholemeal and brown flours their brown colour are removed, resulting in the white flour which is used to make fine-textured white bread and cakes. Most white flour has been chemically bleached. If you want to use untreated flour, then look for the word 'unbleached' on the label. White flour is available in strong, plain and self-raising forms.

Rye flour Used on its own, rye flour produces rather dense, heavy bread since rye lacks sufficient protein for the formation of gluten.

Finely milled rye flour gives the densest texture while bread made with coarse rye flour is rougher and more open-textured. When baking rye bread, combine the rye flour with a strong flour.

Buckwheat flour is a fine and grey-coloured flour. It is most often used for making pancakes. Because it contains no gluten it should be mixed with strong flour when making bread. In a gluten-free diet, buckwheat flour can be used for bread and cakes, although these will not rise in the same way as those made with wheat flour.

Self-raising flour is popular because it eliminates errors; the raising agents are already evenly blended throughout the flour.

Plain flour can be used with a raising agent and the raising agent can be varied to suit individual recipes. If you only have plain flour, use 225 g (8 oz) flour and 15 ml (1 level tbsp) baking powder to replace self-raising flour in scones, 10 ml (2 level tsp) baking powder for a plain cake mixture, e.g. rock buns, and 5 ml (1 level tsp) for a rich fruit cake mixture. Sift the flour and baking powder together before use to ensure even blending.

Barley was one of the earliest grains to be culti-vated but is now seldom used to make bread because when used on its own it produces a moist and heavy loaf. However, if mixed with a strong flour it produces a good, earthy-flavoured result.

Cornmeal is made from dried whole grains. As it lacks gluten it should be mixed with a strong flour for making bread. It has a slightly sweet flavour.

Oatmeal also lacks gluten and should be mixed with strong flour when making bread.

The keeping quality of a flour or meal depends on how much germ it includes, because the germ contains oil which eventually turns rancid. White wheat flour should keep for about a year in a cool, dry, well-ventilated place. Flours and meals containing germ will keep for 2–3 months if kept in a cool, dark place (darkness delays the oil's spoilage).

SUGARS AND SYRUPS

Sugar is one type of carbohydrate that is easily digested and is an important ingredient in all baking. Apart from being the natural sweetener, it is a texture improver and bulking agent.

Caster sugar has a small regular grain size that makes it the most commonly used sugar in cakes, as it blends easily to give an even texture.

Granulated sugar has a larger grain size than caster that makes it a little less suitable for light cakes but it is quite acceptable for rubbed in mixtures.

Icing sugar is the finest of all sugars. It is not generally used for basic cake mixtures as it produces a poor volume and hard crust. It is used for icing and decorating cakes.

Decorating with icing sugar

Light brown soft sugar has a small grain size and it can be used to replace caster sugar where more colour and flavour are required.

Demerara sugar has a unique flavour that makes it particularly popular with coffee. As the grain size is slightly larger than granulated, it is less suitable for creamed mixtures, but it is ideal as a crunchy topping.

Dark brown soft sugar is used where a rich colour and flavour is required, as in celebration cakes or gingerbreads.

Vanilla sugar can be made at home by filling a jar with caster sugar and adding a vanilla pod. Leave the sugar for 2–3 weeks, to absorb the vanilla flavour, before using. Keep the jar topped up with sugar so that you always have some ready for use.

Golden syrup gives a special flavour, which is particularly good with spices. Lyle's golden syrup is a unique product that has been a household favourite since the end of the last century. It may be used to add its own special flavour, colour and moistness to a variety of cakes and puddings.

Black treacle is a dark syrup, which is not as sweet as golden syrup. A little added to rich fruit cakes gives a good dark colour and distinctive flavour. It is also a traditional ingredient for gingerbreads and for the making of malt bread. When measuring treacle by the spoonful first warm the measuring spoon in hot water. 25 g (1 oz) is equal to 15 ml (1 tbsp).

Measuring with a warm spoon

Honey may be used in some recipes. It absorbs and retains moisture, helping to keep the products fresh.

Maple syrup is produced by trapping the sap of the North American maple trees. It contains a high proportion of sugar and is a fairly thin, dark red brown syrup with a distinctive flavour.

Malt extract is a thick, sticky brown syrup produced from germinated barley grains consisting mainly of maltose.

FATS AND OILS

Butter and block margarine are interchangeable in cake, teabread and biscuit making although butter gives the richest flavour and cakes made with butter keep better. Soft tub margarines are only suitable for special all-in-one recipes. Vegetable oil can be used in specially proportioned recipes.

Do not use butter and block margarine direct from the refrigerator. If the fat for a creamed mixture is too firm, beat it alone until softened, then add the sugar and cream them together. If melted fat is required, heat it very gently as it turns brown quickly.

EGGS

Egg whites become foamy by trapping air when whisked; this special property enables them to act as a raising agent for batters and cakes, either alone or in combination with the yolk. When whisked separately egg whites give soufflés and meringues their characteristic lightness.

In creamed mixtures the eggs are beaten in and as long as the correct proportion of egg is used and the mixture is well beaten, little additional raising agent is needed. In plain cakes, where beaten egg is added together with the liquid, the egg helps to bind the mixture but it does not act as the main raising agent.

Buy the freshest eggs possible. Avoid buying eggs that are stored near a sunny window or radiator in the shop. Eggs are graded according to weight; unless otherwise stated, use size 2 in the recipes in this book.

A fresh egg broken on to a flat surface will have an upstanding yolk and the whites adhering to it. Old eggs will have thin runny whites. To test for freshness put the egg into a tumbler of cold water. If the egg is fresh it will lie flat at the bottom of the glass. If the egg tilts slightly it is starting to become old and if it floats it is very likely to be bad.

To separate an egg give the egg a sharp knock against the side of a basin or cup and break the shell in half; tapping the egg several times may cause it to crack in several places and not break evenly. Pass the yolk back and forth from one half of the shell to the other letting the white drop into the basin.

When separating more than one egg it is a good idea to use a third bowl for cracking the eggs as a precaution against a yolk breaking and spoiling the whites. Put the second yolk in with the first one and tip the white in with the first white. Continue using the third bowl in this way.

Egg whites When egg whites are whisked tiny globules of air are trapped in the egg to form an almost tasteless substance, which when added to other ingredients gives them an airy and light texture. If heat is applied to the egg whites the trapped air expands further causing the mixture to rise further as in soufflés. Whisked egg whites can also become firm and hard without losing their shape, as in meringues.

Egg whites will achieve maximum volume when whisked in a metal bowl; copper is best but stainless steel is also good. Use a balloon whisk as a rotary or electric beater cannot be circulated as well throughout the eggs.

Eggs that are 2–3 days old will whisk to a greater volume than new-laid eggs. For best results separate the eggs 24 hours before using them and store them in a covered container in the refrigerator. An acid such as cream of tartar added to the eggs or rubbing the bowl with lemon helps whites hold their shape when whisked.

What is important is that the bowl and the whisk are immaculately clean. If egg whites come into contact with any grease or dirt they will not whisk to maximum volume. Any egg yolk present in the whites and volume also decreases plus the eggs will take much longer to foam. Salt also adversely affects the foaming of egg whites.

Start whisking with a slow circular movement and gradually work faster, lifting the eggs high out of the bowl to help incorporate as much air as possible. Whisk until the egg whites stand in stiff, pointed peaks when lifted from the bowl. Stiffly beaten egg whites should not fall out of the bowl if the bowl is upturned.

If using an electric beater, start on the lowest speed and gradually increase the speed. If the eggs are beaten too much the foam becomes dry and brittle and other ingredients such as sugar will not easily be incorporated.

Folding in egg whites Mixtures combine more easily when their consistency and temperatures are similar. Folding in is best done with a metal spoon or plastic spatula. Use a continuous cutting and lifting movement, scooping right down to the bottom of the bowl. Scoop one way turning the bowl the other. Stop folding as soon as the mixture is blended. Too much folding and the egg white may start to liquefy.

Use leftover egg whites for glazing pies, pastry and breads.

Beaten egg In creamed mixtures the eggs are beaten in and – as long as the correct proportion of egg is used and the mixture is well beaten – little additional raising agent is needed.

In plain cakes, where beaten egg is added together with the liquid, the egg helps to bind the mixture, but it does not act as the main raising agent.

YEAST

Yeast gives bread and yeast cakes their characteristic mouth-watering smell. It is the oldest and for centuries the only form of raising agent. You will find it quite easy to use once you realize that it is a living plant and, like most plants, requires heat, food and water in order to grow. These last two requirements are usually supplied by the carbohydrate in flour and the liquid used when making dough. With their help, plus gentle warmth, the yeast grows rapidly and, like other living plants, 'breathes' out a harmless gas – carbon dioxide. It is the expansion of this gas that makes the dough rise and gives the bread an open texture. Too much heat will kill the yeast altogether and too little will retard its growth – so read the step-by-step instructions on dough making to make quite sure you know what's what before you start cooking with yeast.

Fresh yeast is also known as compressed yeast. It is sold in small blocks and is creamy fawn in colour with a faint winy smell. It should have a smooth, compact texture and crumble easily.

Fresh yeast is usually blended with a tepid

liquid and then added to the flour in one go. It can also be rubbed directly into the flour or added as a batter. The batter method is known as the 'sponge dough process': some of the ingredients are mixed to form a sponge, which is allowed to ferment, then mixed with the remaining ingredients to form a dough.

The best results are obtained when the yeast is very fresh, but it can be stored, wrapped in cling film or foil, in the refrigerator for up to a month. It can also be frozen for up to 3 months, but it is advisable to wrap in 25 g (1 oz) portions. When using yeast that has been frozen, allow it to thaw at room temperature for a couple of hours or add to half of the tepid liquid used in the recipe, leave in a warm place for 15–20 minutes, then add the remaining tepid liquid.

Dried yeast is more concentrated than fresh yeast. It consists of small granules and is sold in small sachets or 100 g (4 oz) tins. It is mixed with a tepid liquid and left in a warm place for 15–20 minutes to become frothy, before being mixed with flour. If the liquid is water, then a pinch of sugar should be added to activate the yeast. This is not necessary if using milk, as milk contains sugar in the form of lactose. If the yeast fails to froth after 15–20 minutes, it is no longer active and should not be used.

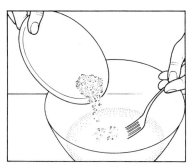

Mixing dried yeast with a tepid liquid

Dried yeast will keep in an airtight container in a cool place for up to 6 months.

Fast-action yeast is also known as 'easy-mix yeast'. It is another form of dried yeast, but the granules are finer and are mixed with bread improvers which make the dough rise more quickly.

Fast action yeast is not mixed with liquid but simply mixed into the flour. The dough requires only one rising when made with this yeast.

The recipes in this book give equivalents for fresh and dried yeast. If you wish to use fast-action yeast read the instructions on the packet, but generally you will need to use 1 sachet or 7.5 ml (1½ level tsp) to each 700 g (1½ lb) strong flour.

Measuring yeast Dried yeast is most easily measured by the teaspoonful (remember to use proper British Standard teaspoon measures). Fresh yeast is easy to measure by weight, but a teaspoon equivalent is useful to know.

WEIGHT	SPOON EQUIVALENT
Fresh Yeast	
7.5 g (¼ oz)	5 ml (1 level tsp)
15 g (½ oz)	10 ml (2 level tsp)
22.5 g (¾ oz)	15 ml (1 level tbsp)
25 g (1 oz)	20 ml (4 level tsp)
Dried Yeast	
7.5 g (⅛ oz)	7.5 ml (1½ level tsp)
15 g (½ oz)	15 ml (1 level tbsp)
22.5 g (¾ oz)	25 ml (1½ level tbsp)
25 g (1 oz)	30 ml (2 level tbsp)
Fast-Action Yeast	
7.5 g (¼ oz)	7.5 ml (1½ level tsp)
25 g (1 oz)	15 ml (1 level tbsp)

RAISING AGENTS

Baking powder is the raising agent most commonly used in cakes, teabreads and scones. It usually consists of bicarbonate of soda and an acid-reacting chemical such as cream of tartar. When moistened, these react together to give off carbon dioxide. Flour contains gluten, which holds this gas in the form of tiny bubbles when it is wet. Since all gases expand when heated, these tiny bubbles formed throughout the mixture become larger during the baking, and thus the cake rises. The heat dries and sets the gluten and so the bubbles are held, giving the cake a light texture. However, cake mixtures can hold only a certain amount of gas, and if too much raising agent is used the cake rises well at first, then collapses, and a heavy, close texture is the result.

Bicarbonate of soda and cream of tartar combined may be used in some cake and teabread recipes to replace baking powder. It is usually in the proportion of one part bicarbonate of soda to 2 parts cream of tartar. It is also used in Soda Bread.

Eggs By including whisked egg in a cake mixture, air is used as a raising agent, instead of carbon dioxide. When a high proportion of egg is used and the mixture is whisked, as in sponge cakes, very little, if any, other raising agent is needed to obtain the desired result.

CHOCOLATE AND CAROB

A lot of cakes, gâteaux and biscuits include chocolate, cocoa and sometimes carob as flavourings or decoration. For chocolate decorations see page 30.

Cocoa powder is made from the cocoa bean. It has a bitter flavour which needs to be tempered by a sweetener.

Chocolate is basically made from cocoa beans, milk and sugar. It must contain at least 35 per cent dry cocoa solids and a minimum of 18 per cent cocoa butter. Chocolate is high in fats and sugar.

Cooking chocolate costs no more than plain chocolate. It is often sold loose in delicatessens broken into large pieces, or in a bar which is marked in measured segments.

Chocolate-flavoured cake covering has very good melting qualities and is used for icings and for making moulded sweets, but because it lacks the true chocolaty flavour it should not be used unless called for in the recipe.

Carob powder is produced from the carob bean (also known as the locust bean) and is naturally sweet. Carob powder contains less fat and sodium than cocoa, fewer calories and no caffeine. Because of its sweet flavour, you need less sugar or other sweeteners than cocoa powder in order to make it taste pleasant.

To melt chocolate break it into small pieces and place in the top of a double saucepan over hot but not boiling water, or in a heatproof basin standing over a pan of hot water.

Alternatively, melt it in a microwave: break it into small pieces (unless using chocolate chips) and cook on LOW just until the chocolate is soft and looks glossy on top. Remove from the cooker and stir until melted. Block cooking chocolate heats more slowly – as a guide, 100 g (4 oz) cooking chocolate takes about 4 minutes to melt in the microwave on LOW. The melting times vary according to the material and shape of the container used, so it is advisable to check every minute during melting. Take care not to overcook and do not melt on HIGH or the chocolate may scorch.

To thin melted chocolate if it thickens or curdles as a result of overheating add a little blended white vegetable fat (do not use butter or margarine). Break the fat into small pieces and stir into the mixture until it reaches the desired consistency.

To substitute cocoa for chocolate if you run out of plain chocolate, use 45 ml (3 level tbsp) cocoa powder and 15 ml (1 level tbsp) softened blended white vegetable fat or vegetable oil (do not use butter or margarine) for every 25 g (1 oz) of chocolate used in the recipe.

NUTS

The term nut is used to describe any seed or fruit with an edible kernel inside a hard shell. Nuts are a highly concentrated food, rich in protein, vitamins, minerals, fats and fibre.

Shelled, flaked, chopped and ground nuts are best bought loose in small quantities, or vacuum packed. Store them in airtight containers, preferably in the refrigerator. Nuts bought in their shells should feel heavy; if they feel light they are likely to be stale. Store them in a cool, dark place for up to 3 months.

When using nuts in a recipe, check first to see whether they are to be blanched or unblanched, whole, split, flaked, chopped or ground. This may seem a small point, but it saves last-minute irritation.

Almonds are the seeds of a tree belonging to the peach family, which grows in countries with hot, dry climates such as Sicily, Spain and California. There are two varieties of almonds – bitter and sweet. Bitter almonds contain prussic acid and are seldom eaten raw (if they are eaten, they must only be eaten in small quantities) and are used mainly for making essences and oils. Sweet almonds are available in their shells at Christmas, and shelled the rest of the year.

Whole and split almonds are used in baking. Flaked almonds are often toasted and used as a garnish or decoration. To toast flaked almonds in the microwave, spread them out on a heat-proof plate and microwave on HIGH for 8–10 minutes until golden brown, stirring frequently. Ground almonds are used to make almond paste as well as to flavour cakes and teabreads.

To blanch almonds, cover with boiling water and leave for 10 seconds, then rinse in cold water and rub off the skin. Alternatively, blanch in a microwave: put in a small bowl with 150 ml (¼ pint) water, microwave on HIGH for 2 minutes then drain and slip off the skins.

Brazil nuts are large, oval, creamy-coloured nuts with a high percentage of fat. They grow grouped together in their individual shells, inside the round fruit of a South American tree. They are available in their shells or shelled.

Cashew nuts are whitish-coloured nuts and come from the tropical cashew tree. The tree bears reddish pear-shaped fruit and one kidney-shaped nut grows from the base of each fruit. As there is toxic oil in the shells of cashews, they are always sold shelled. They are sold whole or in pieces, often salted and roasted. They have a slightly crumbly texture and a delicate sweet flavour.

Chestnuts are the fruit of the sweet chestnut tree, which grows mainly in European countries. Chestnuts are sold fresh in their skins; dried; cooked and canned; as a purée (sweetened or unsweetened) in cans or tubes; or preserved in sugar to make marrons glacés. Chestnuts in their skins must be peeled and cooked before eating.

To peel, make a tiny slit in the skin near the pointed end, then cover with boiling water and leave for 5 minutes. Remove from the water, one at a time, and peel off the thick outer skin and thin inner skin while warm. To cook, simmer the peeled nuts for 30–40 minutes. Alternatively, bake the nuts in their skins in the oven at 200°C (400°F) mark 6 for 20 minutes, then peel.

Coconuts are the nuts of the coconut palm, with hard, hairy brown shells containing sweet white flesh and a liquid called coconut milk which makes a delicious drink. When choosing, test a coconut for freshness by shaking it to make sure it contains liquid.

In addition to the whole coconut, desiccated (dried unsweetened) coconut and shredded (dried sweetened) coconut are also available.

To prepare a coconut, puncture the shell at the eyes with a screwdriver and hammer. Drain off the milk into a jug or bowl. Store, covered, in the refrigerator for up to 2 days. Crack the shell by hitting the widest part of the coconut all around with a hammer or the back of a cleaver. Separate the halves and prise the flesh from the shell with a small sharp knife.

To shred and toast coconut, first remove the rough brown skin using a sharp knife. Shred the white flesh on a coarse grater or grate in a food processor or blender. Freshly grated coconut can be toasted in a 180°C (350°F) mark 4 oven until golden brown. Stir the coconut frequently. Store for up to 4 days.

Chopping nuts

Hazelnuts, filberts and cobs are all fruits of different varieties of the hazel tree. Cobs are less common than the other two nuts. They are all available in their shell, as shelled whole nuts (plain or roasted), flaked or ground. The thin inner covering of shelled hazelnuts is usually removed because it has a bitter taste. To remove, heat the nuts through in the oven or toast under a low grill, then tip the hot nuts on to a clean teatowel and rub until the papery skins slip off. If using a microwave, place them on a layer of absorbent kitchen paper and microwave on HIGH for 30 seconds, then rub off the skins.

Peanuts (ground nuts, monkey nuts) are a type of underground bean which grows in India, Africa and parts of America and the Far East. They consist of two kernels which grow in a crinkly shell. They are available as whole nuts roasted in their shells or as shelled nuts, which may be plain, dry roasted or roasted and salted.

Pecan nuts belong to the walnut family and grow in North America, where they are also known as hickory nuts. They are available in their shells or shelled. They can be used instead of walnuts in any recipe.

Pine nuts (pine kernels, Indian nuts, pignolias, pignoli) are small, pale cream-coloured seeds of the Mediterranean pine tree. They are always sold shelled and may be roasted and salted. They have a strong resinous flavour and a soft oily texture.

Pistachio nuts are the fruit of a small tree native to the Middle East and Central Asia, but now grown in other parts of the world. The bright green kernels have purple skins and beige-coloured shells. The shell splits when the kernels are ripe. They are available in their shells or shelled (plain or salted). Skin as for almonds.

Walnuts are one of the most popular nuts and are grown in many parts of the world. They have a round, crinkly shell with a wrinkled-looking kernel, and have a moist texture and an oily flavour. They are available in their shells, shelled, chopped or ground.

TO TOAST AND ROAST NUTS
The flavour of nuts is often more pronounced if they are first toasted. Pale-coloured almonds

turn a golden colour making them especially attractive for dessert decorations. Spread whole, chopped or slivered nuts on a baking tray and toast them under a medium grill, turning the nuts occasionally, until they have darkened. Alternatively, they can be roasted in a 180°C (350°F) mark 4 oven for 10–12 minutes. Nuts can be dry fried in a frying pan for about 5 minutes. Watch nuts carefully as they can suddenly burn.

TO GRIND NUTS
Nuts ground at home will have more flavour and aroma than bought ones. Almonds and hazelnuts are often used ground (especially almonds, for making marzipan). Ground nuts are good to sprinkle over a flan case before filling with a juicy fruit filling – they absorb the fruit juices and ensure the baked-blind crust remains crisp as well as adding extra flavour.

Grind nuts in a coffee grinder or food processor. Grind for about 1 minute, turning the grinder on and off frequently during grinding. Only grind a few at a time. Be careful that the nuts do not turn to a paste.

PRALINE

Praline is the name given to crushed caramelized almonds. It is useful for adding flavour and texture to butter cream and cream cake fillings, or as a decoration

MAKES ABOUT 100 g (4 oz)

75 g (3 oz) granulated sugar

25 g (1 oz) blanched almonds, chopped and toasted

1 Oil a baking sheet. Place the sugar with 60 ml (4 tbsp) water in a saucepan and heat gently, stirring all the time, until the sugar dissolves. Bring to the boil and boil steadily, without stirring, until golden brown.
2 Add the almonds and pour at once on to the prepared baking sheet. Leave to set for about 10 minutes.
3 Crush the praline finely with a rolling pin or in a food processor or blender. Store in an airtight container.

Pouring praline on to a baking sheet

DRIED FRUIT

Drying fruit is one of the oldest ways of preserving it and, although the methods have changed – much of the dried fruit is now dried by artificial heat rather than the sun – the principle is the same. The water content is drawn out, preventing the growth of mould and bacteria and leaving the natural sugar in the fruit to act as a preservative. Dried fruits such as apricots, figs, bananas, peaches and dates usually need to be soaked in water for at least 3 hours or overnight, before using. Cold strained black tea or fruit juice can be used for extra flavour instead of water. Some 'no-soak' dried fruits are now available and these are useful for cake and teabread making as they can be used straight from the packet. Although dried fruit is most frequently bought in small packages, large packages of raisins and sultanas are a more economical buy, as are dried fruits sold loose or in bulk from some health food shops. Packaged dried fruits are always pre-washed but fruit sold loose should be washed.

Store dried fruit in a cool dark place. Unopened packages will keep for up to one year. Once opened, or if bought loose, store in an airtight tin and use within 3 months.

Apples are one of the few fruits which do not lose any Vitamin C content in the drying process. They are usually sold as rings.

Apricots The flavour of dried apricots is often better than that of the fresh fruit. Some types are specially tenderized so that there is no need to soak them before use.

Bananas are peeled and dried whole or sliced lengthways.

Dates Dried dates are available whole with stones or as pressed blocks of stoned fruit. Whole dates can be stoned and used for tea-breads without soaking. The pressed blocks need to be soaked overnight. Chopped dates rolled in sugar are also available and these can be used without soaking.

Figs Dried figs may be sold loose or in pressed blocks. They should not be too sticky. The compressed blocks need to be soaked before use.

Peaches Unlike apricots, dried peaches lack the flavour of the fresh fruit. They are usually sold in packets of mixed dried fruit and need to be soaked before use.

Pears are also usually sold in packets of mixed dried fruit and can be used in the same way as peaches. Soak before use.

Prunes are whole dried plums with or without the stones. Some varieties are tenderized and do not need soaking before use. Others can be soaked in cold tea or red wine rather than water, for a better flavour.

Vine fruits Currants, raisins and sultanas are all types of dried grapes. They do not need soaking and are often sold pre-washed. Currants are dried small black seedless grapes. Seedless raisins are dried seedless grapes and are the most popular type for cooking. The largest and sweetest raisins come from the Spanish Muscatel grapes. Sultanas are dried small white seedless grapes. Should you find that the fruit has become hard, cover in boiling water, leave to plump up then dry thoroughly. If using a microwave, cover with water and microwave on HIGH for 5 minutes. Stir, leave to stand, then drain and dry.

Glacé fruit and crystallized fruit Fruits which are preserved in sugar syrup and have a glossy coating are known as glacé fruits. Those with a granulated coating are known as crystallized fruits.

The glossy coating on cherries and other glacé fruits should be removed before they are used in baking, otherwise the fruit will sink to the bottom of the pan as it is dragged down by the sugary coating. Rinse the fruit under warm running water and pat dry with absorbent kitchen paper.

Toss the fruit in a little of the recipe flour before adding to the pudding or cake mixture. Glacé fruits used to decorate desserts will lose their lustre if washed, but the sugary coating also tends to seep on the topping if they are applied much in advance of serving.

Candied peel Candied orange or lemon peel can be bought separately, then mixed to definite proportions after shredding, grating, mincing or chopping. Ready-mixed chopped peel is no doubt easier and quicker, but there is extra aroma and flavour to be gained by preparing peel yourself. Ready-cut peel may need further chopping to make it finer.

Angelica is the candied stalk of the angelica herb. Look for angelica with a good green colour. To make it into leaves for decorating small cakes and pastries, cut it into 0.5 cm (¼ inch) strips, then cut each strip into diagonal slices.

SPICES

Allspice is also known as Jamaica pepper, as the seeds of allspice are just slightly larger than peppercorns and dark brown in colour. Despite its alternative name it is not peppery in flavour, but delicately spicy with a tinge of cloves, cinnamon and nutmeg. Allspice can be bought whole or ground and it can be added to both sweet and savoury dishes. Add ground allspice to ginger cakes and scald whole seeds in milk for making puddings and custards.

Aniseed The tiny, purse-shaped seeds of anise have a warm, sweet, pungent flavour and can be used in sweet and savoury dishes.

Caraway The small, elongated, dark brown seeds of caraway have a warming but slightly sharp flavour. Their valuable digestive properties make them particularly suitable for

eating with rich, fatty foods. Most often, however, they are added to cakes and pastries and baked apples.

Cardamom is available as pods and seeds, and comes from a perennial plant related to ginger. The pods (which contain the seeds) can be either green or black. Cardamom seeds should always be bought inside their pods, removed by crushing and discarding the pods, and ground at home as, once ground, their light, sweet, sherbety flavour is quickly lost. Green cardamom has the finer flavour and is added to both sweet and savoury dishes, particularly in Indian cooking.

Cinnamon is native to Sri Lanka, and is the bark of a tree which is a member of the laurel family. The bark is peeled from the young shoots of the tree, then left to dry in the sun so that it curls into quills, known as cinnamon sticks. The bark of the cassia tree is often sold as cinnamon, which it resembles closely, both in flavour and appearance.

Cloves get their name from the Latin word for nail – *clavus* – which the spice resembles in appearance. Cloves are in fact the flower buds of an evergreen shrub native to the Spice Islands, but nowadays the majority are imported from Zanzibar and Madagascar. The volatile oil of cloves is a powerful antiseptic (it is a standard remedy for toothache) and cloves are also used in the making of pomanders. In cooking, cloves are used both in their whole and ground form. Use ground cloves in baking and puddings, particularly with apples.

Coriander are round, light brown seeds with a fresh, spicy flavour. They can be bought whole or ground and are used in many Indian and Pakistani dishes. Their flavour is improved if they are gently dry-roasted before grinding. Ground coriander can be added to bread and cakes.

Nutmeg is the seed of the nutmeg fruit. The outer covering of nutmeg is sold separately as **mace** and has a stronger flavour than nutmeg. Nutmeg is sold whole or ground.

Vanilla pod is the seed pod of a type of orchid. It is yellow-green when picked and dark brown after curing and drying. The pod can be reused several times provided it is dried well and stored in a polythene bag.

Vanilla is essentially a flavouring for sweet dishes, particularly ice creams, custards and pastry cream. Use it to flavour hot chocolate or coffee drinks and infuse it in wine cups. Keep it in a jar of caster sugar to make your own vanilla sugar.

Mixed spice is a mixture of sweet-flavoured ground spices. The main ingredient is nutmeg and included in smaller amounts are cinnamon, cloves, ginger, cardamom, vanilla, allspice and sometimes fennel seeds.

Mixed spice is often used in sweet dishes, cakes, biscuits and confectionery. Buy it ready made or make your own using the following proportions.

30 ml (2 level tbsp) whole cloves
25 ml (5 level tsp) whole allspice berries
12.5 cm (5 inch) cinnamon stick
1.25 ml (¼ tsp) black peppercorns
60 ml (4 level tbsp) freshly grated nutmeg
30 ml (2 level tbsp) ground ginger

Grind the whole spices together and mix with the nutmeg and ginger. Store in an airtight, screw-topped jar. Keeps well for up to 1 month. Use for baking and in puddings.

GRINDING YOUR OWN SPICES

Spices taste better when freshly ground. Peppercorns and allspice berries can have their own peppermills. Small amounts of spice can be crushed with a pestle and mortar or with a rolling pin. Grind large amounts in an electric or hand grinder, remembering to wipe it out well each time with kitchen paper, so that no cross flavouring occurs. Most spices benefit from being gently dry-fried for a few minutes before being ground. This releases extra flavour, especially with spices such as cumin and coriander.

To dry-fry spices Heat a heavy frying pan over moderate heat. Put in the spices and stir them constantly until they are an even brown – do not allow them to burn. Tip the spices out to cool and then grind them in an electric grinder.

FLAVOURINGS AND ESSENCES

True essences are made by naturally extracting the flavour from the food itself. Flavourings, on the other hand, are synthetic and tend to be cheaper. Both flavourings and essences have very strong flavours and usually only a few drops are needed in a recipe.

Almond The essence is made from bitter almonds. It is not widely available but is sold at herbalists. Almond flavouring is sold in most supermarkets. Either can be used in baking.

Coffee essence is bottled coffee concentrate which is used to impart flavour to cakes and icings.

Orange flower water is orange-flavoured water, which can be used in small quantities in baking and sweet dishes.

Peppermint oil is similar to essence as it is made from the natural plant. The oil is mostly used for making sweets but can be used to flavour glacé icing and butter cream.

Rose water is highly fragrant rose-flavoured water, used in Turkish delight, baking and sweet dishes and in many Middle Eastern dishes.

Vanilla True vanilla essence is extracted from vanilla pods. It is not widely available but is sold at some high-class food shops and herbalists. It may be sold as an essence or natural vanilla. Vanilla flavouring, which is made from an ingredient in clove oil, is sold in supermarkets. Both can be used, particularly, to bring out the flavour of coffee and chocolate.

Flavouring with lemon, lime or orange Remember when using the rind of any citrus fruit, to grate it only lightly as the white pith imparts a bitter flavour. If only a few drops of lemon juice are needed, pierce the fruit with a fork and squeeze out the juice. Citrus fruits will yield more juice if microwaved on HIGH for 30 seconds before squeezing.

Flavouring with geranium The geraniums most used for culinary purposes are the rose-, mint- and lemon-scented varieties. Put washed leaves into the base of a cake tin when making a sponge cake and remove them when the cake is cooked. When making custard add them to the pan when scalding the milk.

CAKE MAKING METHODS

·

RUBBING-IN METHOD

'Rubbing in' is a literal description of the method: the fat is lightly 'worked' into the flour between the fingers and thumbs until the mixture resembles fine breadcrumbs.

Some air is incorporated during this process, which helps to make the cake light, but the main raising agents are chemical. The proportion of fat to flour is half or less.

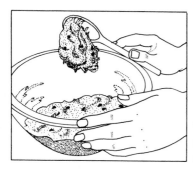

Testing for a dropping consistency

Add the liquid, using just enough to bring the mixture to the right consistency: too much liquid can cause a heavy, doughy texture and insufficient liquid results in a dry cake. The mixture should drop easily from the spoon when the handle is gently tapped against the side of the bowl. For small cakes and buns that are baked on a flat baking sheet, the mixture should be stiff enough to hold its shape without spreading too much during baking. A stiff consistency describes a mixture which will cling to the spoon.

Because they are low in fat, cakes made by the rubbing-in method do not keep well. They are best eaten the day they are made.

CREAMING METHOD

Rich cakes are made by the creaming method. The fat and sugar are beaten together until as pale and fluffy as whipped cream, the eggs are beaten in and the flour is then folded in. In some recipes the egg whites are whisked separately and folded in with the flour.

You need a mixing bowl large enough to accommodate vigorous beating without any danger of the ingredients overflowing. If beating by hand, use a wooden spoon and warm the bowl first to make the process easier.

Scrape the mixture down from the sides of the bowl from time to time to ensure no sugar crystals are left. An electric mixer or electric hand whisk is a time- and labour-saving alternative to creaming by hand, but remember it cannot be used for incorporating the flour.

Use eggs at room temperature and beat thoroughly after each addition to reduce the risk of the mixture curdling. (A mixture that curdles holds less air and produces a heavy, dense cake.)

As an extra precaution against the mixture curdling, add a spoonful of the sifted flour with the second and every following addition of egg and beat thoroughly. To keep the mixture light, fold in the remaining flour gradually, using a metal spoon.

ALL-IN-ONE METHOD

The one-stage method is based on soft tub margarine and this type of cake is wonderfully quick and easy to prepare. There is no need for any creaming or rubbing in: all the ingredients are simply beaten together with a wooden spoon for 2–3 minutes, until well blended and slightly glossy.

This method is also ideal for making cakes in an electric mixer, but be careful not to overbeat.

Self-raising flour is invariably used – often with the addition of a little extra baking powder to boost the rise. You can use either caster or light brown soft sugar for these quick cakes because their fine crystals dissolve easily.

These cakes are similar to those made by the

creaming method, but their texture is more open and they do not keep as well. Wrap them in foil as soon as they are cold to prevent them going stale.

MELTING METHOD

Gingerbreads and other cakes made by the melting method have a deliciously moist and sticky texture.

The inviting texture and rich dark colour of these cakes are due to the high proportion of sugary ingredients, including liquid sweeteners such as golden syrup or black treacle. To ensure the liquid sweetener is easily incorporated, it is warmed with the fat and sugar until blended and then added to the dry ingredients together with any eggs and the liquid.

Bicarbonate of soda is often used to raise these cakes – it reacts with natural acids present in liquid sweeteners. Spices are frequently added to enhance the flavour and also counteract the faintly bitter taste of bicarbonate of soda.

Measure the liquid sweetener carefully; too much can cause a heavy, sunken cake. Put the saucepan on the scales, set the dial to zero, then spoon in the required amount of syrup or treacle, or weigh the pan, then add the sweetener until the scales register the weight of the pan plus the required weight of syrup. Warm it very gently, just until the sugar has dissolved and the fat has melted. If allowed to boil, the mixture will become an unusable toffee-like mass.

Allow the mixture to cool slightly before pouring it on to the dry ingredients, or it will begin to cook the flour and a hard, tough cake will result. The blended mixture should have the consistency of heavy batter; it can be poured into the prepared tin and will find its own level.

Most cakes made by the melting method should be stored for a day or so before cutting, to allow the crust to soften and give the flavour time to mellow.

WHISKING METHOD

Most sponges and gâteaux are made by the whisking method. This produces the lightest of all cakes. The classic sponge is light and feathery and is made by whisking together eggs

and caster sugar, then folding in the sifted flour. There is no fat in the mixture, and the cake rises simply because of the air incorporated during whisking. For an even lighter cake, the egg yolks and sugar can be whisked together, with the whites whisked separately and folded in afterwards. Because cakes made by this method contain no fat, they always require a filling and do not keep well. A sponge cake should be baked on the day you wish to eat it.

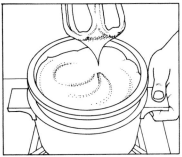

Whisking eggs and sugar

To make a really good sponge, the eggs and sugar must be whisked until thick enough to leave a trail when the whisk is lifted from the surface. If you use a rotary whisk or a hand-held electric mixer, place the bowl over a saucepan of hot water to speed the thickening process. Do not let the bottom of the bowl touch the water or the mixture will become too hot. When the mixture is really thick and has doubled in volume, take the bowl off the heat and continue to whisk until the mixture is cool. When whisking in an electric table-top mixer, additional heat is not required. Add the sifted flour carefully, adding a little at a time to the whisked mixture, folding it in with a metal spoon until evenly blended. Do not stir or you will break the air bubbles and the cake will not rise.

A moister version of the whisked sponge is a Genoese sponge. This is also made by the whisking method, but melted butter is added with the flour. This gives a delicate sponge, lighter than a Victoria sandwich, but with a moister texture than the plain whisked sponge. When adding melted butter, make sure it is just liquid and pour into the mixture around the sides of the bowl and fold in very lightly. Don't try to substitute margarine for butter in this recipe or the flavour and texture will be lost. A Genoese sponge keeps better than a plain whisked sponge and will keep for 2–3 days.

CAKES MADE USING OIL

Cakes made using oil (corn oil, for example) are very easy to mix and very successful. When using oil for making sandwich cakes, it is essential to add an extra raising agent or to whisk the egg whites until stiff and fold them into the mixture just before baking. This counteracts the heaviness of the cake that sometimes occurs when oil is used.

MERINGUE

Meringue is a mixture of whisked egg white and sugar, which is very slowly baked in the oven so that it dries out and becomes crisp and firm. The light texture of meringue is the perfect foil to creamy fillings and soft fruit, and this combination produces some of the most delicious gâteaux. Making meringues is the ideal way of using up leftover egg whites and the meringues will keep for up to six weeks in an airtight tin.

There are three basic types of meringue:

Meringue Suisse is made by incorporating caster or caster and granulated sugar into stiffly whisked egg white. Half the sugar is very gradually added, about 15 ml (1 tbsp) at a time, whisking after each addition, until the sugar is fully mixed in and partially dissolved. Sugar added in large amounts at this stage may result in a sticky meringue. The remaining sugar is added by sprinkling it over the whisked egg white then folding it in with a metal spoon. The mixture should be firm and have a glossy appearance. This is the type of meringue most used in home baking.

Meringue cuite is made by cooking the egg whites over boiling water while whisking them. This means that the meringue can be stored, if necessary, before shaping. Meringues made this way are harder, whiter and more powdery than Meringue Suisse and are made mostly by professional bakers as they require great care and long whisking.

Italian meringue is made by adding a hot sugar syrup to egg whites. It requires a sugar thermometer and is rarely used at home as the above types of meringue are easier to make.

BAKING TINS

Choose good-quality, strong tins in a variety of shapes and sizes. Non-stick surfaces clean most easily and are particularly useful in small awkwardly shaped tins. Some cake tins have a loose bottom or a loosening device to make it easier to remove the cake.

Use the size of tin specified in the recipe. Using too large a tin will tend to give a pale, flat and shrunken-looking cake; cakes baked in too small a tin will bulge over and lose their contours. If you do not have the tin specified, choose a slightly larger one. The mixture will be shallower and will take less time to cook, so test if the cake is ready 5–10 minutes early.

Flan rings and tins come in many forms. Round tins with plain or fluted sides and removable bases are primarily for pastry flan cases. For sponge flans, use a flan tin with a raised base.

Loaf tins are used for cakes as well as bread. The two most useful sizes are 900 ml (1½ pints), also known as a 450 g (1 lb) loaf tin, and 1.7 litres (3 pints), known as a 900 g (2 lb) loaf tin. Where reference is made to a 900 ml (1½ pint) loaf tin, the approximate sized tin to use is one with 16.5 × 10.5 cm (6½ × 4 inch) top measurements, and for a 1.7 litre (3 pint) loaf tin, use one with 20.5 × 12.5 cm (8 × 5 inch) top measurements.

Sandwich tins are shallow round tins with straight sides for making sandwich and layer cakes, in sizes 18–25 cm (7–10 inches).

Moule à manqué tins are deep sandwich tins with sloping sides.

Small cake tins and moulds come in sheets of 6, 9 and 12, or as individual tins. There are shapes for buns, sponge fingers, madeleines, etc.

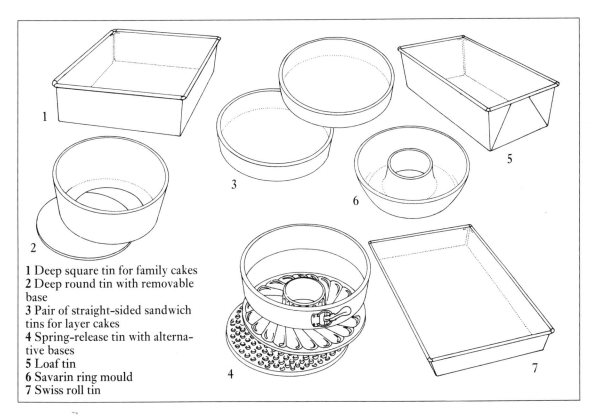

1 Deep square tin for family cakes
2 Deep round tin with removable base
3 Pair of straight-sided sandwich tins for layer cakes
4 Spring-release tin with alternative bases
5 Loaf tin
6 Savarin ring mould
7 Swiss roll tin

Springform tins come complete with different loose bottoms.

Standard cake tins For everyday use, 15 cm (6 inch), 18 cm (7 inch) and 20.5 cm (8 inch) tins are adequate. For celebration cakes you may need larger sizes that are available in a variety of shapes.

PREPARING TINS

·

Follow the manufacturer's special directions regarding non-stick (silicone-finished) tins, which do not usually require greasing or lining.

GREASING

When greasing tins, brush lightly with melted margarine or butter (preferably unsalted). They may also be dredged with flour as an additional safeguard against sticking; sprinkle a little flour in the tin and shake until coated, then shake out any surplus.

For fatless sponges, use a half-and-half mixture of flour and caster sugar sifted together, for sprinkling over the greased tin. You can do the same to a sponge flan tin to produce a crisper crust.

LINING

With most cakes it is necessary to line the tins with greaseproof paper, which is usually greased before the mixture is put in, or with non-stick paper, which does not require greasing, and can be used several times.

For a Victoria sandwich cake mixture, it is sufficient to line just the base of the tin. For rich mixtures and fruit cakes, line the whole tin. The paper is usually doubled to prevent the outside of the cake from overbrowning and drying out. With the extra rich fruit mixtures used for wedding and other formal cakes, which require a long cooking time, it is also advisable to pin a double strip of thick brown paper or newspaper around the outside of the tin, to help prevent the outside of the cake overcooking.

To line a deep tin Cut a piece (or two pieces, if necessary) of greaseproof paper long enough to reach around the tin and overlap slightly, and high enough to extend about 2.5 cm (1 inch) above the top edge. Fold up the bottom edge of the strip about 2.5 cm (1 inch), creasing it firmly, then open out and snip into this folded portion with scissors; this snipped edge enables the paper band to fit a square, oblong, round or oval tin neatly.

Grease the inside of the paper. Place the strip in position in the greased tin, with the cut edge flat against the base. In a rectangular tin, make sure the paper fits snugly into the corners.

Cut a double round of paper to fit inside the base of the tin. (Stand the tin on the paper, draw round it and then cut.) Put the rounds in place – they will keep the snipped edge of the band in position and make a neat lining; brush the base of the lining with melted lard.

Lining a deep cake tin

To line a sandwich tin Cut a round of grease-proof paper to fit the bottom of the tin exactly. If the tin's sides are shallow and you want to raise them, fit a band of paper inside the tin, coming about 2.5 cm (1 inch) above the rim.

To line a Swiss roll tin Cut a piece of paper about 5 cm (2 inches) larger all around than the tin. Place the tin on it and in each corner make a cut from the angle of the paper as far as the corner of the tin. Grease the tin and put in the paper so that it fits closely, overlapping at the corners. Grease the paper and dust with a half-and-half mixture of flour and sugar sifted together. Non-stick paper is very satisfactory for lining this type of tin.

To line a loaf tin It is not usually necessary to line a loaf tin fully. To do so, grease the inside, line the base only with an oblong of greaseproof paper and grease the paper.

To line a sponge flan tin Grease the inside well, and place a round of greased greaseproof paper over the raised part of the tin only.

HEATING THE OVEN
•

Preheat the oven before starting to bake so that it will be at the correct temperature by the time the cake or loaf is ready to go in. Check that the shelves are in the centre of the oven where possible, unless otherwise stated.

TO TEST WHETHER A CAKE IS COOKED
Small cakes should be well risen, golden brown in colour and firm to the touch – both on top and underneath – and they should begin to shrink from the sides of the tin on being taken out of the oven.

Larger cakes present more difficulty, especially for beginners, although the oven heat and time of cooking give a reasonable indication, but the following tests are a guide:
● Press the centre top of the cake very lightly with the fingertip. The cake should be spongy and should give only very slightly to the pressure then rise again immediately, re-taining no impression.
● In the case of a fruit cake, lift it gently from the oven and 'listen' to it, putting it closely to the ear. A continued sizzling sound indicates that the cake is not cooked through.
● Insert a warmed long skewer (never use a cold knife) in the centre of the cake. If any mixture is sticking to it, the cake requires longer cooking.

TO TEST WHETHER BREAD IS COOKED
Bread should be well risen and golden brown when cooked, and it should sound hollow when tapped underneath with the knuckles. Larger loaves may need to be turned out of the tin and returned to the oven upside down for the last 10–15 minutes of the cooking time to ensure they are cooked through.

COOLING
Allow cakes a few minutes to cool before turning them out of the tin; they will shrink away from the sides and are more easily

removed. Turn out on to a wire rack. Allow fruit cakes to cool completely in the tin.

Bread should be removed from the tin and allowed to cool on a wire rack.

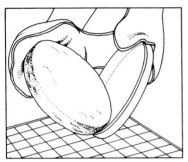

Cooling a cake on a wire rack

WHAT WENT WRONG?

•

There are many reasons for a disappointing result when baking. Here are some of them, with their suggested causes. For scones, see page 111.

CAKES, SPONGES AND FRUIT CAKES
Too close a texture
1 Too much liquid.
2 Too little raising agent.
3 Insufficient creaming of the fat and sugar – air should be well incorporated at this stage.
4 Curdling of the creamed mixture when the eggs are added (a curdled mixture holds less air than one of the correct consistency).
5 Over-stirring or beating the flour into a creamed mixture when little or no raising agent is present.

Uneven texture with holes
1 Over-stirring or uneven mixing in of the flour.
2 Putting mixture into the tin in small amounts – pockets of air trapped in the mixture.

DRY AND CRUMBLY TEXTURE
1 Too much raising agent.
2 Too long a cooking time in too cool an oven.

Fruit cakes dry and crumbly
1 Cooking at too high a temperature.
2 Too stiff a mixture.
3 Not lining the tin thoroughly – for a large cake, use double greaseproof paper.

Fruit sinking to the bottom of the cake
1 Damp fruit.
2 Sticky glacé cherries.
3 Too soft a mixture: a rich fruit cake mixture should be fairly stiff, so that it can support the weight of the fruit.
4 Opening or banging the oven door while the cake is rising.
5 Using self-raising flour where the recipe requires plain, or using too much baking powder – the cake over-rises and cannot carry the fruit with it.

'Peaking' and 'cracking'
1 Too hot an oven.
2 The cake being placed too near the top of the oven.
3 Too stiff a mixture.
4 Too small a cake tin.

Close, heavy-textured whisked sponge
1 The eggs and sugar being insufficiently beaten, so that not enough air is enclosed.
2 The flour being stirred in too heavily or for too long – very light folding movements are required and a metal spoon should be used.

Cakes sinking in the middle
1 Too soft a mixture.
2 Too much raising agent.
3 Too cool an oven, which means that the centre of the cake does not rise.
4 Too hot an oven, which makes the cake appear to be done on the outside before it is cooked through, so that it is taken from the oven too soon.
5 Insufficient baking.

Burnt fruit on the outside of a fruit cake
1 Too high a temperature.
2 Lack of protection: as soon as the cake begins to colour, a piece of brown paper or a double thickness of greaseproof

paper should be placed over the top for the remainder of the cooking time to prevent further browning.

A heavy layer at the base of a Genoese sponge

1 The melted fat being too hot – it should be only lukewarm and just flowing.
2 Uneven or insufficient folding in of fat or flour.
3 Pouring the fat into the centre of the mixture instead of round the edge.

DISGUISING THE DAMAGE

If a cake goes wrong in the baking, there is no way of going back and putting it right without baking a new cake. But there are ways of disguising the damage so that only you will know.

- If a chocolate cake turns out rather too moist, call it a pudding and serve it with a fluffy sauce.
- If biscuits crumble badly, use them to make a biscuit crumb flan case.
- If the top of a fruit cake gets burnt, cut it off and use a well-flavoured almond paste to disguise it.
- If meringues break as you lift them off the baking sheet, serve large pieces on top of fruit and cream.
- If a sponge cake turns out a thin, flat layer, cut into fancy shapes with a biscuit cutter and sandwich together with jam and cream.
- If your cake rises unevenly, level the top, turn it over and ice the bottom.
- If a cake breaks as you take it out of the tin, disguise it as a pudding with custard sauce or fruit.
- If a cake sinks in the middle, cut out the centre and turn it into a ring cake. Ice it with butter cream or almond paste and royal icing, according to type, or decorate with whipped cream and fill the centre with fruit for a dessert.
- If a sponge or plain cake is dry, crumbly or heavy, use it as the base for a trifle and soak it in plenty of booze!

BREADS AND YEAST CAKES

A 'flying top' (when the top crust breaks away from the loaf):

1 Under-proving.
2 Dough surface allowed to dry out during proving.
3 Oven too hot.

Loaf has a flat top:

1 Flour too soft.
2 Too little salt.
3 Dough too wet.
4 Poor shaping of dough.

Crust surface cracks after removal from the oven:

1 Over-proving.
2 Oven too hot.
3 Cooling in a draught after baking.

Dough collapses when put into the oven:

1 Over-proving.

Heavy, close texture; poor volume:

1 Flour too soft.
2 Too much salt.
3 Insufficient kneading or proving.
4 Yeast killed by rising in too hot a place.

Coarse, open texture:

1 Too much liquid.
2 Over-proving.
3 Oven too cool.

Uneven texture with large holes:

1 Dough not knocked back properly.
2 Dough left uncovered during rising.

Sour, yeasty flavour and smell of alcohol:

1 Over-proving.
2 Too much yeast.
3 Stale yeast, or fresh yeast creamed with sugar.

Bread stales quickly and is crumbly:

1 Too much yeast.
2 Flour too soft.
3 Rising too quickly in too hot a place.
4 Under-rising.
5 Over-proving.

BUTTER CREAMS, GLACÉ ICING AND FROSTINGS

·

Cakes can be covered with a variety of toppings, each of which can be flavoured to suit the cake. Choose from butter cream, glacé icing, crème au beure or frosting. For royal icing see pages 151–3.

BUTTER CREAM

This quantity is sufficient to coat the sides of a 20.5 cm (8 inch) cake and provide a topping or a filling. To coat the sides and provide a thicker topping and filling, increase the amounts of butter and sugar to 150 g (5 oz) and 275 g (10 oz) respectively.

·

225 g (8 oz) icing sugar

100 g (4 oz) butter

vanilla flavouring

15–30 ml (1–2 tbsp) milk or water

Sift the icing sugar into a bowl. Cream the butter until soft and gradually beat in the icing sugar, adding a few drops of vanilla flavouring and the milk or water.

VARIATIONS

Orange or Lemon Butter Cream
Omit the vanilla flavouring and add a little **finely grated orange** or **lemon rind** and a little of the **juice**, beating well to avoid curdling the mixture.

Walnut Butter Cream
Stir **30 ml (2 level tbsp) very finely chopped walnuts** into the butter cream.

Almond Butter Cream
Stir **30 ml (2 level tbsp) very finely chopped toasted almonds** into the butter cream.

Coffee Butter Cream
Omit the vanilla flavouring and flavour with **10 ml (2 level tsp) instant coffee powder** dissolved in some of the liquid, heated. Alternatively, use **15 ml (1 tbsp) coffee flavouring** to replace an equal amount of the liquid.

Chocolate Butter Cream
Flavour by adding **25–40 g (1–1½ oz) melted chocolate**, omitting 15 ml (1 tbsp) of the milk or water. Alternatively, dissolve **15 ml (1 level tbsp) cocoa powder** in a little hot water taken from the measured amount of liquid. Allow to cool before adding to the mixture.

Mocha Butter Cream
Dissolve **5 ml (1 level tsp) cocoa powder** and **10 ml (2 level tsp) instant coffee powder** in a little warm water taken from the measured amount of liquid. Cool before adding to the mixture.

CRÈME AU BEURRE

On more elaborate cakes, use Crème au Beurre in place of butter cream.

·

MAKES ABOUT 275 g (10 oz)

75 g (3 oz) caster sugar

2 egg yolks, beaten

175 g (6 oz) butter, softened

1 Place the sugar in a heavy-based saucepan with 60 ml (4 tbsp) water and heat very gently to dissolve the sugar without boiling.
2 When completely dissolved, bring to boiling point and boil steadily for 2–3 minutes to reach a temperature of 107°C (225°F).
3 Put the egg yolks in a deep bowl and pour on the syrup in a thin stream, whisking all the time. Continue to whisk until the mixture is thick and cold.
4 In another bowl, cream the butter until very soft and gradually beat in the egg yolk mixture.

VARIATIONS see overleaf

Chocolate

Melt **50 g (2 oz) plain chocolate** with 15 ml (1 tbsp) water. Cool slightly and beat into the Crème au Beurre mixture.

Fruit

Crush **225 g (8 oz) fresh strawberries** or other fresh fruit, or thaw, drain and crush frozen fruit. Beat into the Crème au Beurre mixture.

Orange or Lemon

Add the **freshly grated rind and juice** to taste to the Crème au Beurre mixture.

Coffee

Beat **15–30 ml (1–2 tbsp) coffee essence** into the Crème au Beurre mixture.

COFFEE FUDGE FROSTING

·

MAKES ABOUT 400 g (14 oz)

50 g (2 oz) butter or margarine
125 g (4 oz) light brown soft sugar
45 ml (3 tbsp) coffee essence
30 ml (2 tbsp) single cream or milk
200 g (7 oz) icing sugar, sifted

1 Put the butter, light brown soft sugar, coffee essence and cream in a saucepan and heat gently until the sugar dissolves. Boil briskly for 3 minutes.
2 Remove from the heat and gradually stir in the icing sugar. Beat with a wooden spoon until smooth, then continue to beat for 2 minutes until the icing is thick enough to spread. Use immediately, spreading with a wet palette knife.

VARIATION

Chocolate Fudge Frosting

Omit the coffee essence and add **75 g (3 oz) plain chocolate or plain chocolate flavoured cake covering** with the butter in the pan.

VANILLA FROSTING

·

MAKES ABOUT 175 g (6 oz)

150 g (5 oz) icing sugar
25 ml (1½ tbsp) vegetable oil
15 ml (1 tbsp) milk
few drops of vanilla flavouring

1 Put the icing sugar in a bowl and beat in the oil, milk and vanilla flavouring. Beat until smooth.

CHOCOLATE FROSTING

·

MAKES ABOUT 200 g (7 oz)

25 g (1 oz) plain chocolate or plain chocolate flavoured cake covering
150 g (5 oz) icing sugar
1 egg, beaten
2.5 ml (½ tsp) vanilla flavouring
25 g (1 oz) butter or margarine, softened

1 Break the chocolate into pieces and place in a bowl over a pan of simmering water. Heat gently until chocolate has melted.
2 Stir in the icing sugar, add the egg, vanilla flavouring and butter and beat until smooth.

AMERICAN FROSTING

·

MAKES ABOUT 225 g (8 oz)

1 egg white
225 g (8 oz) caster or granulated sugar
pinch of cream of tartar

1 Whisk the egg white until stiff. Gently heat the sugar with 60 ml (4 tbsp) water and the cream of tartar, stirring until dissolved. Then without stirring, bring to the boil and boil to 120°C (240°F).

2 Remove the syrup from the heat and immediately when the bubbles subside, pour it on the egg white in a thin stream, beating the mixture. Leave it to cool slightly.

3 When the mixture starts to go dull around the edges and is almost cold, pour quickly over the cake and spread evenly with a palette knife.

SEVEN-MINUTE FROSTING

•

MAKES ABOUT 175g (6oz)

1 egg white
175 g (6 oz) caster sugar
pinch of salt
pinch of cream of tartar

1 Put all the ingredients into a bowl with 30 ml (2 tbsp) water and whisk lightly.

2 Place the bowl over a pan of hot water and heat, whisking continuously, until the mixture thickens sufficiently to stand in peaks. This will take about 7 minutes.

3 Pour the frosting over the top of the cake and spread with a palette knife.

GLACÉ ICING

This quantity is sufficient to cover the top of a 20.5 cm (8 inch) cake or about 8 small cakes.

•

100–175 g (4–6 oz) icing sugar
flavouring
colouring

Sift the icing sugar into a bowl and gradually add 15–30 ml (1–2 tbsp) warm water until the icing is thick enough to coat the back of a spoon. Stir in the chosen flavouring. If necessary, add more sugar or water to obtain the correct consistency. Add a few drops of colouring, if required, and use at once.

VARIATIONS

Extra-smooth Glacé Icing
For icing of a finer texture place the sugar, water, flavouring and colour in a small pan and heat, stirring, until the mixture is warm – do not allow it to get too hot. The icing should coat the back of a wooden spoon and look smooth and glossy.

Orange or Lemon Icing
Substitute **15–30 ml (1–2 tbsp) strained orange juice or 15 ml (1 tbsp) strained lemon juice** for the same amount of measured water.

Chocolate Icing
Blend **10 ml (2 level tsp) cocoa powder** in a little hot water and use to replace the same amount of measured water.

Coffee Icing
Flavour with either **5 ml (1 tbsp) coffee flavouring** or **10 ml (2 level tsp) instant coffee powder** dissolved in a little of the measured water, heated.

Mocha Icing
Flavour with **5 ml (1 tsp) cocoa powder** and **10 ml (2 level tsp) instant coffee powder**, dissolved in a little of the measured water, heated.

Liqueur Icing
Replace **10–15 ml (2–3 tsp)** of the measured water by a chosen **liqueur**.

Fondant Icing
See pages 150–1.

Royal Icing
See page 151.

ICING AND DECORATING SPONGE CAKES AND GÂTEAUX

PREPARING A CAKE FOR DECORATING

Cool the cake completely. Make sure the surface is quite level for icing – if necessary, turn the cake upside down and use the flat underside. With a pastry brush, brush away any crumbs or loose bits which might stick to the icing and spoil the effect.

If making a sandwich or layer cake, first put in the filling. Slice the cake horizontally in half and spread the bottom layer with the filling – if using butter cream, spread it over the cut surface of both cakes – then put the layers together again and press down to prevent them sliding apart when you cut the cake.

If the sides are to be coated with chopped nuts, desiccated coconut, etc, do this before icing the top (see below).

Place the cake on a wire rack so it can be easily moved when finished, as newly applied icing may crack if you transfer the cake from one plate to another. Prepare any decoration required – chop nuts, toast flaked almonds, grate chocolate and so on.

DECORATING THE SIDES OF A CAKE

Covering the sides with chopped nuts, grated chocolate, chocolate vermicelli or desiccated coconut is a quick and easy way to give a cake a professional look. To make sure the decoration will stick, brush the sides of the cake with apricot glaze (see page 150) or coat with butter cream.

To coat with butter cream, spread evenly round the sides of the cake with a palette knife, making sure there are no gaps. Then hold the knife upright, at an angle of 45° to the cake, and draw it towards you to smooth the surface. Spread a fairly thick layer of chopped nuts or other decoration down the centre of a piece of greaseproof paper. Hold the cake on its side between the palms of your hands and roll it in the nuts until the sides are completely coated.

DECORATING THE TOP OF A CAKE

Using Butter Cream Pile butter cream on top of the cake and spread it smoothly and evenly, with a palette knife, right to the edges. For a more interesting effect, draw the prongs of a fork across the butter cream or make pronounced swirl marks with the flat blade of a knife before adding any other decoration.

Using Glacé Icing If coating both the top and sides of a cake, stand the cake on a wire rack with a large plate or tray underneath to catch the drips. As soon as the icing reaches a coating consistency and looks smooth and glossy, pour it from the bowl on to the centre of the cake. Allow the icing to run down the sides, guiding the flow with a palette knife. Keep a little icing in reserve to fill any gaps. An attractive effect – particularly suited to unfilled cakes and loaf cakes – can be achieved simply by allowing the icing to dribble down the sides of the cake, and leaving the gaps unfilled.

If the sides are decorated and only the top is to be glacé-iced, pour the icing on to the centre of the cake. Use a palette knife to spread the icing evenly over the surface, stopping just inside the top edges to prevent it dripping down the sides.

If the top of the cake is to be glacé-iced but you wish to leave the sides plain, secure a double band of greaseproof paper around the cake – the band should project about 2.5 cm (1 inch) above the top of the cake. Pour the icing on to the cake and allow it to find its own level. Leave until set, then carefully peel away the paper with the aid of a palette knife.

FEATHER ICING

Feather icing is one of the easiest ways to decorate a child's birthday cake. Make a quantity of glacé icing and mix to a coating consistency. Make up a second batch of icing using half the quantity of sugar and enough warm water to mix it to a thick piping consistency. Tint the second batch with food colouring. Spoon the coloured icing into a greaseproof paper piping bag (see page 153).

Coat the top of the cake with the larger quantity of icing. Work quickly, before the icing has time to form a skin. Snip the end off the

CROQUEMBOUCHE (page 185)

piping bag and pipe parallel lines of coloured icing about 1–2 cm (½–¾ inch) apart, over the surface. Then quickly draw the point of a skewer or a sharp knife across the piped lines, first in one direction then in the other, spacing these new lines evenly apart.

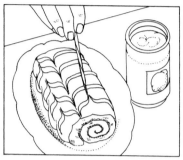

Feather icing a Swiss roll

CAKE DECORATIONS

·

Arrange any prepared decorations in position as soon as the icing has thickened and formed a slight skin. If added while the icing is still wet, decorations will slide out of position. If added when the icing is completely dry, they will cause the surface to crack. If you have to add decorations at the last minute, when the icing is hard, stick them on with a little extra icing or some apricot glaze.

FROSTED FRUITS AND FLOWERS
Whisk together the white of 1 egg with 2 teaspoonfuls of cold water to give a frothy mixture. Brush the mixture on to fruits or flowers, then dip these in caster sugar. Shake off any excess, then spread out on greaseproof paper and leave in the air to dry for at least 24 hours. Use to decorate cakes, mousses and soufflés.

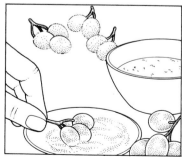

Frosting grapes

MARZIPAN 'ORANGES'
Colour batches of marzipan with orange and green food colouring. With your fingers, shape small amounts of the orange marzipan into balls. Stick a trimmed whole clove in the end for the 'eye' of the fruit. Roll on the fine side of a conical or box grater to give the texture of orange skin, then roll in caster sugar. Attach 'leaves' made from the green-coloured marzipan.

CITRUS JULIENNE
Remove very thin strips of rind from citrus fruit with a cannelle knife or vegetable peeler, making sure that the strips contain no traces of pith. Blanch the strips in boiling water for about 3 minutes, then drain and rinse under cold running water. Dry thoroughly and cut into julienne strips about 0.5 cm (¼ inch) thick and about 5 cm (2 inches) long. Use to sprinkle over desserts; looks especially good on rosettes of whipped cream or buttercream icing.

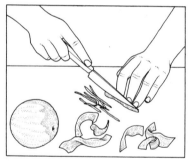

Making citrus julienne

CHOCOLATE DECORATIONS
Chocolate caraque Melt 100 g (4 oz) chocolate (see page 12). Pour it in a thin layer on to a

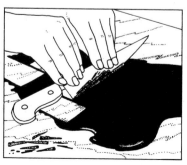

Making chocolate caraque

marble slab or cold baking tray and leave to set until it no longer sticks to your hand when you touch it. Holding a large knife with both hands push the blade across the surface of the chocolate to roll pieces off in long curls. Adjust the angle of the blade to get the best curls.

Chocolate shapes Make a sheet of chocolate as above and cut into neat triangles or squares with a sharp knife, or stamp out circles with a small round cutter.

Chocolate curls Using a potato peeler, pare thin layers from the edge of a block of chocolate.

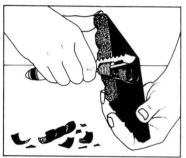

Making chocolate curls

Chocolate leaves Melt 100 g (4 oz) chocolate (see page 12). Using leaves which have been thoroughly washed and dried, drag the upper surface of each leaf through the chocolate, making sure that the underside of the leaf does not become chocolate-coated too. For small leaves, use a small clean paint brush to brush on the chocolate. Turn the leaves chocolate-side up and place on greaseproof paper to set. When the chocolate has set, carefully peel off the leaf.

SPUN SUGAR

These fine threads of sugar are useful for decorating special cakes or pastries.

•

225 g (8 oz) granulated sugar

15 ml (1 tbsp) liquid glucose

1 Lightly oil a rolling pin. Cover the work surface with newspaper, and also cover the floor immediately below. Cover the newspaper on the work surface with greaseproof paper.

2 Put the sugar, 90 ml (6 tbsp) water and the liquid glucose into a saucepan and heat gently until every granule of sugar has dissolved, brushing down the sides of the pan with a little hot water. Boil the sugar syrup to a temperature of 160°C (320°F). Immediately plunge the base of the pan into cold water to prevent further cooking.

3 Dip two forks, held together, into the syrup then hold them up high until a fine thread starts to fall. Gently spin the sugar threads around a rolling pin until a good quantity of threads accumulate. Remove from the rolling pin and set aside. Repeat until all the syrup has been used.

CARAMEL SUGAR

Caramel sugar can range from straw-coloured to a deep brown; this depends on how long the sugar is cooked. It tastes much less sweet than ordinary sugar and has a distinctive flavour.

•

75 g (3 oz) granulated sugar

1 Dissolve the sugar very gently in 75 ml (3 fl oz) water. Increase the heat and boil rapidly without stirring until the syrup turns a rich-brown caramel colour. Pour at once into a greased shallow tin (a Swiss roll tin is ideal), then leave until cold and set.

2 Crush with a mallet or rolling pin into fine pieces and sprinkle over cakes and gâteaux.

SAVOURY BREADS

There is nothing more evocative than the smell of new-baked bread filling every corner of the kitchen and much has been written in its praise. Bread has a long and fascinating history going right back to the Neolithic age. Tombs of the Pharaohs have pictures showing what is thought to be the fermenting of yeast (a process they probably discovered).

Each country has its own version of the daily bread, based on local crops. Flat, unleavened breads of barley, millet, maize or buckwheat belong to Asia and Africa, for example, while rye breads are popular in Germany, Scandinavia and Russia. In Great Britain and in the United States we favour wheat.

A SELECTION OF SAVOURY BREADS (pages 37–55)

INGREDIENTS FOR BREAD MAKING

FLOUR

Strong flour has a high gluten content and is used for making bread. See pages 7–8 for information on the different types of flour and their gluten content.

Generally, bread made with wholemeal rye or buckwheat flour has a closer texture and a stronger, more distinctive taste than bread made with white flour. If making bread with rye or buckwheat flour, remember to combine it with a strong flour to increase the gluten content (see page 7).

If you wish to eat a bread high in fibre, choose a flour with a high percentage of the wheat grain (see page 7). Extra fibre can be added in the form of bran, branflakes or oatmeal. Add in small quantities and use a little extra liquid for mixing.

YEAST

Yeast is a living plant available fresh or dried. When mixed with flour and liquid it gives off carbon dioxide, which expands, making the dough rise. For more information on the different types of yeast and how to measure then, see pages 10–11.

SALT

Salt is important for the flavour and texture of bread. It should be measured accurately, as too little causes the dough to rise too quickly and too much kills the yeast and gives the bread an uneven texture. Salt is used in the proportions of 5–10 ml (1–2 level tsp) to 450 g (1 lb) flour. Low-sodium salts may also be used.

FAT

Adding fat to the dough enriches it and gives a moist, close-textured loaf with a soft crust. It also helps keep the bread fresh and soft for a longer time. It is often rubbed into the flour and salt or, if a large quantity is used, it is melted and added with the liquid ingredients. If using margarine, block margarine is better than soft tub margarine as it is easier to rub in. Oil may be used instead of fat.

LIQUID

Water is suitable for plain bread, producing a loaf with an even texture and a crisp crust. Milk and water, or milk alone, will give a softer, golden crust and the loaf will stay soft and fresh for longer.

The amount of liquid used will vary according to the absorbency of the flour. Too much will give the bread a spongy and open texture, and too little will give a dry and crumbly dough that won't mix well. Wholemeal and brown flours are usually more absorbent than white.

The liquid is generally added to the yeast at a tepid temperature, i.e. 43°C (110°F). Boiling liquid will kill the yeast.

GLAZES AND FINISHES

If a crusty finish is desired, bread or rolls can be brushed before baking with a glaze made by dissolving 10 ml (2 level tsp) salt in 30 ml (2 tbsp) water.

For a shiny finish, the surface should be brushed with beaten egg or beaten egg mixed with milk.

For a soft finish, dust the bread or rolls with flour before baking.

Some bread and yeast buns are glazed *after* baking to give them a sticky finish. To do this, brush the bread with warmed honey or a golden syrup made by dissolving 30 ml (2 level tbsp) sugar in 30 ml (2 tbsp) water and bringing to the boil.

MAKING BREAD

MIXING THE DOUGH

Warm ingredients and a warm bowl will help to speed up the first rising process. Measure all the ingredients carefully into a large bowl. Add the yeast liquid and mix with the dry ingredients, using a wooden spoon or fork, until blended. Work the dough, using your hands, until the mixture is smooth and leaves the sides of the bowl clean.

KNEADING THE DOUGH

Kneading is essential to strengthen the gluten in the flour, thus making the dough elastic in texture and enabling it to rise more easily.

By hand Turn the dough on to a floured work surface, knead the dough by folding it towards you and quickly and firmly pushing down and away from you with the heel of the hand. Give the dough a quarter turn and continue kneading for about 10 minutes, until it is firm, elastic and no longer sticky.

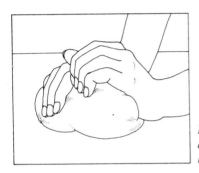

Kneading dough by hand

Using a dough hook If you have a mixer with a dough hook attachment, it can take the hard work out of kneading. Follow manufacturer's instructions. Working with small amounts of dough is more successful than attempting a large batch all at once. Place the yeast liquid in the bowl, add the dry ingredients, begin at the lowest speed and mix to form the dough. Increase the speed for the recommended time.

Using a food processor A food processor also takes the hard work out of mixing and kneading yeast mixtures. Follow the manufacturer's instructions on quantities as it is important that the bowl is not overfilled. You may need to halve the recipe and prepare two batches of dough.

RISING
The kneaded dough is now ready for rising. Unless otherwise stated, place in an oiled bowl and cover with oiled cling film. This will prevent a skin forming during rising. Rising times vary with temperature. Allow 1½–2 hours at room temperature for the dough to rise. It should have doubled in size and the risen dough should spring back when gently pressed with a lightly floured finger. The dough can be made to rise in about 45 minutes–1 hour if placed in a warm place such as an airing cupboard or above a warm cooker.

Good results are obtained by allowing the covered dough to rise in the refrigerator overnight or for up to 24 hours. The dough must be allowed to return to room temperature (which will take several hours) before it is shaped.

PREPARING TINS
Unless a recipe states otherwise, tins and baking sheets should be greased. This can be done while the dough is rising.

KNOCKING BACK
The best texture is obtained by kneading the dough for a second time, after rising. This knocks out any large bubbles and ensures an even texture. Turn the risen dough on to a lightly floured work surface and knead for 2–3 minutes. The dough is then shaped as required (see pages 38–9), placed in the prepared tins or on baking sheets, covered with oiled cling film or a clean tea towel and left to rise again.

PROVING OR SECOND RISE
This is the last process before baking. The shaped dough should be allowed to prove – in other words left at room temperature until it has doubled in size and will spring back when lightly pressed with a floured finger. The dough is now ready for glazing (see page 34) and baking.

BAKING
Breads are baked in a very hot oven. When cooked, the bread should be well risen and golden brown and it should sound hollow when tapped underneath with the knuckles. Larger loaves may need to be turned out of the tin and

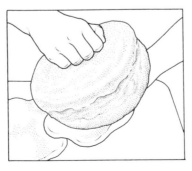

Cooked bread sounds hollow when tapped

returned to the oven upside down for the last 10–15 minutes of the cooking time to ensure they are cooked through. When cooked, remove from the tin and allow to cool on wire racks.

STORING BREAD

If you intend to keep bread for more than one day, put it into a dry, well-ventilated bread bin. The length of time it will keep depends on the ingredients in the dough. An egg and butter enriched bread will keep for longer than a plain loaf. In general, a plain bread will keep for 3–4 days, and a rich dough a few days more.

Bread freezes very well. Wrapped tightly in cling film, foil or sealed in a freezer bag it will keep for several months. It takes about 3–6 hours for a large loaf to thaw. Bread that has been frozen is nicer if refreshed in a hot oven before serving. Slices can be toasted from frozen.

Unbaked bread dough can also be frozen. Although frozen dough will not result in the perfect loaf, it is possible to freeze some for an emergency. The best time to freeze dough is when it has risen once, been knocked back and shaped and is in the tin ready to rise for the second time. Just place each tin in a good-sized, oiled plastic bag, squeeze out the air, tie the bag leaving 2.5 cm (1 inch) space above the dough, and put it into the freezer. To thaw, place the frozen loaf, still in its bag, in a warm – not too hot – place and leave to thaw and rise to double its size. It will then be ready for baking.

BREAD IN THE MICROWAVE COOKER

A microwave cooker is useful for speeding up some of the bread making processes. Milk and water can be warmed by pouring them into a heatproof jug and then cooking on HIGH for 1–2 minutes or until tepid.

Speed up the rising process by putting the dough in a large bowl, covering with a clean tea towel and cooking on HIGH for 15 seconds. Leave to stand for 5 minutes. Repeat the cooking and standing process 5 or 6 times until the dough springs back when pressed lightly.

Bread cooked in a microwave cooker will not have the characteristic crisp crust of conventionally baked bread, because when bread is cooked in the microwave, moisture is drawn to the surface preventing it from becoming crisp. This can be overcome by browning under a hot grill after cooking.

When cooking bread in the microwave, stand the dish on a microwave roasting rack and cook on HIGH. A 450 g (1 lb) loaf will take about 6 minutes and should be left to stand in the dish for 10 minutes after cooking.

To warm bread rolls, place the rolls in a wicker serving basket and cook on HIGH. Six rolls will take about 30 seconds–1 minute.

The microwave is also useful for thawing bread (see the chart below). To absorb the moisture produced, stand on a piece of absorbent kitchen paper (remove the paper as soon as the bread is thawed). For greater crispness, stand the bread on the paper on a microwave rack to allow the air to circulate.

Thawing Times for Bread in the Microwave Cooker

Type	Quantity	Approximate Time on LOW Setting	Special Instructions
Loaf, whole	1 large	6–8 minutes	Uncover and place on absorbent kitchen
Loaf, whole	1 small	4–6 minutes	paper. Turn over during thawing. Stand for 5–15 minutes.
Loaf, sliced	1 large	6–8 minutes	Thaw in wrapper but remove any metal
Loaf, sliced	1 small	4–6 minutes	tags. Stand for 10–15 minutes.
Slice of bread	25 g (1 oz)	10–15 seconds	Place on absorbent kitchen paper. Time carefully. Stand for 1–2 minutes.
Bread rolls	2	15–20 seconds	Place on absorbent kitchen paper. Time carefully. Stand for 2–3 minutes.

BREAD ROLLS (below and pages 38–40)

BASIC BREAD AND ROLLS

Shape into the loaf or rolls on page 38.

•

MAKES 1 LARGE LOAF OR 8 ROLLS

15 g (½ oz) fresh yeast or 7.5 ml (1½ level tsp) dried

about 300 ml (½ pint) tepid milk

450 g (1 lb) strong wholemeal flour or strong white flour

5 ml (1 level tsp) salt

beaten egg, to glaze

poppy, caraway, fennel or sesame seeds

1 Dissolve the fresh yeast in the milk. If using dried yeast, sprinkle it into the milk and leave in a warm place for 15 minutes or until frothy.

2 Put the flour and salt in a bowl. Make a well in the centre, then pour in the yeast liquid. Beat well together until the dough leaves the sides of the bowl clean. If using wholemeal flour, you will need to add a little extra milk.

3 Turn on to a lightly floured surface and knead for about 10 minutes, until smooth and elastic. Place in an oiled bowl. Cover with oiled cling film and leave in a warm place for about 1 hour, until doubled in size.

4 Turn the dough on to a floured surface and knead lightly. Shape into the desired shape or make into rolls (see overleaf). Cover with oiled cling film and leave in a warm place for about 30 minutes or until doubled in size.

5 Brush with beaten egg to glaze and sprinkle with seeds. Bake in the oven at 230°C (450°F) mark 8 for 10 minutes, then reduce the temperature to 200°C (400°F) mark 6 and bake loaves for a further 20–25 minutes or rolls for a further 10 minutes. Cool on a wire rack.

LOAF SHAPES

·

LOAF
For a perfect shape, only fill the tin two-thirds full. Fold the dough in 3, smooth over the top and tuck in the ends.

TIN
Roll out the dough to an oblong and roll up like a Swiss roll. Tuck the ends under and place in the prepared tin. Before baking, score the top of the loaf with a sharp knife if wished.

BATON
Divide the dough into 2 and shape each piece into a long roll with tapering ends, about 35.5 cm (14 inches) long.

COB
Knead the dough into a ball by drawing the sides down and tucking them underneath.

CROWN
Divide the dough into 7 pieces. Knead and shape into rounds, and place in a greased round sandwich tin. To serve, pull apart into rolls.

COTTAGE
Cut one-third off the dough. Knead both pieces well and shape into rounds, place the smaller round on top of the larger one, and place on a baking sheet. Using the handle of a wooden spoon, make a hole through the middle of the smaller piece, pushing down into the larger piece beneath to secure them. Glaze with salt water before baking.

BLOOMER
Flatten the dough and roll up like a Swiss roll. Tuck the ends under and place on a baking sheet. When proved to double its size, make diagonal slits on top with a sharp knife.

PLAIT
Divide the dough into 3 and shape each into a roll about 30.5 cm (12 inches) long. Pinch the ends together and plait loosely, then pinch the other ends together.

ROLL SHAPES

·

COTTAGE ROLLS
Divide the dough into 8 then cut off one-third of each piece. Shape the rolls as for cottage loaf.

PLAITS
Divide the dough into 8 then divide each piece into 3. Shape the pieces into long rolls about 30.5 cm (12 inches) long. Place three of these together. Pinch the ends together to secure and plait loosely, then pinch the other ends together. Repeat with the remaining pieces of dough, to make 8 plaits in all.

KNOTS
Divide the dough into 8. Shape each piece into a thin roll 15 cm (6 inches) long and tie into a knot.

TWIST
Divide the dough into 8, then divide each piece of dough into 2. Shape into thin rolls about 15 cm (6 inches) long. Place 2 strips side by side and hold one set of ends together. Twist the pieces of dough together. Damp the ends and tuck under.

ROUNDS
Divide the dough into 8. Place the pieces on a very lightly floured surface and roll each into a ball: hold the hand flat almost at table level and move it round in a circular motion, gradually lifting the palm to get a good round shape.

RINGS
Divide the dough into 8. Make a thin roll, about 15 cm (6 inches) long, with each piece of dough and bend it round to form a ring. Dampen the ends and mould them together.

FLOURY BAPS
Divide the dough into 8. Shape each piece into a ball, place on a baking sheet and flatten slightly. Cover with oiled cling film and leave in a warm place for about 30 minutes or until doubled in size. Dredge with flour before baking at 200°C (400°F) mark 6 for 15–20 minutes.

BRIDGE ROLLS

Make the dough using white flour. Divide into 24 pieces then shape each into a tapered roll shape and place close together in rows on a baking sheet. Cover with oiled cling film and leave in a warm place for about 30 minutes or until doubled in size. Brush with beaten egg and bake at 220°C (425°F) mark 7 for 15 minutes. Cool on a wire rack before separating into rolls.

POPPY SEED ROLLS

Black poppy seeds add texture and flavour to the bread.

•

MAKES 8

450 g (1 lb) strong white flour
45 ml (3 level tbsp) poppy seeds
5 ml (1 level tsp) salt
5 ml (1 level tsp) sugar
15 g (½ oz) fresh yeast or 7.5 ml (1½ level tsp) dried
325 ml (11 fl oz) tepid milk
beaten egg and milk, to glaze

1   Dissolve the fresh yeast in the milk. If using dried yeast, sprinkle it into the milk and leave in a warm place for 15 minutes or until frothy.
2   Mix the flour, 30 ml (2 level tbsp) poppy seeds, salt and sugar together in a bowl. Pour the yeast mixture and mix well to form a firm dough.
3   Knead the dough for at least 10 minutes until smooth and elastic. Place in an oiled bowl, cover with oiled cling film and leave in a warm place to rise until doubled in size.
4   Knead again for 5 minutes. Divide the dough into 24 pieces. Shape each piece into a ball. On a floured baking sheet, place the dough balls in triangular groups of three.
5   Cover with oiled cling film and leave in a warm place until risen and puffy. Glaze with a mixture of beaten egg and milk. Sprinkle with the remaining poppy seeds.
6   Bake in the oven at 200°C (400°F) mark 6 for about 20 minutes. Cool on a wire rack.

GRANARY BREAD

Granary flour is produced by only one manufacturer but is fairly widely available in most supermarkets. It has a deliciously nutty texture and is well worth seeking out. If you can't find it make your own by mixing 450 g (1 lb) plain wholemeal flour with 175 g (6 oz) strong white plain flour and 175 g (6 oz) soaked, dried cracked wheat. Increase the salt in the basic recipe to 10 ml (2 level tsp).

•

MAKES 2 LARGE LOAVES

450 g (1 lb) Granary flour
175 g (6 oz) strong white plain flour
7.5 ml (1½ level tsp) salt
25 g (1 oz) butter or margarine
25 g (1 oz) fresh yeast or 15 ml (1 level tbsp) dried and 5 ml (1 level tsp) sugar
15 ml (1 level tbsp) malt extract

1   Grease two 1.3 litre (2¼ pint) loaf tins.
2   Mix the flours and salt in a bowl and rub in the butter.
3   Cream the fresh yeast with the malt extract and 150 ml (¼ pint) water and add to the flour with a further 250 ml (9 fl oz) tepid water. If using dried yeast, sprinkle it into the water with the sugar, add the malt extract and a further 250 ml (9 fl oz) tepid water and leave in a warm place for 15 minutes or until frothy.
4   Add the yeast mixture to the flour and butter mixture, and mix to a soft dough. Turn on to a floured surface and knead for 10 minutes, until firm and elastic and no longer sticky.
5   Place in an oiled bowl and cover with oiled cling film. Leave to rise in a warm place until doubled in size. Turn on to a lightly floured surface and knead for 2–3 minutes.
6   Divide the dough into two pieces and knead each piece until smooth and elastic. Shape into oblongs and place in the tins. Cover with oiled cling film and leave in a warm place until the dough is 1 cm (½ inch) above the top of the tins.
7   Bake in the oven at 220°C (425°F) mark 7 for 30–35 minutes or until well risen and hollow-sounding when tapped on the base. Cover lightly with greaseproof paper if browning too quickly. Turn out and cool on a wire rack.

HEDGEHOG ROLLS

Children will have fun helping to make these rolls.

· —————

M A K E S 8

25 g (1 oz) fresh yeast or 15 ml (1 level tbsp) dried and 10 ml (2 tsp) honey
350 g (12 oz) strong wholemeal flour
350 g (12 oz) strong white flour
5 ml (1 level tsp) ground cinnamon
1 egg
16 currants
30 ml (2 tbsp) clear honey, to glaze

1   Dissolve the fresh yeast in 450 ml (¾ pint) tepid water. If using dried yeast, sprinkle it into the tepid water with the honey and leave in a warm place for 15 minutes or until frothy.

2   Put the flours and cinnamon into a large mixing bowl. Make a well in the centre of the flour and pour in the yeast mixture. Mix to form a fairly firm dough.

3   Turn the dough on to a floured surface and knead for about 10 minutes until smooth and elastic. Divide into 8 pieces. Form each piece into an oval-shaped roll and shape one end into a point to form a 'nose'. Arrange on a greased baking sheet and cover with oiled cling film. Leave in a warm place until doubled in size.

4   Lightly beat the egg with 5 ml (1 tsp) water and brush over the rolls. Using the points of kitchen scissors, snip each roll to create 'spikes', leaving the nose end plain. Insert 2 currants for eyes. Cover with oiled cling film and leave in a warm place for about 30 minutes or until doubled in size.

5   Bake in the oven at 230°C (450°F) mark 8 for 15–20 minutes, until cooked through and golden brown. Warm the honey and brush over the hot rolls to give a sticky glaze.

BRIDGE ROLLS AND FLOURY BAPS (page 38–39)

FRENCH BREAD (below)

FRENCH BREAD

A roasting tin full of hot water placed in the oven during cooking produces steam and gives a light airy crumb.

•

MAKES 2 STICKS

15 g (½ oz) fresh yeast or 7.5 ml (1½ level tsp) dried and 5 ml (1 level tsp) sugar
350 g (14 oz) plain flour
50 g (2 oz) cornflour
5 ml (1 level tsp) salt
1 egg

1 Blend the fresh yeast with 250 ml (½ pint) tepid water. If using dried yeast, sprinkle it into the tepid water with the sugar and leave in a warm place for 15 minutes or until frothy.

2 Sift the plain flour and cornflour with the salt into a large bowl. Make a well in the centre of the dry ingredients and pour in the yeast liquid. Using a wooden spoon gradually beat the flour into the liquid until a firm dough is formed.

3 Turn the dough on to a lightly floured surface and knead for about 10 minutes or until the dough is smooth and elastic. Place in an oiled bowl, cover with oiled cling film and leave in a warm place for about 1 hour or until doubled in size.

4 Divide the dough in two and knead each piece until just smooth. On a well-floured surface roll each piece out to an oblong about 35.5 × 15 cm (14 × 6 inches) leaving the ends rounded off. Carefully roll up the dough from the long side like a Swiss roll. Place the rolls, seam side down, on well-floured baking sheets.

5 Using a sharp knife slash along the top of the dough at 4 cm (1½ inch) intervals. Make these diagonal cuts to a depth of 5 mm (¼ inch) only. Beat the egg with a good pinch of salt until well mixed. Brush all over the surface of the loaves, making sure it doesn't collect in the grooves.

6 Place the loaves in a warm place for about 1 hour until well puffed up. They should feel springy to the touch and have doubled in size. The dough is not covered so that a skin will form. This gives the traditional hard crust.

7 Preheat the oven to 220°C (425°F) mark 7 and place a roasting tin of hot water in the base. Bake the loaves for 15 minutes then remove the pan of water. Continue baking the loaves for a further 8–10 minutes or until well browned and really crisp. The loaves should sound hollow when tapped. Cool on a wire rack.

41

EMMENTAL PUFF ROLLS

These rich, cheese-flavoured rolls are delicious served warm with soups and salads.

•

MAKES 8

15 g (½ oz) fresh yeast or 7.5 ml (1½ level tsp) dried

50 ml (2 fl oz) tepid milk

225 g (8 oz) strong white flour

5 ml (1 level tsp) salt

75 g (3 oz) butter

1 egg, beaten

15 ml (1 tbsp) mild wholegrain mustard

50 g (2 oz) Emmental cheese, coarsely grated

45 ml (3 level tbsp) freshly grated Parmesan cheese

milk, to glaze

1 Blend the fresh yeast with the milk and 30 ml (2 tbsp) tepid water. If using dried yeast, sprinkle it into the milk and water and leave in a warm place for 15 minutes or until frothy.

2 Mix the flour and salt together in a large bowl. Rub in 25 g (1 oz) of the butter. Make a well in the centre and pour in the yeast liquid. Mix to a firm dough. Knead for 10 minutes or until smooth then place in an oiled bowl, cover with oiled cling film and leave in a warm place for 1 hour or until doubled in size.

3 Knead the dough again for 2–3 minutes then roll out on a lightly floured surface to a 38 × 15 cm (15 × 6 inch) rectangle.

4 Beat together the remaining butter with the mustard and the Emmental cheese. Dot one-third of the butter mixture over the bottom two-thirds of the dough. Fold the top third down and the bottom third up. Press to seal. Repeat twice more until all the butter mixture is used. Wrap and chill for 30 minutes.

5 Roll the dough out to a 30.5 cm (12 inch) square and sprinkle with half of the Parmesan. Cut into four equal strips and place these on top of each other. Slice through the pieces of dough into eight equal pieces.

6 Lay the slices on their side so that the four layers show and place in patty or bun tins. Cover and leave in a warm place for 10 minutes or until slightly puffy.

7 Brush with milk, sprinkle with the remaining Parmesan and bake in the oven at 200°C (400°F) mark 6 for about 25 minutes or until golden brown. Serve warm.

QUICK PEANUT LOAF

This bread, which is given only one rising, has a slightly closer texture than the traditionally prepared loaf.

•

MAKES 1 LOAF

15 g (½ oz) fresh yeast or 7.5 ml (1½ level tsp) dried and 5 ml (1 level tsp) sugar

450 g (1 lb) strong plain white flour

5 ml (1 level tsp) salt

60 ml (4 level tbsp) crunchy peanut butter

milk for glazing

sea salt

1 Dissolve the fresh yeast in 325 ml (11 fl oz) tepid water. If using dried yeast, sprinkle it into the tepid water with the sugar and leave in a warm place for 15 minutes or until frothy.

2 Place the flour and salt in a bowl, then using a fork 'cut' in the peanut butter. Make a well in the centre and pour in the yeast liquid and mix to a soft dough.

3 Turn out on to a lightly floured surface and knead for about 10 minutes until smooth and no longer sticky.

4 Lightly grease two 900 ml (1½ pint)/450 g (1 lb) loaf tins. Divide the dough in two and knead into oblong shapes to fit the tins. Place the dough seam-side down in the prepared tins. Cover loosely with oiled cling film and leave in a warm place for about 1 hour or until doubled in size.

5 Using a large sharp knife, make a shallow cut along each loaf. Brush with milk and sprinkle over a little sea salt.

6 Bake at 230°C (450°F) mark 8 for about 20 minutes or until well risen, golden brown and hollow-sounding when tapped. Cool on a wire rack.

ZIGZAG BATON

The zigzag shape is easy to do and is very effective.

•

MAKES 1 LOAF

15 g (½ oz) fresh yeast or *7.5 ml (1½ level tsp) dried*
about 300 ml (½ pint) tepid milk
225 g (8 oz) plain wholemeal flour
225 g (8 oz) strong white flour
10 ml (2 level tsp) salt
25 g (1 oz) butter
beaten egg, to glaze
poppy seeds, to decorate

1 Blend the fresh yeast with the milk. If using dried yeast, sprinkle it into the milk and leave in a warm place for 15 minutes or until frothy.
2 Mix together the flours and salt in a large bowl then rub in the butter.
3 Make a well in the centre, add the yeast liquid and mix with a wooden spoon. If too dry, add a little lukewarm water.
4 Turn the dough on to a floured surface and knead for 10 minutes until smooth and elastic. Place in a bowl, cover with oiled cling film and leave in a warm place for 1 hour or until doubled in size.
5 Turn on to a floured surface and knead for 2–3 minutes. Using both hands, roll the dough into a sausage shape, about 40.5 cm (16 inches) long. Place on a greased baking sheet.
6 With a pair of sharp scissors held at a 30° angle to the top surface of the dough, make V-shaped cuts about three-quarters of the way through it at 5 cm (2 inch) intervals.
7 Pull each section of dough out to alternate sides to give a 'zigzag' appearance. Leave to prove in a warm place for about 1 hour or until doubled in size.
8 Brush the dough with beaten egg, then sprinkle with poppy seeds. Bake in the oven at 230°C (450°F) mark 8 for 30 minutes until golden. Cool on a wire rack before serving.

PARSNIP BREAD

The parsnips give a hint of sweetness and add moisture to the loaf.

•

MAKES 1 LOAF

450 g (1 lb) parsnips
25 g (1 oz) butter or margarine
15 g (½ oz) fresh yeast or *7.5 ml (1½ level tsp) dried*
225 ml (8 fl oz) tepid milk
450 g (1 lb) Granary flour
5 ml (1 level tsp) salt
milk, to glaze
30 ml (2 level tbsp) cracked wheat

1 Peel the parsnips, cut into chunks and boil for about 20 minutes or until tender. Drain well then mash with the butter until smooth. Leave to cool.
2 Blend the fresh yeast with the milk. If using dried yeast, sprinkle it into the milk and leave in a warm place for 15 minutes or until frothy.
3 Place the flour and salt in a bowl and stir in the parsnip purée. Make a well in the centre and pour in the yeast liquid. Mix to a soft dough. Turn out on to a lightly floured surface and knead for about 10 minutes until the dough is smooth and no longer sticky.
4 Place the dough in a lightly oiled bowl, cover loosely with oiled cling film and leave in a warm place for 1 hour or until doubled in size.
5 Knead the dough, divide into three, then knead and roll out each piece into a 35.5 cm (14 inch) long sausage shape. Place the strips on a lightly greased baking sheet, pinching them together at one end to join. Working carefully and without stretching the dough, plait the loaf. Make sure that the bottom edges are well sealed.
6 Brush with a little milk and sprinkle over the cracked wheat. Leave in a warm place until it has doubled in size and is spongy to the touch.
7 Bake in the oven at 200°C (400°F) mark 6 for about 30 minutes or until golden brown and hollow-sounding when tapped. Cover lightly with greaseproof paper if browning too quickly.

SAGE AND ONION BREAD

This is a mouth-watering savoury bread that fills the kitchen with an aroma of herbs as it bakes. Serve it warm with soup, or well buttered with cheese or pâté and salad, for a simple lunch. Using dried sage will still give good results.

· • ·

M A K E S   2   S M A L L   L O A V E S

15 g (½ oz) fresh yeast or 7.5 ml (1½ tsp) dried
300 ml (½ pint) tepid milk
1 large onion, skinned and finely chopped
25 g (1 oz) butter
225 g (8 oz) strong white flour
225 g (8 oz) strong wholemeal flour
5 ml (1 level tsp) salt
pepper
30 ml (2 tbsp) chopped fresh sage or 5 ml (1 level tsp) dried
milk, to glaze
cracked wheat for sprinkling

SAGE AND ONION BREAD (below)

1 Dissolve the fresh yeast in the milk. If using dried yeast, sprinkle it into the milk and leave in a warm place for 15 minutes or until frothy.
2 Meanwhile, put the onion and the butter in a small saucepan, cover and cook gently for about 5 minutes, until the onion is soft and transparent but not browned.
3 Put the flours, salt, pepper and sage in a large bowl and mix together. Make a well in the centre, then pour in the softened onion and the butter and the yeast liquid. Beat well together until the dough leaves the sides of the bowl clean.
4 Turn on to a lightly floured surface and knead well for about 10 minutes, until smooth and elastic. Place in an oiled bowl, cover with oiled cling film and leave in a warm place for about 1 hour, until doubled in size.
5 Turn the dough on to a floured surface and knead lightly. Divide into two, shape into rounds and place on a large greased baking sheet.
6 Brush with a little milk and sprinkle with cracked wheat. Cover and leave in a warm place for about 30 minutes, until doubled in size. Bake in the oven at 230°C (450°F) mark 8 for 15 minutes, then reduce the oven temperature to 200°C (400°F) mark 6 and bake for a further 15 minutes. When cooked the loaves will be well risen and golden brown, and sound hollow if tapped on the bottom. Cool slightly and serve warm, or turn on to a wire rack and leave to cool completely.

ONION LOAF

A basic milk dough which is topped with golden onion slices. It is delicious served with just a hint of warmth.

•

MAKES 1 LOAF

15 g (½ oz) fresh yeast or 7.5 ml (1½ level tsp) dried
225 ml (8 fl oz) tepid milk
350 g (12 oz) strong white flour
5 ml (1 level tsp) salt
pinch cayenne pepper
25 g (1 oz) butter or margarine
15 ml (1 tbsp) olive oil
2 medium onions skinned and sliced
1 egg yolk

1 Dissolve the fresh yeast in the milk. If using dried yeast, sprinkle it into the milk and leave in a warm place for 15 minutes or until frothy.
2 Put the flour, salt and cayenne pepper in a bowl, then rub in the butter. Make a well in the centre of the flour and pour in the yeast liquid. Mix to a soft dough then turn out on to a lightly floured surface and knead for about 10 minutes until smooth and no longer sticky.
3 Place the dough in a lightly oiled bowl, cover loosely with oiled cling film and leave in a warm place for 1 hour or until doubled in size.
4 Knead the dough then shape into a flat round, about 18 cm (7 inches) in diameter. Place on a floured baking sheet and with a sharp knife slash the dough into six wedges. Cover loosely with oiled cling film and leave in a warm place until doubled in size and spongy to the touch.
5 Meanwhile heat the oil in a frying pan, then add the onions, cover and cook until they are beginning to soften but not colour. Drain well.
6 Uncover the dough, brush with the lightly beaten egg yolk and spoon over the onions. Bake in the oven at 220°C (425°F) mark 7 for 15–20 minutes, then reduce the temperature to 200°C (400°F) mark 6 for a further 15–20 minutes or until well risen, hollow-sounding when tapped and the onions are golden brown. Cover lightly with greaseproof paper if the onions brown too quickly. Serve warm.

SESAME MALT RING

The malt extract gives depth to the flavour of this bread, you'll find it in health food stores and some chemists.

•

MAKES 2 RINGS

25 g (1 oz) fresh yeast or 15 ml (1 level tbsp) dried and 5 ml (1 level tsp) sugar
60 ml (4 tbsp) malt extract
700 g (1½ lb) plain wholemeal flour
10 ml (2 level tsp) salt
30 ml (2 level tbsp) sesame seeds

1 Dissolve the fresh yeast in 150 ml (¼ pint) tepid water. If using dried yeast, sprinkle it into the tepid water with the sugar and leave in a warm place for 15 minutes or until frothy. Dissolve the malt extract in a further 300 ml (½ pint) tepid water.
2 Place the flour and half of the salt in a bowl. Make a well in the centre and pour in the yeast and malt liquids. Mix to a soft dough then turn out on to a lightly floured surface and knead for about 10 minutes until smooth and no longer sticky.
3 Place the dough in a lightly oiled bowl, cover loosely with oiled cling film and leave to rise in a warm place for about 1 hour or until it has doubled in size.
4 Knead the dough and divide into twelve. Knead each piece into a small smooth round and flatten slightly. Flour two baking sheets and arrange six rounds on each, overlapping slightly to form a circle. Cover loosely with oiled cling film and leave until doubled in size and spongy to the touch.
5 Dissolve the remaining salt in 30 ml (2 tbsp) boiling water and brush over the rolls. Sprinkle with the sesame seeds.
6 Bake in the oven at 220°C (425°F) mark 7 for about 25 minutes or until well risen, golden brown and hollow-sounding when tapped. Cover lightly with greaseproof paper if browning too quickly.

BEER BREAD

A substantial Danish bread – known as øllebrød – that is delicious served with slices of cheese.

·

MAKES 3 LOAVES

25 g (1 oz) fresh yeast or 15 ml (1 level tbsp) dried and 5 ml (1 level tsp) sugar

350 ml (12 fl oz) light ale

150 ml (5 fl oz) molasses or *black treacle*

450 g (1 lb) plain rye flour

700 g (1½ lb) strong white flour

15 ml (1 level tbsp) salt

1 Dissolve the fresh yeast in 375 ml (13 fl oz) tepid water. If using dried yeast, sprinkle it into the tepid water with the sugar and leave in a warm place for 15 minutes or until frothy.

2 Mix the yeast liquid with the light ale and molasses and stir into the flours and salt, beating well to form a soft dough. Turn out on to a lightly floured surface and knead until the dough is elastic and smooth.

3 Place the dough in a large oiled bowl, and cover with oiled cling film. Leave to rise in a warm place for about 1 hour or until doubled in size.

4 Turn out on to a lightly floured surface and knead again for about 5 minutes. Divide into three and shape each into an oblong. Place on greased baking sheets and cover loosely with oiled cling film. Leave in a warm place until doubled in size – about 20 minutes.

5 Bake in the oven at 200°C (400°F) mark 6 for 10 minutes and then reduce the temperature to 170°C (325°F) mark 3 for a further 30 minutes, or until the loaf is brown and sounds hollow when tapped on the bottom. Cool on wire racks.

POPPY SEED AND HONEY BAGELS

Bagels or beigels, are Jewish ring-shaped rolls.

·

MAKES 12

15 g (½ oz) fresh yeast or 7.5 ml (1½ level tsp) dried and 5 ml (1 level tsp) sugar

50 g (2 oz) butter or margarine

30 ml (2 tbsp) runny honey

275 g (10 oz) strong plain white flour

175 g (6 oz) plain wholemeal flour

5 ml (1 level tsp) salt

30 ml (2 level tbsp) poppy seeds

milk for glazing

1 Blend the fresh yeast with 225 ml (8 fl oz) tepid water. If using dried yeast, sprinkle it into the water with the sugar and leave in a warm place for 15 minutes or until frothy. Heat the butter with the honey then cool.

2 Place the flours, salt and 10 ml (2 level tsp) poppy seeds in a bowl. Make a well in the centre and pour in the yeast liquid and cooled margarine. Mix to a soft dough.

3 Turn the dough out on to a floured surface and knead until smooth and no longer sticky.

4 Place in lightly oiled bowl, cover loosely with oiled cling film and leave in a warm place until doubled in size.

5 Knead for 5 minutes then divide the dough into 12. Knead each piece until smooth then roll to a sausage shape about 18 cm (7 inches) long. Dampen the ends and seal together to form a ring.

6 Place the rings well apart on lightly greased baking sheets, cover loosely with oiled cling film and leave until doubled in size.

7 Half fill a frying pan with water, heat to simmering point then add the bagels a few at a time. Simmer for 20 seconds only (the bagels will puff up), drain well then place on well-greased baking sheets.

8 Brush each bagel with milk and sprinkle over the remaining poppy seeds. Bake at 200°C (400°F) mark 6 for about 20 minutes or until well risen and golden brown.

PUMPKIN BREAD

A shiny amber-coloured loaf with an unusual flavour.

· · ·

M A K E S   1   L O A F

450 g (1 lb) pumpkin

15 g (½ oz) fresh yeast or 7.5 ml (1½ level tsp) dried

275 ml (½ pint) tepid milk

2.5 ml (½ level tsp) sugar

450 g (1 lb) plain wholemeal flour

2.5 ml (½ level tsp) salt

beaten egg to glaze

30 ml (2 level tbsp) dried pumpkin seeds

1 Roughly chop the pumpkin, discarding the seeds. Cook in boiling water for 20–25 minutes until very tender. Drain well, cool and peel. Put in a blender or food processor and purée until smooth.

2 Blend the fresh yeast with a little of the measured milk. Add the remaining milk and sugar. If using dried yeast, sprinkle it into the milk with the sugar and leave in a warm place for 15 minutes or until frothy.

3 Rub the pumpkin purée into the flour and salt. Pour in the yeast mixture. Mix to a firm dough. Knead for 10 minutes until smooth. Place in an oiled bowl, cover with oiled cling film and leave in a warm place for 30–40 minutes or until doubled in size.

4 Knead the dough again for 5 minutes. Divide into 12 pieces, then knead each piece into a smooth ball.

5 Grease a 900 g (2 lb) loaf tin. Dust lightly with flour. Place 6 balls of dough evenly in the tin. Brush with beaten egg. Place the remaining dough on top. With a sharp knife cut down straight through both lines of dough. Cover and leave in a warm place for 15–20 minutes or until doubled in size.

6 Brush with beaten egg. Sprinkle with roughly chopped pumpkin seeds.

7 Bake in the oven at 200°C (400°F) mark 6 for about 50 minutes until well risen and golden brown. Cool on a wire rack.

DARK RYE BREAD

Rye flour used on its own produces rather dense, heavy bread, as rye lacks sufficient protein for the formation of gluten. It is therefore always mixed with a strong flour in bread making.

· · ·

M A K E S   1   L O A F

350 g (12 oz) rye flour

50 g (2 oz) plain wholemeal flour

finely grated rind of 1 lemon

5 ml (1 level tsp) salt

25 g (1 oz) butter

5 ml (1 level tsp) caraway seeds, lightly crushed (optional)

125 g (4 oz) cool mashed potato

15 g (½ oz) fresh yeast or 7.5 ml (1½ level tsp) dried and 5 ml (1 level tsp) sugar

5 ml (1 level tsp) sugar

50 g (2 oz) molasses or black treacle

1 Mix together the flours, lemon rind and salt. Rub in the butter, caraway seeds and mashed potato.

2 Blend the fresh yeast with 150 ml (¼ pint) tepid water. If using dried yeast, sprinkle it into the water with 5 ml (1 tsp) sugar and leave in a warm place for 15 minutes or until frothy. Heat the other 5 ml (1 tsp) sugar, molasses and 30 ml (2 tbsp) water together. Cool until tepid.

3 Pour the yeast liquid and molasses mixture on to the dry ingredients. Beat well to form a firm dough.

4 Knead on a lightly floured surface for 10 minutes until smooth and no longer sticky. Place in an oiled bowl, cover with oiled cling film and leave to rise in a warm place for about 1½ hours until doubled in size.

5 Knead again for 5 minutes then shape into a large round, about 18 cm (7 inches) in diameter. Place on a baking sheet. Cut a criss-cross pattern on the surface of the loaf to a depth of 5 mm (¼ inch). Dust with a little more flour. Leave to rise in a warm place for 10–15 minutes.

6 Bake in the oven at 200°C (400°F) mark 6 for about 50 minutes. Cool on a wire rack.

OLIVE BREAD

This loaf is bursting with olives. For a less rich dough, use half the quantity of olives; chop them a little more finely and knead into the risen dough. Shape into an oblong and prove as before.

·

MAKES ABOUT 2 LOAVES

25 g (1 oz) fresh yeast or 15 ml (1 level tbsp) dried and 5 ml (1 level tsp) sugar

400 g (14 oz) strong white flour

50 g (2 oz) buckwheat flour

2.5 ml (½ level tsp) salt

freshly ground black pepper

15 ml (1 tbsp) olive oil

225 g (8 oz) pitted black olives, roughly chopped

1 Blend the fresh yeast with 300 ml (½ pint) tepid water. If using dried yeast, sprinkle it into the water with the sugar and leave in a warm place for 15 minutes or until frothy.

2 Put the flours, salt and pepper in a bowl then add the yeast liquid and mix to a moist dough, adding a little more water if necessary.

3 On a lightly floured surface, knead the dough for 10–12 minutes, or until smooth. Place in a large oiled bowl and cover with oiled cling film. Leave in a warm place for about 1 hour until doubled in size.

4 Turn out the dough on to a floured surface, punch down and press out until quite flat. Drizzle over the olive oil and knead again until smooth.

5 Halve the dough, roll out each piece to a 30.5 × 20.5 cm (12 × 8 inch) rectangle. Spread with the olives. Roll up tightly from the longest edge and place on an oiled baking sheet. Brush with water and make 3 or 4 slashes across the top of each loaf. Leave to rise for about 15 minutes.

6 Bake in the oven at 230°C (450°F) mark 8 for 15 minutes. Reduce the temperature to 190°C (375°F) mark 5 and continue to bake for a further 45 minutes or until the loaves sound hollow when tapped on the base. Cool on a wire rack.

BRIOCHE

The French traditionally serve brioche warm for breakfast, with a large cup of milky coffee or chocolate and homemade fruit preserves.

·

MAKES 1 LOAF

15 g (½ oz) fresh yeast or 7.5 ml (1½ level tsp) dried yeast and a pinch of sugar

225 g (8 oz) strong white flour

a pinch of salt

15 ml (1 level tbsp) caster sugar

2 eggs, beaten

50 g (2 oz) butter or block margarine, melted

beaten egg, to glaze

1 Brush a 1.1 litre (2 pint) fluted mould with oil.

2 Blend the fresh yeast with 25 ml (5 tsp) tepid water. If using dried yeast, sprinkle it into the water with the pinch of sugar and leave in a warm place for 15 minutes or until frothy.

3 Mix together the flour, salt and sugar. Stir the yeast liquid into the flour, with the eggs and melted butter. Work to a soft dough, turn out on to a floured board and knead for about 5 minutes, until smooth and elastic.

4 Put the dough in a large oiled bowl, cover with oiled cling film and leave in a warm place for about 1 hour until doubled in size.

5 Knead the dough well on a lightly floured surface. Shape three-quarters of it into a ball and place in the bottom of the mould. Press a hole in the centre as far as the tin base. Shape the remaining dough into a 'knob', put into the hole and press down lightly.

6 Cover with oiled cling film and leave in a warm place until the dough is light and puffy and nearly reaches the top of the mould.

7 Brush lightly with beaten egg and bake in the oven at 230°C (450°F) mark 8 for 15–20 minutes, until golden. Turn out and serve at once or cool on a wire rack.

Brioche (opposite)

VARIATIONS

Individual Brioches

For small brioches divide the dough into 12 pieces, put into deep 7.5 cm (3 inch) oiled fluted patty tins, and bake as above for about 10 minutes. Serve hot or cool on wire racks.

Saucisson en Brioche

Roll the dough out to a 25.5 cm (10 inch) square keeping a 7.5 cm (3 inch) strip across the centre twice the thickness of the strips on either side. Skin a 450 g (1 lb) piece of garlic sausage about 14 cm (5½ inches) long and place on the centre of the dough. Brush the dough and the sausage with beaten egg then fold it to cover the sausage completely. Place the loaf, seam side down, in a 1.1 litre (2 pint) loaf tin. Cover and leave in a warm place for 30–40 minutes or until the dough comes to the top of the tin. Brush with beaten egg and bake at 190°C (375°F) mark 5 for 35 minutes. Prepare 200 ml (7 fl oz) aspic jelly. When it is just on the point of setting, make two holes on the top of the loaf and pour in the jelly. Leave to set.

GOLDEN CORNMEAL BREAD

Cornmeal, which is, as the name suggests, ground corn, gives this bread a bright yellow colour and a distinctive flavour and texture. Don't be surprised by the addition of sugar; it helps bring out the flavour but still produces a savoury bread. Add other flavourings such as chopped chillis or coriander, if you like.

•

MAKES 2 LOAVES

15 g (½ oz) fresh yeast or 7.5 ml (1½ level tsp) dried

about 375 ml (13 fl oz) tepid milk

350 g (12 oz) cornmeal

450 g (1 lb) strong white flour

100 g (4 oz) light brown soft sugar

10 ml (2 level tsp) salt

50 g (2 oz) butter or margarine

corn or maize meal for sprinkling

1 Blend the fresh yeast with the milk. If using dried yeast, sprinkle it into the milk and leave in a warm place for 15 minutes or until frothy.
2 Put the cornmeal, flour, sugar and salt in a bowl. Rub in the butter. Make a well in the centre then pour in the yeast liquid to make a soft dough, adding a little more milk if necessary.
3 Knead on a floured surface for 10 minutes or until smooth and elastic. Place in an oiled bowl, cover with oiled cling film and leave to rise in a warm place for about 1 hour or until doubled in size.
4 Knead the dough for 5 minutes then divide into two. Shape each piece into a 15 cm (6 inch) round and place on two greased baking sheets. Cover and leave in a warm place until doubled in size.
5 Using a sharp knife mark the top of each loaf in squares. Brush with water then sprinkle generously with corn or maize meal. Bake in the oven at 230°C (450°F) mark 8 for 15 minutes, then reduce the temperature to 190°C (375°F) mark 5 for 15 minutes or until well risen and the loaves sound hollow if tapped on the bottom. Cool on a wire rack.

BROWN SODA BREAD

Soda bread is quick to make as it does not require the long preparation of a yeast dough. However, it must be eaten quickly, preferably warm from the oven, as it stales much quicker than yeast bread.

•

MAKES 8 WEDGES

225 g (½ lb) plain wholemeal flour

125 g (4 oz) plain white flour

50 g (2 oz) medium oatmeal

7.5 ml (1½ level tsp) bicarbonate of soda

7.5 ml (1½ level tsp) cream of tartar

3.75 ml (¾ level tsp) salt

40 g (1½ oz) butter or margarine

about 200 ml (7 fl oz) milk

30 ml (2 tbsp) lemon juice

milk, for glazing

oatmeal, for sprinkling

1 In a large bowl thoroughly mix the flours, oatmeal, the bicarbonate of soda, cream of tartar and salt. Rub in the butter.
2 Mix the milk with the lemon juice. Stir into the dry ingredients until a soft dough is formed. Add a little more milk if necessary. Knead *lightly* until just smooth.
3 Pat out the dough to an 18 cm (7 inch) round and place on a greased baking sheet. Mark the top into eight wedges. Brush with a little milk and sprinkle lightly with oatmeal.
4 Bake in the oven at 220°C (425°F) mark 7 for about 30 minutes. Serve warm.

VARIATIONS

Cheese Soda Bread
At the end of stage 1, add **75 g (3 oz) grated Cheddar cheese, 45 ml (3 level tbsp) chopped fresh herbs** and **25 g (1 oz) grated onion.** Complete as above.

Sultana Tea Bread
At the end of stage 1, add **75 g (3 oz) sultanas, 25 g (1 oz) cut mixed peel** and **30 ml (2 level tbsp) soft brown sugar.** Complete as above.

NAN

In India, this flat, tear-drop-shaped bread is traditionally baked on the side of a tandoor oven.

•

MAKES 6

15 g (½ oz) fresh yeast or 7.5 ml (1½ tsp) dried

about 150 ml (¼ pint) tepid milk

450 g (1 lb) plain white flour

5 ml (1 level tsp) baking powder

2.5 ml (½ level tsp) salt

10 ml (2 level tsp) caster sugar

1 egg, beaten

30 ml (2 tbsp) vegetable oil

60 ml (4 tbsp) natural yogurt

1   Blend the fresh yeast with the milk. If using dried yeast, sprinkle it into the milk and leave in a warm place for 15 minutes or until frothy.
2   Sift the flour, baking powder and salt into a large bowl. Make a well in the centre and stir in the sugar, egg, oil and yogurt.
3   Add the yeast liquid and mix well to a soft dough, adding more milk if necessary. Turn the dough on to a lightly floured surface and knead well for 10 minutes until smooth and elastic.
4   Place the dough in a bowl, cover with oiled cling film and leave to rise in a warm place for about 1 hour until doubled in size.
5   Knead the dough on a lightly floured surface for 2–3 minutes, then divide into 6 equal pieces. Roll out each piece on a lightly floured surface and shape into a large tear-drop about 25 cm (10 inches) long.
6   Place a nan on a baking sheet and put under a preheated hot grill. Cook for 1½–2 minutes on each side until golden brown and puffy. Cook the remaining nan in the same way. Serve warm.

VARIATION

Peshawari Nan (Nan with sultanas and almonds)

Follow the recipe above to the beginning of step 5. To make the filling, mix together **175 g (6 oz) sultanas, 45 ml (3 tbsp) chopped fresh coriander, 175 g (6 oz) ground almonds** and **90 ml**

(6 tbsp) melted butter. Knead the dough on a lightly floured surface and divide into 6 equal pieces. Roll out into a round about 15 cm (6 inches) in diameter. Spoon the filling into the centre of the Nan and fold over the dough to completely enclose the filling. Press the edges well together to seal. Roll out each piece on a lightly floured surface and shape into a large tear-drop about 25 cm (10 inches) long. Cook as in step 6 of the recipe above.

OAT SQUARES

Oatmeal gives an interesting texture and flavour.

•

MAKES ABOUT 10

50 g (2 oz) fine oatmeal

125 g (4 oz) Granary flour

125 g (4 oz) strong white flour

2.5 ml (½ level tsp) salt

15 g (½ oz) fresh yeast or 7.5 ml (1½ level tsp) dried and 5 ml (1 level tsp) sugar

coarse oatmeal for sprinkling

1   Mix together the oatmeal, flours and salt.
2   Blend the fresh yeast with 175 ml (6 fl oz) tepid water. If using dried yeast, sprinkle it into the tepid water with the sugar and leave in a warm place for 15 minutes or until frothy.
3   Gradually beat the yeast liquid into the dry ingredients. Mix together to form a firm dough.
4   Turn on to a lightly floured surface and knead for at least 10 minutes until smooth and elastic. Place in an oiled bowl, cover with oiled cling film and leave to rise in a warm place until doubled in size.
5   Knead again for 5 minutes. With a lightly floured rolling pin, roll the dough out until 1 cm (½ inch) thick. Cut into 6 cm (2½ inch) squares. Continue until all the dough is used.
6   Place the dough squares on a lightly floured baking sheet, cover and leave to rise in a warm place for 10 minutes.
7   Brush the dough with salt water and sprinkle with coarse oatmeal. Bake in the oven at 200°C (400°F) mark 6 for 20–25 minutes. Cool on a wire rack.

PITTA BREAD

Homemade pitta bread is not quite the same as the perfectly pocketed manufactured kind. However, if you follow this recipe exactly most of your pittas, if not all, should have a pocket, and they will all retain a soft, pliable crust.

MAKES 16

15 g (½ oz) fresh yeast or 7.5 ml (1½ level tsp) dried and 5 ml (1 level tsp) sugar

700 g (1½ lb) strong white flour

5 ml (1 level tsp) salt

15 ml (1 level tbsp) sugar

15 ml (1 tbsp) olive oil

1   Blend the fresh yeast with 450 ml (¾ pint) tepid water. If using dried yeast, sprinkle it into the water with the sugar and leave in a warm place for 15 minutes or until frothy.
2   Put the flour, salt and sugar in a bowl, make a well in the centre and pour in the yeast liquid with the olive oil. Mix to a smooth dough, then turn out on to a floured surface and knead for 10 minutes until smooth and elastic.
3   Place the dough in a large bowl, cover with oiled cling film and leave to rise in a warm place until doubled in size.
4   Divide the dough into 16 pieces and roll each into an oval shape about 20.5 cm (8 inches) long. Place on floured baking sheets, cover with oiled cling film and leave in a warm place for about 30 minutes or until slightly risen and puffy.
5   Bake in batches at 240°C (475°F) mark 9 for 5–8 minutes only. The pittas should be just lightly browned on top. Remove from the oven and wrap in a clean tea towel.
6   Repeat with the remaining pittas. When the pittas are warm enough to handle, but not completely cold, transfer them to a plastic bag and leave until cold. This will ensure that they have a soft crust.
7   To serve, warm in the oven, or toast lightly. Split and fill with salads, cheese, cold meats or your favourite sandwich filling. Or, cut into strips and serve with dips.

SESAME AND CUMIN BREAD STICKS

These crisp, slightly spicy bread sticks are perfect for serving with taramasalata, hummus or your favourite dip.

MAKES ABOUT 32

15 g (½ oz) fresh yeast or 7.5 ml (1½ level tsp dried) and 5 ml (1 level tsp) sugar

450 g (1 lb) strong white flour

7.5 ml (1½ level tsp) salt

5 ml (1 level tsp) ground cumin

50 g (2 oz) butter or margarine

30 ml (2 tbsp) sesame oil

30 ml (2 tbsp) vegetable oil

1 egg, beaten

45 ml (3 tbsp) sesame seeds

30 ml (2 tbsp) cumin seeds

1   Blend the fresh yeast with 200 ml (7 fl oz) tepid water. If using dried yeast sprinkle it into the water with the sugar and leave in a warm place for 15 minutes or until frothy.
2   Put the flour, salt and cumin in a large bowl. Put the butter and oils in a small saucepan and heat gently until the butter is melted. Make a well in the centre of the dry ingredients and pour in the fat with the yeast liquid. Mix to make a dough, adding a little extra water if necessary.
3   Turn the dough out on to a floured surface and knead for 10 minutes until smooth and elastic. Place in an oiled bowl, cover with oiled cling film and leave in a warm place for 1 hour or until doubled in size.
4   Knead the dough for 2–3 minutes then divide into 32 pieces. Roll each piece into a sausage shape about 20.5 cm (8 inches) long. Place on greased baking sheets.
5   Brush with beaten egg and sprinkle with the sesame and cumin seeds. Bake in the oven at 200°C (400°F) mark 6 for 15–20 minutes or until golden brown. Turn off the oven and leave the breadsticks to cool in the oven. When cold they should be crisp. Store in an airtight container.

Sesame and Cumin Bread Sticks and Pitta Bread (opposite)

CROISSANTS

Croissants should always be served warm and crisp from the oven. To reheat, place on a baking sheet and cook at 200°C (400°F) mark 6 for 5–10 minutes or until hot.

·

MAKES 12

25 g (1 oz) fresh yeast or 15 ml (1 level tbsp) dried yeast and 5 ml (1 level tsp) sugar
2 eggs
450 g (1 lb) strong white flour
10 ml (2 level tsp) salt
25 g (1 oz) lard
225 g (8 oz) unsalted butter, at cool room temperature
2.5 ml (½ level tsp) caster sugar

1 Blend the fresh yeast with 225 ml (8 fl oz) tepid water. If using dried yeast, sprinkle it into the water with the sugar and leave in a warm place for 15 minutes or until frothy.

2 Whisk one egg into the yeast liquid. Sift the flour and salt into a large bowl and rub in the lard. Make a well in the centre and pour in the yeast liquid. Mix and then beat in the flour until the bowl is left clean. Turn on to a lightly floured surface, knead well for about 10 minutes until the dough is firm and elastic.

3 Roll out the dough on a floured surface to an oblong about 51 × 20.5 cm (20 × 8 inches). Keep the edges as square as possible, gently pulling out the corners to stop them rounding off. Dust the rolling pin with flour to prevent it sticking to the dough.

4 Divide the butter into three. Dot one portion over the top two-thirds of the dough but clear of the edge. Turn up the bottom third of the dough over half the butter, then fold down the remainder. Seal the edges with a rolling pin. Turn the dough so that the fold is on the right.

5 Press the dough lightly at intervals along its length, then roll out to an oblong again. Repeat rolling and folding with the other two portions of butter. Rest dough in refrigerator for 30 minutes, loosely covered with a clean tea towel. Repeat 3 more times, cover and chill for 1 hour.

6 Roll out the dough to an oblong about 48 × 33 cm (19 × 13 inches), lay a clean tea towel over the top and leave to rest for 10 minutes. Trim off 1 cm (½ inch) all around and divide the dough in half lengthways, then into three squares, then across into triangles.

7 Beat the remaining egg, 15 ml (1 tbsp) water and sugar together for the glaze and brush it over the triangles. Roll each triangle up from the long edge finishing with the tip underneath. Curve into crescents and place well apart on ungreased baking sheets, allowing room to spread. Cover loosely with a clean tea towel.

8 Leave at room temperature for about 30 minutes, or until well risen and 'puffy'. Brush carefully with more glaze. Bake in the oven at 220°C (425°F) mark 7 for about 15 minutes, until crisp and well browned.

PUMPERNICKEL

Pumpernickel is characteristically moist and dense.

·

MAKES 2 LOAVES

700 g (1½ lb) rye flour
225 g (8 oz) plain wholemeal flour
20 ml (4 level tsp) bran
7.5 ml (1½ level tsp) salt
60 ml (4 tbsp) molasses or black treacle

1 Grease and base line two 1.1 litre (2 pint) pudding basins. Place the flours, bran and salt in a bowl. Make a well in the centre.

2 Dissolve the molasses in 150 ml (¼ pint) boiling water. Pour this into the well with a further 600 ml (1 pint) tepid water.

3 Using a wooden spoon, gradually mix together and beat until evenly blended. The mixture will be very soft. Divide between the prepared basins, cover with greased greaseproof paper and foil. Secure with string.

4 Steam for 4½ hours or until dark brown and firm to touch. Check the water level regularly.

5 Turn out the bread and allow to cool. When cold wrap in greaseproof paper and foil and store in the refrigerator for 4 days before eating. Before serving refresh, covered, in a hot oven for about 20 minutes.

CRUMPETS

Crumpets are satisfying to make. To serve, they should be toasted on both sides until a light golden brown, spread generously with butter and served while still warm.

·

MAKES ABOUT 24

350 g (12 oz) strong white flour

15 g (½ oz) fresh yeast or 7.5 ml (1½ level tsp) dried yeast and a pinch of sugar

2.5 ml (½ level tsp) salt

2.5 ml (½ level tsp) bicarbonate of soda

225 ml (8 fl oz) milk

vegetable oil

1   Sieve 175 g (6 oz) flour into a mixing bowl and crumble in the fresh yeast. Make a well in the centre of the flour and pour in 300 ml (½ pint) tepid water. Gradually mix together until smooth, beating well as the flour is worked into the liquid. Cover and leave to stand in a warm place for about 15 minutes or until frothy.
2   If using dried yeast, sprinkle it into the water with the pinch of sugar and leave in a warm place for 15 minutes or until frothy.
3   Meanwhile, sieve the remaining flour, salt and bicarbonate of soda into a large bowl (if dried yeast is being used, all the flour will be added at this stage). Make a well in the centre, then pour in the yeast mixture and the milk. Mix to give a thick batter consistency.
4   Using a wooden spoon, vigorously beat the batter for about 5 minutes to incorporate air. Cover and leave in a warm place for about 1 hour, until sponge-like in texture. Beat the batter for a further 2 minutes to incorporate more air.
5   Place a large, preferably non-stick frying pan on to a high heat and, using absorbent kitchen paper, rub a little oil over the surface. Grease the insides of three crumpet rings or three 8 cm (3¼ inch) plain metal pastry cutters. Place the rings blunt edge down on to the hot surface and leave for about 2 minutes, or until very hot.
6   Pour the batter into a large measuring jug. Pour a little batter into each ring to a depth of 1 cm (½ inch). Cook the crumpets for 5–7

minutes until the surface of each appears dry and is honeycombed with holes.
7   When the batter has set, carefully remove each metal ring. Flip the crumpet over and cook the second side for 1 minute only. Cool on a wire rack.
8   Continue cooking the crumpets until all the batter is used. It is important that the frying pan and metal rings are well oiled each time, and heated before the batter is poured in.

CHEESE LOAF

Use a strong-flavoured Cheddar, such as Farmhouse, for the best flavour.

·

MAKES 2 LOAVES

450 g (1 lb) strong white flour

salt and pepper

5 ml (1 level tsp) mustard powder

100–175 g (4–6 oz) Cheddar cheese, grated

15 g (½ oz) fresh yeast or 7.5 ml (1½ level tsp) dried and a pinch of sugar

1   Mix together the flour, salt, pepper and mustard in a large bowl. Stir in three-quarters of the cheese.
2   Blend the fresh yeast and 300 ml (½ pint) tepid water together. If using dried yeast, sprinkle it into the water with the pinch of sugar and leave in a warm place for 15 minutes or until frothy. Add the yeast liquid to the dry ingredients and mix to a soft dough.
3   Turn on to a floured surface and knead for about 10 minutes, until the dough feels firm and elastic and no longer sticky. Cover with a clean tea towel and leave to rise in a warm place for about 45 minutes, until doubled in size. Turn on to a floured surface and knead for 5 minutes.
4   Divide the dough into two and shape to fit two greased 450 g (1 lb) loaf tins. Cover with oiled cling film and leave to prove in a warm place, until the dough reaches the top of the tins. Sprinkle with the remaining cheese.
5   Bake in the oven at 190°C (375°F) mark 5 for 40–45 minutes, until well risen and golden brown on top. Turn out and cool on a wire rack.

SWEET BREADS

These special breads are yeast mixtures enriched with fat, eggs and sugar. Fruit and spices are usually added too and the dough then moulded into fancy shapes or baked in decorative tins.

Adding eggs and butter makes the dough rich, light and moist with a soft crust and a moist yellow crumb. The more of these ingredients that are added, the nearer the bread comes to having a cake-like taste and texture. Once the enriched dough is made, the possibilities for fillings and flavourings are endless. The dough can be layered with a rich filling of chocolate and poppy seeds as in the famous Viennese Gugelhupf; or rolled with a purée of dried apricots as in Iced Apricot Buns.

All the instructions for savoury breads apply, so read pages 34–36 before starting.

ICED APRICOT BUNS (*page 58*), DEVONSHIRE SPLITS
(*page 63*)

ICED APRICOT BUNS

These delicious, sticky buns can also be made with other dried fruit such as pears, peaches, figs or dates. Amaretto in the icing is not essential but gives it a certain kick!

·

M A K E S   1 0

FOR THE DOUGH

20 g (¾ oz) fresh yeast or 10 ml (2 level tsp) dried

300 ml (½ pint) tepid milk

450 g (1 lb) strong white flour

50 g (2 oz) caster sugar

2.5 ml (½ level tsp) salt

100 g (4 oz) butter or margarine, melted

1 egg, beaten

FOR THE FILLING

225 g (8 oz) no-soak dried apricots

25 g (1 oz) caster sugar

1.25 ml (¼ level tsp) ground cinnamon

25 g (1 oz) ground almonds

25 g (1 oz) toasted flaked almonds

FOR THE ICING

50 g (2 oz) icing sugar

15 ml (1 tbsp) Amaretto

25 g (1 oz) toasted flaked almonds, to decorate

1   To make the dough, blend the fresh yeast with the milk. If using dried yeast, sprinkle it into the milk and leave in a warm place for 15 minutes or until frothy.

2   Put the flour, sugar and salt in a bowl. Make a well in the centre then pour in the yeast liquid with the butter and egg. Beat well to make a soft dough that leaves the sides of the bowl clean.

3   Turn the dough on to a floured surface and knead for about 10 minutes, until smooth, elastic and no longer sticky. Put the dough in a large oiled bowl and cover with oiled cling film. Leave in a warm place until doubled in size.

4   To make the filling, put the apricots and 300 ml (½ pint) water in a saucepan and bring to the boil. Cover and simmer gently for about

30 minutes. Leave to cool. Blend the apricots and their cooking water with the sugar and cinnamon to make a smooth purée or rub through a sieve. Stir in the ground almonds and flaked almonds.

5   Turn the dough on to a floured surface and knead again lightly. Grease a 24 cm (9½ inch) springform cake tin. Roll out the dough on a floured surface to a 38 cm (15 inch) square. Spread the apricot mixture over the dough. Carefully roll the dough up and cut into 10 slices. Arrange in the prepared tin, cut side down.

6   Cover with oiled cling film and leave in a warm place for 30 minutes or until doubled in size.

7   Bake in the oven at 190°C (375°F) mark 5 for about 45 minutes or until golden brown and firm to the touch. Turn out and cool on a wire rack for 20 minutes.

8   To make the icing, sieve the icing sugar into a bowl and blend with the Amaretto to make a thin icing. Drizzle over the buns and sprinkle with the almonds. Leave to cool completely.

LONDON BUNS

These little, orange-flavoured yeast buns became popular in the 18th century at the fashionable Old Chelsea Bun House in Pimlico.

·

M A K E S   1 2

15 g (½ oz) fresh yeast or 7.5 ml (1½ level tsp) dried

300 ml (½ pint) tepid milk

450 g (1 lb) strong white flour

pinch of nutmeg

50 g (2 oz) caster sugar

40 g (1½ oz) butter, melted

30 ml (2 level tbsp) chopped mixed peel

finely grated rind of 1 orange

beaten egg, to glaze

coarse sugar, to decorate

1   Blend the fresh yeast with the milk. If using dried yeast, sprinkle it on to the milk and leave in a warm place for 15 minutes or until frothy.

2 Sift the flour and nutmeg into a large bowl and stir in the sugar. Make a well in the centre, pour in the yeast liquid and the butter, add the peel and orange rind and mix to a soft dough.
3 Turn on to a floured surface and knead well, until the dough feels firm and elastic. Place in an oiled bowl, cover with oiled cling film and leave to rise for about 1 hour until doubled in size.
4 Turn on to a floured surface and knead well, divide into twelve pieces and knead each piece into a round bun. Put them on a greased baking sheet and leave to prove until doubled in size.
5 Bake in the oven at 200°C (400F) mark 6 for 25 minutes. Brush the buns with beaten egg, sprinkle with sugar and return to the oven for 5 minutes to glaze. Cool on a wire rack.

SCENTED FRUIT LOAF

The combination of scented honey, lemon and orange rind, and spices gives this bread a delicious aroma.

·

MAKES 10–12 SLICES

FOR THE FILLING

450 g (1 lb) mixed dried fruit such as apples, peaches, apricots, chopped

30 ml (2 tbsp) orange or other scented honey

50 ml (2 fl oz) dark rum

45 ml (3 tbsp) lemon juice

7.5 ml (1½ tsp) grated lemon rind

7.5 ml (1½ tsp) grated orange rind

1.25 ml (¼ tsp) ground cardamom

2.5 ml (½ tsp) ground coriander

FOR THE DOUGH

15 g (½ oz) fresh yeast or 7.5 ml (1½ level tsp) dried

75–100 ml (3–4 fl oz) tepid milk

40 g (1½ oz) butter or margarine, chopped

50 g (2 oz) caster sugar

about 275 g (10 oz) strong plain flour

large pinch of salt

2 egg yolks, beaten

FOR THE ICING

50 g (2 oz) icing sugar

toasted flaked almonds, to decorate

1 To make the filling bring 450 ml (¾ pint) of water to the boil in a heavy-based saucepan. Add the dried fruits and simmer until they are very soft, stirring frequently. Stir in the honey, rum, lemon juice, fruit rinds and spices. Simmer, stirring frequently, until the liquid has been absorbed by the fruit. Leave to cool.
2 Meanwhile, to make the dough, blend the fresh yeast with half of the milk. If using dried yeast, sprinkle it into half of the milk and leave in a warm place for 15 minutes or until frothy. Gently warm the remaining milk with the butter and sugar until the butter has melted and the sugar dissolved. Leave to cool.
3 Sift the flour and salt into a bowl. Make a well in the centre. Pour the egg yolks into the well, followed by the milk and then the yeast liquid. Gradually draw the dry ingredients into the liquids to give a smooth dough.
4 Beat well, then turn on to a lightly floured surface and knead for 10 minutes. Transfer the dough to a lightly oiled bowl, cover with lightly oiled cling film and leave to rise in a warm place for about 1 hour or until doubled in size.
5 Knock the dough down and knead for 2–3 minutes then press out into a large rectangle, about 1 cm (½ inch) thick. Spread the fruit filling over the dough leaving a narrow border around the edges. Dampen the edges and roll up the dough like a Swiss roll. Press the edges firmly together to seal.
6 Transfer the roll to a large buttered baking sheet, placing the seam underneath, and forming the roll into a horse-shoe shape if necessary. Cover with oiled cling film and leave to rise in a warm place until puffy.
7 Bake at 180°C (350°F) mark 4 for about 20–25 minutes, until golden brown and the loaf sounds hollow when tapped on the bottom. Transfer to a wire rack and cool to lukewarm.
8 Blend the icing sugar with about 15 ml (1 tbsp) water to make a smooth paste. Brush the loaf with the icing, allowing it to trickle down the sides, and sprinkle with the nuts. Leave to cool and set.

CHELSEA BUNS

The London shop from which these buns originated would, in its heyday, sell as many as 250,000 buns in one day. The owner, Richard Hand, was known as 'Captain Bun'. The buns are easily recognized, as the dough is baked in a flat coil and given a shiny sugar glaze.

•

MAKES 12

15 g (½ oz) fresh yeast or 7.5 ml (1½ tsp) dried
100 ml (4 fl oz) tepid milk
225 g (8 oz) strong white flour
2.5 ml (½ level tsp) salt
40 g (1½ oz) butter, diced
1 egg, beaten
100 g (4 oz) mixed dried fruit
50 g (2 oz) light brown soft sugar
clear honey, to glaze

1 Blend the fresh yeast with the milk. If using dried yeast, sprinkle it on to the milk and leave in a warm place for 15 minutes or until frothy.
2 Put the flour and salt in a bowl, then rub in 25 g (1 oz) of the butter until the mixture resembles fine breadcrumbs. Make a well in the centre, pour in the yeast liquid and the egg, then beat together until the mixture forms a dough that leaves the sides of the bowl clean.
3 Turn on to a lightly floured surface and knead well for 10 minutes, until smooth and elastic. Place in an oiled bowl, cover with oiled cling film and leave in a warm place for about 1 hour, until doubled in size.
4 Knead the dough lightly on a floured surface, then roll out to a large rectangle, measuring about 30 × 23 cm (12 × 9 inches). Mix the dried fruit and sugar together. Melt the remaining butter, then brush over the dough. Scatter with the fruit mixture, leaving a 2.5 cm (1 inch) border around the edges.
5 Roll the dough up tightly like a Swiss roll, starting at a long edge. Press the edges together to seal, then cut the roll into 12 slices. Place the rolls cut side uppermost in a greased 17.5 cm (7 inch) square tin. Cover with oiled cling film and leave in a warm place for 30 minutes, until doubled in size.
6 Bake in the oven at 190°C (375°F) mark 5 for 30 minutes, until well risen and golden brown. Brush them with the honey while still hot. Leave to cool slightly in the tin before turning out. Serve warm.

YORKSHIRE TEA CAKES

To make spicy tea cakes, add 5 ml (1 level tsp) ground mixed spice to the flour.

•

MAKES 8

15 g (½ oz) fresh yeast or 7.5 ml (1½ level tsp) dried
300 ml (½ pint) tepid milk
450 g (1 lb) strong white flour
5 ml (1 level tsp) salt
50 g (2 oz) butter or margarine
25 g (1 oz) caster sugar
100 g (4 oz) currants
25 g (1 oz) chopped mixed peel
milk, to glaze

1 Blend the fresh yeast with the milk. If using dried yeast, sprinkle it on to the milk and leave in a warm place for 15 minutes or until frothy.
2 Mix together the flour and salt, rub in the butter and stir in the sugar, currants and peel. Add the yeast liquid and mix to give a fairly soft dough.
3 Beat well and knead on a lightly floured surface for about 10 minutes, until smooth. Place in an oiled bowl, cover with oiled cling film and leave in a warm place for about 1 hour or until doubled in size.
4 Turn on to a lightly floured surface, knead lightly and divide into 8 equal pieces. Roll each out to a 10 cm (4 inch) round. Put on two greased baking sheets and brush with milk.
5 Cover with oiled cling film and leave to rise for 30 minutes, until doubled in size. Bake in the oven at 200°C (400°F) mark 6 for about 20 minutes or until risen and golden brown. Cool on a wire rack. To serve, split in two and butter or split, toast and serve hot and buttered.

YORKSHIRE TEA CAKES (opposite)

PLAITED HAZELNUT BREAD

Serve with hot chocolate for a delicious breakfast.

·

MAKES 1 LARGE LOAF

FOR THE DOUGH

25 g (1 oz) fresh yeast or 15 ml (1 tbsp) dried
300 ml (½ pint) tepid milk
700 g (1½ lb) strong white flour
2.5 ml (½ level tsp) salt
50 g (2 oz) butter or margarine
finely grated rind of 1 lemon
1 egg

FOR THE FILLING

100 g (4 oz) butter
100 g (4 oz) ground hazelnuts
75 g (3 oz) dark brown soft sugar
75 g (3 oz) fresh wholemeal breadcrumbs
finely grated rind and juice of 1 lemon
10 ml (2 level tsp) ground mixed spice
5 ml (1 level tsp) ground cardamom
beaten egg, to glaze

1 To make the dough, blend the fresh yeast with the milk. If using dried yeast, sprinkle it on to the milk and leave in a warm place for 15 minutes or until frothy.

2 Meanwhile, put the flour and salt in a bowl and rub in the butter. Beat the lemon rind, the egg and 150 ml (¼ pint) tepid water into the yeast liquid then pour into the dry ingredients. Beat well, then turn out on to a floured surface and knead for 10 minutes until smooth. Put into an oiled bowl, cover with oiled cling film and leave in a warm place for 1 hour or until doubled in size.

3 To make the filling, beat the butter until soft then beat in the remaining ingredients.

4 Knead the dough for 2–3 minutes then divide into 3. Roll each piece into a 20.5 × 35.5 cm (8 × 14 inch) rectangle. Spread the dough evenly with the filling.

5 Starting from a long edge roll each piece of dough into a long sausage. Press the ends together to seal. Using a sharp knife make 4 deep cuts along the length of each piece of dough to reveal the filling.

6 Join the 3 pieces together at the top then plait together. Press the ends together. Transfer to a baking tray. Cover and leave in a warm place for about 30 minutes or until puffy.

7 Brush with beaten egg to glaze, then bake in the oven at 200°C (400°F) mark 6 for about 30–35 minutes or until golden brown.

WHOLEMEAL APPLE ROLLS

Grated apple gives these rolls a slightly sweet flavour.

·

MAKES 8

15 g (½ oz) fresh yeast or 7.5 ml (1½ tsp) dried and 5 ml (1 tsp) clear honey
225 g (8 oz) plain wholemeal flour
225 g (8 oz) strong white flour
75 g (3 oz) eating apple, peeled and grated
wholemeal flour, for dusting

1 Blend the fresh yeast with 150 ml (¼ pint) tepid water. If using dried yeast, sprinkle it on to the tepid water mixed with the honey, and leave in a warm place for 15 minutes or until frothy.

2 Mix together the flours, then add the yeast liquid, apple and 150 ml (¼ pint) tepid water and mix to a soft dough. Knead on a lightly floured surface for 10 minutes until smooth and no longer sticky. Place in an oiled bowl, cover with oiled cling film and leave to rise in a warm place for 1 hour or until doubled in size.

3 Turn out on to a lightly floured surface, knead for a few minutes, then divide the dough into 8 pieces. Shape into rolls about 7.5 cm (3 inches) long. Place on a greased baking sheet, cover with oiled cling film and leave in a warm place for 30 minutes, until doubled in size.

4 Dust with flour and bake at 230°C (450°F) mark 8 for 15–20 minutes, until the rolls sound hollow when the bases are tapped.

SCANDINAVIAN SAFFRON COFFEE BREAD

Saffron gives this dough a subtle flavour and a warm yellow colour. Serve sliced with coffee.

MAKES 1 LOAF

15 g (½ oz) fresh yeast or 7.5 ml (1½ level tsp) dried
90 ml (3½ fl oz) milk
large pinch of saffron stamens
75 g (3 oz) butter or margarine
50 g (2 oz) caster sugar
2 eggs
350 g (12 oz) strong white flour
pinch of salt
5 ml (1 level tsp) ground cardamom
25 g (1 oz) soft brown sugar
40 g (1½ oz) blanched almonds
10 ml (2 level tsp) ground cinnamon
beaten egg, to glaze
chopped almonds, to decorate
brown sugar, to decorate

1 Crumble the fresh yeast into a bowl. Warm the milk with the saffron until tepid, strain then pour on to the yeast. If using dried, sprinkle it into the warmed milk and leave in a warm place for 15 minutes until frothy. Stir well.
2 Meanwhile, melt 50 g (2 oz) of the butter and leave to cool. Stir into the yeast liquid with the caster sugar and the eggs.
3 Place the flour, salt and cardamom in a large bowl. Make a well in the centre and pour in the liquid ingredients and mix until smooth.
4 Turn on to a floured surface and knead thoroughly until smooth and elastic. Place the dough in a lightly oiled bowl, cover with oiled cling film and leave until doubled in size.
5 Knead the dough for 5 minutes, then roll into an oblong about 51 × 30.5 cm (20 × 12 inches). Cover the surface with pats of the remaining butter then sprinkle with the brown sugar, almonds and cinnamon.

6 Roll the dough up tightly to form a long sausage, pinching the edges together to seal. Curl the ends around to form a ring, join and seal together. Place on a greased baking sheet and cut the dough from above three-quarters of the way through, at 2.5 cm (1 inch) intervals. Gently ease alternate cut sections forward and back to show the layers in the dough.
7 Cover lightly with oiled cling film and leave for about 15–20 minutes until puffy. Glaze with beaten egg, sprinkle with a few chopped nuts and a little brown sugar. Bake in the oven at 200°C (400°F) mark 6 for about 20–25 minutes.

DEVONSHIRE SPLITS

When eaten with cream and treacle Devonshire Splits are known as 'thunder and lightning'.

MAKES 16

15 g (½ oz) fresh yeast or 7.5 ml (1½ level tsp) dried
about 300 ml (½ pint) tepid milk
450 g (1 lb) strong plain flour
5 ml (1 level tsp) salt
50 g (2 oz) butter
30 ml (2 level tbsp) sugar

1 Blend the fresh yeast with half of the milk. If using dried yeast, sprinkle it into half of the milk and leave in a warm place for 15 minutes or until frothy.
2 Mix the flour and salt and make a well in the centre. Heat the butter and sugar in the remaining milk until tepid. Stir into the flour with the yeast liquid. Beat to an elastic dough, turn it out on to a floured surface and knead until smooth. Place in an oiled bowl, cover with oiled cling film and leave in a warm place for about 1 hour or until doubled in size.
3 Turn the dough on to a lightly floured surface and divide into 16 pieces. Knead each lightly into a ball then flatten slightly. Place on a greased baking sheet, cover with oiled cling film and leave in a warm place for about 20 minutes or until risen and puffy.
4 Bake in the oven at 220°C (425°F) mark 7, for 15–20 minutes until well risen and golden.

HONEY HAZELNUT TWIST

A highly-glazed, coiled bread packed with honey and nuts.

·

MAKES 10–12 SLICES

60 ml (4 tbsp) tepid milk

15 g (½ oz) fresh yeast or 5 ml (1 tsp) dried

175 g (6 oz) strong white flour

2.5 ml (½ level tsp) salt

75 g (3 oz) butter or block margarine, diced

15 ml (1 tbsp) caster sugar

1 egg, size 6

50 g (2 oz) shelled hazelnuts

75 ml (5 tbsp) thick honey

1 Grease a 18 cm (7 inch) straight-sided sandwich tin. Line the base with greaseproof paper and grease the paper.

2 Blend the fresh yeast with the milk. If using dried yeast, sprinkle on to the milk and leave in a warm place for about 15 minutes or until frothy.

3 Sift the flour with the salt into a bowl and rub in 50 g (2 oz) of the butter until the mixture resembles fine breadcrumbs. Stir in the sugar and beat in the egg and the yeast liquid to form a soft dough.

4 Turn out on to a lightly floured surface and

Honey Hazelnut Twist (above)

knead for about 5 minutes until smooth. Put into an oiled bowl, cover with oiled cling film and leave in a warm place for about 1 hour until doubled in size.

5   Meanwhile, spread the nuts out on a baking sheet and brown in the oven at 200°C (400°F) mark 6 for 5–10 minutes. Put into a clean tea towel and rub off the skins. Grind the nuts in an electric blender or food processor.

6   Beat the remaining butter with the nuts and 45 ml (3 tbsp) honey to a smooth paste.

7   Turn the dough out on to a floured surface, knead again lightly and roll out to an oblong 61 × 20 cm (24 × 8 inches). Spread the honey mixture over the surface.

8   Roll up from a long edge. Coil into the prepared sandwich tin starting in the middle of the tin. Press down firmly. Cover with oiled cling film and leave for about 45 minutes until doubled in size.

9   Bake in the oven at 200°C (400°F) mark 6 for 20–25 minutes until golden brown. Turn out on to a wire rack and brush at once with the remaining honey. Leave to cool completely.

STRAWBERRY SAVARIN

A savarin is an open-textured, spongy yeast cake. Once cooked it is soaked in a sugar or liqueur syrup and the centre is usually filled with fruit. Serve as a delicious dessert for a dinner party with lashings of lightly whipped cream.

•

M A K E S   6   S L I C E S

15 g (½ oz) fresh yeast or 7.5 ml (1½ tsp) dried
45 ml (3 tbsp) tepid milk
2 eggs, lightly beaten
50 g (2 oz) butter, melted and cooled
100 g (4 oz) plain white flour
15 ml (1 level tbsp) caster sugar
25 g (1 oz) desiccated coconut
90 ml (6 tbsp) redcurrant jelly or sieved strawberry jam
75 ml (5 tbsp) lemon juice
450 g (1 lb) strawberries, hulled

1   Lightly oil a 1.3 litre (2¼ pint) savarin tin or ring mould and turn it upside down on absorbent kitchen paper to drain off the excess oil.

2   Blend the fresh yeast with the milk. If using dried yeast, sprinkle it on to the milk and leave in a warm place for 15 minutes or until frothy. Gradually beat the eggs and butter into the yeast liquid.

3   Mix the flour in a bowl with the sugar and coconut. With a wooden spoon, gradually stir in the yeast mixture to form a thick smooth batter. Beat together thoroughly.

4   Turn into the prepared tin, cover with oiled cling film and leave in a warm place for about 30 minutes or until the savarin is nearly doubled in size.

5   Bake in the oven at 190°C (375°F) mark 5 for 35–40 minutes until golden. Turn out on to a wire rack placed over a large plate. Put the jelly and lemon juice into a small pan over low heat.

6   When the jelly is melted spoon over the warm savarin until well glazed, allowing any excess to collect on the plate under the wire rack. Transfer the savarin to a serving plate.

7   Return the excess jelly mixture to the pan and add the strawberries; stir to coat. Remove from heat and cool for 15–20 minutes or until almost set, then spoon into the middle of the savarin. Serve warm or cold with soured cream.

VARIATIONS

Strawberry Babas

Divide the yeast batter between six 9 cm (3½ inch) ring tins. Leave to rise until the moulds are nearly two-thirds full then bake for 15–20 minutes. Replace the lemon juice with **brandy** or **kirsch**, soak each baba well and place on individual serving plates. Finish with strawberries and soured cream as above.

Rum Babas

Make as strawberry babas but soak the warm babas in a rum syrup made with **120 ml (8 tbsp) clear honey, 120 ml (8 tbsp) water and rum** or **rum essence** to taste. Serve filled with **whipped cream**.

DANISH PASTRIES

*The basic dough can be made into any of the classic
shapes below, or be adventurous and invent your own.*

———————————— • ————————————

M A K E S   1 6

FOR THE DOUGH

25 g (1 oz) fresh yeast or 15 ml (1 level tbsp)
dried and 5 ml (1 level tsp) sugar

450 g (1 lb) plain flour

5 ml (1 level tsp) salt

50 g (2 oz) lard

30 ml (2 level tbsp) sugar

2 eggs, beaten

300 g (11 oz) butter or margarine, softened

50 g (2 oz) sultanas

beaten egg, to glaze

FOR THE ALMOND PASTE

15 g (½ oz) butter or margarine

75 g (3 oz) caster sugar

75 g (3 oz) ground almonds

1 egg, beaten

FOR THE CINNAMON BUTTER

50 g (2 oz) butter

50 g (2 oz) caster sugar

10 ml (2 level tsp) ground cinnamon

FOR THE GLACÉ ICING

100 g (4 oz) icing sugar

about 15 ml (1 tbsp) warm water

flaked almonds to decorate

1 Blend the fresh yeast with 150 ml (¼ pint)
tepid water. If using dried yeast, sprinkle it on to
the water with the sugar and leave in a warm
place for 15 minutes, until frothy.
2 Mix the flour and salt, rub in the lard and
stir in the sugar. Add the yeast liquid and beaten
eggs and mix to an elastic dough, adding a little
more water if necessary. Knead well for
5 minutes on a lightly floured surface, until
smooth. Return the dough to the rinsed-out

bowl, cover with a clean tea towel and leave the
dough to 'rest' in the refrigerator for
10 minutes.
3 Shape the butter into an oblong. Roll out the
dough on a floured board to an oblong about
three times as wide as the butter. Put the butter
in the centre of the dough and fold the sides of
the dough over the butter. Press the edges to
seal.
4 With the folds at the sides, roll the dough
into a strip three times as long as it is wide; fold
the bottom third up, and the top third down,
cover and leave to 'rest' for 10 minutes. Turn,
repeat, rolling, folding and resting twice more.
5 To make the almond paste, cream the butter
and sugar, stir in the almonds and add enough
egg to make a soft and pliable consistency.
6 Make the cinnamon butter by creaming the
butter and sugar and beating in the cinnamon.
7 Roll out the dough into the required shapes
and fill with almond paste or cinnamon butter.
8 After shaping, cover the pastries with a
clean tea towel and leave to prove in a warm
place for 20–30 minutes. Brush with beaten egg
and bake in the oven at 220°C (425°F) mark 7
for about 15 minutes.
9 Meanwhile sift the icing sugar into a basin
and add enough water to make a smooth, thin
glacé icing.
10 While the pastries are hot brush with the
icing and sprinkle with flaked almonds.

Shaping Danish Pastries

Crescents Cut out a 23 cm (9 inch) round.
Divide into four segments and put a little
almond paste at the base of each. Roll up from
the base and curl round to form a crescent.
Imperial stars Cut into 7.5 cm (3 inch) squares
and make diagonal cuts from each corner to
within 1 cm (½ inch) of the centre. Put a piece of
almond paste in the centre of the square and
fold one corner of each cut section down to the
centre, securing the tips with beaten egg.
Foldovers and cushions Cut into 7.5 cm (3 inch)
squares and put a little almond paste in the
centre. Fold over two opposite corners to the
centre. Make a cushion by folding over all four
corners, securing the tips with beaten egg.
Pinwheels Cut into a rectangle 25.5 × 10 cm

(10 × 4 inches). Spread with cinnamon butter and sultanas, roll up like Swiss rolls and cut into 2.5 cm (1 inch) slices. Bake cut side upwards.

Twists Cut into rectangles as for pinwheels. Cut each rectangle lengthways to give four pieces. Spread with cinnamon butter and fold the bottom third of each up and the top third down, seal and cut each across into thin slices. Twist these slices and put on a baking sheet.

BOSTON BROWN BREAD

This dense rich bread is cooked in clean, empty cans. You will need cans which contained 397 g (14 oz) of tomatoes, baked beans or something similar. The bread is perfectly round and ideal for children's sandwiches. Try it thinly sliced and filled with cream cheese and smoked salmon.

MAKES 3 SMALL LOAVES

100 g (4 oz) plain wholemeal flour
100 g (4 oz) rye flour
175 g (6 oz) corn or maize meal
7.5 ml (1½ level tsp) bicarbonate of soda
7.5 ml (1½ level tsp) salt
300 ml (½ pint) milk
150 ml (¼ pint) natural yoghurt
225 g (8 oz) black treacle
175 g (6 oz) seedless raisins

1   Line three 450 ml (¾ pint) tins or pudding basins with greaseproof paper. Grease well.

2   Put all the ingredients into a large bowl and beat thoroughly together.

3   Pour into the tins, cover with greaseproof paper and foil then secure with string.

4   Place the tins on a trivet or an upturned heatproof plate, in a large deep saucepan, and add boiling water to come halfway up the tins.

5   Cover the saucepan and simmer gently for 1½ hours or until a skewer inserted comes out clean. Don't forget to top up the water, as necessary, during cooking. Turn out on to a wire rack and cool.

BATH BUNS

These were created in Bath in the 18th century at the time when it was fashionable for the rich to 'take the waters' at Bath Spa.

MAKES ABOUT 18

25 g (1 oz) fresh yeast or 15 ml (1 level tbsp) dried
150 ml (¼ pint) tepid milk
450 g (1 lb) strong white flour
5 ml (1 level tsp) salt
50 g (2 oz) caster sugar
50 g (2 oz) butter, melted and cooled
2 eggs, beaten
175 g (6 oz) sultanas
30–45 ml (2–3 level tbsp) chopped mixed peel
beaten egg, to glaze
crushed sugar lumps, to decorate

1   Blend the fresh yeast with the milk and 60 ml (4 tbsp) tepid water. If using dried yeast, sprinkle it on to the water and leave in a warm place for 15 minutes or until frothy.

2   Sift together the flour and salt and add the sugar. Make a well in the centre and stir in the butter, eggs, yeast mixture, sultanas and peel and mix well. The dough should be fairly soft.

3   Turn on to a floured surface and knead until smooth. Place in an oiled bowl, cover with oiled cling film and leave in a warm place for about 1 hour or until doubled in size. Knead well. Divide into 18 pieces, roll each into a ball and place on 2 greased baking sheets. Cover with oiled cling film and leave in a warm place for about 1 hour or until doubled in size.

4   Brush with egg and sprinkle with crushed sugar. Bake in the oven at 190°C (375°F) mark 5, for about 15 minutes, until golden brown. Cool on a wire rack and serve buttered.

STRAWBERRY SAVARIN (page 65)

RUM AND CHOCOLATE GUGELHUPF (page 70)

LARDY CAKE

Warm or cold, lardy cake is sweet, filling and delicious. It originates from Wiltshire, and in the West Country local bakers still make it to their own recipes, cramming in as much lard, sugar and fruit as they or their customers choose.

•

MAKES 8 PIECES

25 g (1 oz) fresh yeast or 15 ml (1 level tbsp) dried

5 ml (1 level tsp) caster sugar

450 g (1 lb) strong white flour

10 ml (2 level tsp) salt

175 g (6 oz) lard, chilled

175 g (6 oz) mixed sultanas and currants

50 g (2 oz) chopped mixed peel

175 g (6 oz) sugar

caster sugar, for sprinkling

1 Grease a 20.5 × 25 cm (8 × 10 inch) tin. Blend the fresh yeast with the sugar and 300 ml (½ pint) tepid water. If using dried yeast, sprinkle it on to the water with the sugar and leave in a warm place for 15 minutes or until frothy.

2 Sift the flour and salt together into a bowl. Dice 15 g (½ oz) of the lard, toss in the flour, then rub it in. Form a well in the centre, pour in the yeast liquid, then draw in the dry ingredients and mix to a dough that leaves the sides of the bowl clean.

3 Turn on to a lightly floured work surface and knead well for 10 minutes until smooth and elastic. Place in a clean bowl. Cover with oiled cling film and leave in a warm place for about 1 hour or until doubled in size.

4 Turn the dough on to a floured surface and roll out to a rectangle about 0.5 cm (¼ inch) thick. Cut the remaining lard into small pieces and dot one-third of it over the surface of the dough and sprinkle over one-third of the fruit, peel and sugar. Fold the dough in three, folding the bottom third up and the top third down. Give a half turn and roll out as before, repeating the process twice more.

6 Grease a 20.5 × 25 cm (8 × 10 inch) tin. Roll the dough out to fit the tin, cover with oiled cling film and leave in a warm place for 20–30 minutes until puffy.

7 Score the top into 8 rectangles, then bake in the oven at 220°C (425°F) mark 7 for about 45 minutes until golden brown. Cool on a wire rack. When cold sprinkle with caster sugar.

RUM AND CHOCOLATE GUGELHUPF

This famous Austrian cake has as many variations in the spelling of its name as it does in the ingredients included. Basically, it is a rich bread baked in a fancy ring-shaped mould. This version is a very rich mixture indeed, flavoured with rum, fruit and chocolate and filled with poppy seeds. Because the dough is so rich you need to add extra yeast to make it rise, so don't be tempted to reduce the amount. Serve with strong freshly made coffee.

•

MAKES ABOUT 20 SLICES

25 g (1 oz) fresh yeast or 15 ml (1 level tbsp) dried

300 ml (½ pint) tepid milk

700 g (1½ lb) strong white flour

75 g (3 oz) caster sugar

100 g (4 oz) sultanas

75 g (3 oz) chopped mixed peel

100 g (4 oz) dark chocolate, roughly chopped

45 ml (3 tbsp) dark rum

5 ml (1 tsp) vanilla flavouring

2 eggs, beaten

75 g (3 oz) butter, melted

FOR THE FILLING

50 g (2 oz) poppy seeds

50 g (2 oz) dark brown soft sugar

5 ml (1 level tsp) ground mixed spice

25 g (1 oz) butter

75 g (3 oz) dark chocolate

FOR THE ICING

100 g (4 oz) icing sugar plus extra for dusting

about 30 ml (2 tbsp) dark rum

5 ml (1 level tsp) cocoa powder

1   Blend the fresh yeast with half of the milk. If using dried yeast, sprinkle it on to the milk and leave in a warm place for 15 minutes or until frothy.

2   Put the flour, sugar, sultanas, peel and chocolate in a bowl and mix together. Make a well in the centre. Pour in the yeast liquid with the rum, vanilla flavouring, eggs, butter and most of the remaining milk. Beat together to make a very soft dough, adding a little extra milk if necessary.

3   Turn on to a floured surface and knead for about 10 minutes to make an elastic dough. Place in an oiled bowl, cover with oiled cling film and leave in a warm place for about 1 hour or until doubled in size.

4   Meanwhile, make the filling. Put the poppy seeds, sugar, spice and butter in a blender or food processor and purée until smooth. Grease a 2.8 litre (5 pint) gugelhupf mould.

5   Turn the dough on to a floured surface and knead again for 5 minutes. Cut into 12 pieces, shape each piece into a ball and flatten slightly.

6   Melt the chocolate in a small bowl over a pan of simmering water and add to the filling. Spread the filling on one side of each piece of dough. Overlap 6 pieces of dough, filling side uppermost, in the prepared tin. Arrange the remaining pieces on top, filling side down. Make sure that the dough overlaps, to avoid a holey bread, and that the top is level.

7   Cover with oiled cling film and leave in a warm place for 45 minutes or until the dough has almost risen to the top of the tin.

8   Bake in the oven at 190°C (375°F) mark 5 for 1¼ hours or until firm to the touch. Cover with greaseproof paper if it browns too quickly. Cool on a wire rack.

9   When the gugelhupf is cold, dust lightly with icing sugar, then make the icing. Sieve the icing sugar into a bowl and blend with enough rum to make a thin icing. Drizzle half of the icing over the guglehupf. Sieve the cocoa powder into the remaining icing and add a little more rum to thin it down. Drizzle over the gugelhupf. Leave to set. Serve in slices.

FOUGASSE

Fougasse is a kind of dry, usually sweet, dough, pitted with holes. You can find these pastries in French boulangeries in every conceivable size and flavour. Try making them at home and serve with large cups of steaming café au lait.

•

MAKES 2

7.5 g (¼ oz) fresh yeast or 5 ml (1 level tsp) dried and a pinch of sugar

225 g (8 oz) strong white flour

1.25 ml (¼ level tsp) salt

75 g (3 oz) caster sugar

1–2 drops orange flower water

30 ml (2 level tbsp) olive oil

1 egg

milk, to glaze

5 ml (1 level tsp) fennel seeds

1   Blend the fresh yeast with 75 ml (3 fl oz) tepid water. If using dried yeast, sprinkle it on to the water with the sugar and leave in a warm place for 15 minutes or until frothy.

2   Mix together the flour, salt and sugar. Add the yeast liquid with the orange flower water, olive oil and beaten egg. Stir until the mixture forms a soft dough.

3   Knead on a lightly floured surface for 10 minutes until soft and smooth. Place in an oiled bowl, cover with oiled cling film and leave in a warm place for about 2 hours or until doubled in size.

4   Knead the dough again for 2–3 minutes, halve, then roll each piece into an oval about 5 mm (¼ inch) thick. Make several small cuts with scissors right through the dough and pull apart to form holes. Transfer to a baking sheet. Cover with oiled cling film and leave in a warm place for about 10 minutes or until risen and puffy.

5   Brush the dough lightly with milk and sprinkle with fennel seeds. Bake in the oven at 200°C (400°F) mark 6 for 20–25 minutes or until golden brown. Cool on a wire rack.

TEABREADS

Teabreads are so called because they were once part of the traditional British tea, which was taken between 4 and 5 pm and consisted of scones and sandwiches as well as a teabread.

Teabreads are quick and easy to make as they are made either by the rubbing-in method, or the all-in-one method. With the former, the fat is rubbed into the flour before other ingredients (such as dried fruit, nuts, spices, or even chopped, grated or puréed fresh fruit) are added. With the all-in-one method, all the ingredients are simply beaten together.

Serve teabreads fresh, sliced and thickly buttered. The plain ones can also be eaten spread with jam or honey or with cheese.

Teabreads can be frozen whole, or in slices. Whole teabreads will take 2–3 hours to thaw at room temperature.

The notes and information on cake making apply to teabreads too, so turn to pages 7–20 before starting.

Left to right: BRAN AND CURRANT TEABREAD *(page 79)*, CIDER LOAF *(page 82)*, PEANUT AND ORANGE TEABREAD *(page 80)*, LEMON ALMOND TEABREAD *(page 74)*

MARMALADE TEABREAD

For the best result use a well-flavoured, preferably home-made chunky-cut marmalade. Serve sliced and spread with softened butter flavoured with a little orange rind.

•

MAKES 8 – 10 SLICES

200 g (7 oz) plain flour

5 ml (1 level tsp) ground ginger

5 ml (1 level tsp) baking powder

50 g (2 oz) butter or margarine

50 g (2 oz) light brown soft sugar

60 ml (4 tbsp) marmalade

1 egg, beaten

75 ml (3 tbsp) fresh milk

25 g (1 oz) candied peel, chopped

1 Grease a 750 ml (1½ pint) loaf tin, then line the base with greaseproof paper and grease the paper.
2 Put the flour, ginger and baking powder in a bowl and rub in the butter until the mixture resembles fine breadcrumbs. Stir in the sugar.
3 Mix together the marmalade, egg and most of the milk. Stir into the dry ingredients and mix to a soft dough. Add the rest of the milk, if necessary.
4 Turn the mixture into the prepared tin, level the surface and press the candied peel on top. Bake at 170°C (325°F) mark 3 for about 1¼ hours or until well risen and firm to the touch. Turn out on to a wire rack to cool.

LEMON ALMOND TEABREAD

The courgettes add moist sweetness in this recipe. There's no need to mature the teabread before eating because the flavours develop during baking.

•

MAKES 6 – 8 SLICES

150 g (5 oz) butter or margarine

150 g (5 oz) light brown soft sugar

3 eggs, beaten

175 g (6 oz) self-raising wholemeal flour

5 ml (1 level tsp) baking powder

2.5 ml (½ level tsp) ground allspice

175 g (6 oz) courgettes, coarsely grated

finely grated rind of 1 lemon

25 g (1 oz) fresh brown breadcrumbs

50 g (2 oz) flaked almonds

30 ml (2 tbsp) runny honey

1 Grease a 1.3 litre (2¼ pint) loaf tin and line with greaseproof paper.
2 Cream the butter and sugar together until pale and fluffy. Gradually beat in the eggs. Fold in the flour, baking powder and allspice.
3 Stir in the courgettes, grated lemon rind, breadcrumbs and most of the almonds. Spoon the mixture into the prepared tin.
4 Bake at 180°C (350°F) mark 4 for 50 minutes.
5 Brush the teabread with honey and sprinkle over the remaining almonds. Return to the oven and bake for a further 30 minutes or until well browned and firm to the touch. A skewer inserted into the teabread should come out clean.
6 Allow the teabread to cool slightly in the tin, then turn out on to a wire rack to cool completely.

ORANGE TEABREAD

When mandarins and tangerines are in season, take advantage of their strong sweet flavours and use them in this teabread in place of the orange.

•

MAKES 10 – 12 SLICES

50 g (2 oz) butter or margarine

175 g (6 oz) caster sugar

1 egg, beaten

finely grated rind of 1 orange

30 ml (2 tbsp) orange juice

30 ml (2 tbsp) milk

225 g (8 oz) plain flour

12.5 ml (2½ level tsp) baking powder

1 Grease a 1.3 litre (2¼ pint) loaf tin and line with greaseproof paper.
2 Cream the butter and sugar together until pale and fluffy. Gradually beat in the egg. Slowly add the orange rind and juice: do not worry if the mixture curdles. Lightly beat in the milk alternately with the sifted flour and baking powder.
3 Turn into the prepared tin and bake in the oven at 190°C (375°F) mark 5, for 40–50 minutes or until well risen and firm to the touch. Turn out and cool on a wire rack.

HONEY TEABREAD

The easiest way to measure large quantities of honey, syrup or treacle is to weigh the tin or jar, without the lid, then from this weight deduct the amount needed in the recipe. Spoon out from the container until the scales register the calculated amount.

•

MAKES 10 – 12 SLICES

50 g (2 oz) butter or margarine

150 g (5 oz) honey

150 g (5 oz) demerara sugar

275 g (10 oz) plain flour

pinch of salt

5 ml (1 level tsp) bicarbonate of soda

5 ml (1 level tsp) baking powder

5 ml (1 level tsp) ground mixed spice

5 ml (1 level tsp) ground ginger

5 ml (1 level tsp) ground cinnamon

50–100 g (2–4 oz) finely chopped mixed peel

1 egg, beaten

150 ml (¼ pint) milk

flaked almonds, to decorate

1 Grease a 1.3 litre (2¼ pint) loaf tin and line with greaseproof paper.
2 Melt the fat in a small saucepan. Remove from the heat and stir in the honey and sugar. Leave to cool.
3 Sift the flour, salt, raising agents and spices into a bowl and mix in the chopped peel.
4 Beat the egg and milk together and mix thoroughly with the cooled honey mixture. Pour into the dry ingredients and beat until smooth. Pour the mixture into the prepared tin and scatter flaked almonds over it.
5 Bake in the oven at 180°C (350°F) mark 4, for 1¼ hours or until well risen and firm to the touch. Turn out and cool on a wire rack. When completely cold wrap in greaseproof paper and foil and keep for 24 hours before serving sliced and buttered.

APPLE AND WALNUT TEABREAD

Serve this quick-mix, all-in-one teabread thickly sliced and spread with butter, or omit the icing sugar and serve topped with thin slices of cheese.

•

MAKES 10 – 12 SLICES

100 g (4 oz) butter or margarine
100 g (4 oz) caster sugar
2 eggs
15 ml (1 tbsp) golden syrup or honey
100 g (4 oz) sultanas
50 g (2 oz) walnuts, chopped
225 g (8 oz) self-raising flour
5 ml (1 level tsp) ground mixed spice
1 medium cooking apple, peeled, cored and chopped
icing sugar, for dredging

1 Grease a 1.3 litre (2¼ pint) loaf tin and line with greaseproof paper.
2 Place all the ingredients except the icing sugar in a large bowl and beat with a wooden spoon until well combined.
3 Turn into the prepared tin and level the surface. Bake in the oven at 180°C (350°F) mark 4, for 1 hour. Reduce the oven temperature to 170°C (325°F) mark 3 for a further 20 minutes or until well risen and firm to the touch. Turn out and cool on a wire rack. When cold, dredge with icing sugar.

APRICOT TEA LOAF

The flavour of dried apricots is very concentrated and is often better than that of fresh fruit. No-soak dried apricots are specially tenderized so they do not need soaking before use.

•

MAKES 12 SLICES

225 g (8 oz) no-soak dried apricots
300 ml (½ pint) water
175 g (6 oz) caster sugar
75 g (3 oz) butter or margarine
2.5 ml (½ level tsp) ground cinnamon
2.5 ml (½ level tsp) ground cloves
1.25 ml (¼ level tsp) ground nutmeg
2.5 ml (½ level tsp) salt
225 g (8 oz) plain flour
5 ml (1 level tsp) bicarbonate of soda
2 eggs, beaten

1 Grease a 1.7 litre (3 pint) loaf tin and line with greaseproof paper.
2 Cut the apricots into small pieces and place in a pan with the water, sugar, butter, spices and salt. Simmer for 10 minutes, then leave until cold.
3 Sift together the flour and bicarbonate of soda. Make a well in the centre, stir in the apricot mixture and egg, mix well, then pour into the prepared tin.
4 Bake in the oven at 180°C (350°F) mark 4, for about 1–1¼ hours or until well risen and firm to the touch. Turn out and cool on a wire rack.

MARMALADE TEABREAD (page 74), MARBLED CHOCOLATE TEABREAD (opposite)

MARBLED CHOCOLATE TEABREAD

The Victorians were very fond of marbled cakes. The recipe is so called because the feathery swirls of chocolate that are revealed when it is sliced make a pattern similar to that of Italian marble.

•

MAKES ABOUT 10 SLICES

225 g (8 oz) butter or margarine

225 g (8 oz) caster sugar

4 eggs, beaten

225 g (8 oz) self-raising flour

finely grated rind of 1 large orange

15 ml (1 tbsp) orange juice

few drops orange flower water (optional)

75 g (3 oz) plain chocolate

15 ml (1 level tbsp) cocoa powder

1 Grease a 900 ml (2 pint) loaf tin and line with greaseproof paper.

2 Cream the butter and sugar together until pale and fluffy, then gradually beat in the eggs, beating well after each addition. Fold in the flour.

3 Transfer half of the mixture to another bowl and beat in the orange rind, juice and orange flower water, if using.

4 Break the chocolate into pieces, put into a small bowl and place over a pan of simmering water. Stir until the chocolate melts. Stir into the remaining cake mixture with the cocoa powder.

5 Put alternate spoonfuls of the two mixtures into the prepared tin. Use a knife to swirl through the mixture to make a marbled effect, then level the surface.

6 Bake at 180°C (350°F) mark 4 for 1¼–1½ hours, until well risen and firm to the touch. Turn out on to a wire rack to cool.

BANANA AND HONEY TEABREAD

Ripe bananas give the best flavour in cake making. Choose fruit which are yellow and slightly flecked with brown. Speed up the ripening by storing in a paper bag at room temperature.

·

MAKES 10 – 12 SLICES

450 g (1 lb) bananas
225 g (8 oz) self-raising flour
2.5 ml (½ level tsp) salt
1.25 ml (¼ level tsp) freshly grated nutmeg
100 g (4 oz) butter or block margarine
100 g (4 oz) caster sugar
grated rind of 1 lemon
2 large eggs
120 ml (8 tbsp) thick honey
8 sugar cubes, to decorate

1   Grease a 1.3 litre (2¼ pint) loaf tin and line with greaseproof paper.

2   Peel the bananas, then mash the flesh using a fork or potato masher. Mix the flour, salt and nutmeg together. Rub in the fat until the mixture resembles fine breadcrumbs.

3   Stir in the sugar, lemon rind, eggs, 90 ml (6 tbsp) honey and mashed banana. Beat well until evenly mixed. Turn the mixture into the prepared tin.

4   Bake in the oven at 180°C (350°F) mark 4 for about 1¼ hours, covering lightly if necessary. Test with a fine skewer, which should come out clean when the teabread is cooked.

5   Cool slightly, then turn out on to a wire rack to cool completely. Gently warm the remaining honey, then brush over the teabread. Roughly crush the sugar cubes and scatter over the top.

PINEAPPLE TEABREAD

Glacé pineapple is available from good delicatessens and supermarkets. It may seem expensive but the price reflects the amount of time and labour involved in producing it. The fruit is lightly cooked, then preserved by the process of slow impregnation with sugar. If done at home this takes at least 14 days.

·

MAKES 12 SLICES

175 g (6 oz) butter or margarine
350 g (12 oz) self-raising flour
175 g (6 oz) caster sugar
50 g (2 oz) sultanas
175 g (6 oz) glacé pineapple, chopped
2 eggs
45 ml (3 tbsp) milk
2.5 ml (½ tsp) pineapple essence (optional)
12 sugar cubes, to decorate

1   Grease a 1.7 litre (3 pint) loaf tin and line with greaseproof paper.

2   Rub the fat into the flour, add the sugar, sultanas and pineapple. Beat the eggs, milk and essence (if using) together. Pour on to the dry ingredients and mix to a soft dropping consistency.

3   Turn into the prepared tin and level the surface. Roughly crush the sugar cubes and scatter over the top. Bake in the oven at 180°C (350°F) mark 4, for about 1¼ hours or until well risen and firm to the touch. Turn out and cool on a wire rack. When completely cold, wrap in greaseproof paper and foil and keep for 2 days before cutting to allow the flavours to mature.

DATE AND RAISIN TEABREAD

This teabread looks good if you decorate the top with rows of dates and walnut halves. Once cooled brush the top with a little golden syrup or honey, to glaze.

MAKES 12 SLICES

100 g (4 oz) butter or margarine

225 g (8 oz) plain flour

100 g (4 oz) stoned dates, chopped

50 g (2 oz) walnut halves, chopped

100 g (4 oz) seedless raisins

100 g (4 oz) demerara sugar

5 ml (1 level tsp) baking powder

5 ml (1 level tsp) bicarbonate of soda

about 150 ml (¼ pint) milk

1 Grease a 1.7 litre (3 pint) loaf tin and line with greaseproof paper.
2 Rub the fat into the flour until it resembles fine breadcrumbs. Stir in the dates, walnuts, raisins and sugar. Mix the baking powder, bicarbonate of soda and milk together and pour into the centre of the dry ingredients. Mix well together to give a stiff dropping consistency, adding a little extra milk if necessary.
3 Turn the mixture into the prepared tin and bake in the oven at 180°C (350°F) mark 4, for about 1 hour, until well risen and just firm to the touch. Turn out and cool on a wire rack.

BRAN AND CURRANT TEABREAD

Some of the ingredients for this teabread require soaking overnight – start your preparations the day before you plan to bake it. It definitely improves with keeping – leave it at least a day before eating. Serve sliced and spread with butter and golden syrup or honey.

MAKES 10–12 SLICES

75 g (3 oz) All Bran-type cereal

150 g (5 oz) currants

50 g (2 oz) light brown soft sugar

50 g (2 oz) desiccated coconut

400 ml (14 fl oz) milk

polyunsaturated margarine

175 g (6 oz) self-raising flour

5 ml (1 level tsp) baking powder

1 Grease a 1.3 litre (2¼ pint) loaf tin and line with greaseproof paper.
2 Place the cereal, currants, sugar and coconut in a bowl. Pour over the milk, cover and leave to soak overnight.
3 Stir the flour and baking powder into the bran mixture then spoon the mixture into the prepared tin.
4 Bake at 190°C (375°F) mark 5 for about 1¼ hours or until well risen and firm to the touch. Cover lightly with foil if the teabread browns too quickly.
5 Allow to cool slightly in the tin, then turn out on to a wire rack to cool completely. Wrap in greaseproof paper and foil and leave for 1–2 days to mature before eating.

PEANUT AND ORANGE TEABREAD

Chunky peanut butter gives the best flavour and texture. If you only have the smooth variety, roughly chop a few nuts and stir into the cake mixture.

———————— • ————————

M A K E S   1 2   S L I C E S

225 g (8 oz) chunky peanut butter
50 g (2 oz) butter or margarine
225 g (8 oz) self-raising flour
100 g (4 oz) light brown soft sugar
2 eggs
finely grated rind and juice of 1 orange
about 150 ml (¼ pint) milk
50 g (2 oz) unsalted peanuts

1 Grease a 1.7 litre (3 pint) loaf tin and line with greaseproof paper.
2 Put the peanut butter, fat, flour, salt, sugar, eggs and grated orange rind in a large bowl. Squeeze the juice from the orange and make up to 225 ml (8 fl oz) with milk. Add to the bowl and beat all together with a wooden spoon for about 3 minutes.
3 Turn into the prepared loaf tin. Level the surface, sprinkle with the peanuts and press them in lightly. Bake in the oven at 180°C (350°F) mark 4, for about 1¼ hours or until well risen and firm to the touch. Leave in the tin for 10 minutes before turning out to cool on a wire rack.

Wholemeal Date and Banana Bread (opposite), Apricot Oat Crunchies (page 215)

ROSEHIP TEABREAD

A subtle change in flavour could be made by varying the type of tea, try Earl Grey or Darjeeling.

———————— • ————————

M A K E S   6 – 8   S L I C E S

300 ml (½ pint) strained cold rosehip tea
100 g (4 oz) seedless raisins
100 g (4 oz) sultanas
100 g (4 oz) mixed peel
1 egg
75 g (3 oz) plain wholemeal flour
75 g (3 oz) plain flour
50 g (2 oz) light brown soft sugar
5 ml (1 tsp) baking powder

1 Mix together the tea, raisins, sultanas and mixed peel and leave to soak at least 8 hours or overnight.
2 Lightly grease a 900 ml (1½ pint) loaf tin and line with greaseproof paper.
3 Add the egg, flours, sugar and baking powder to the tea and plumped fruit. Mix well and pour into the prepared tin.
4 Bake in the oven at 180°C (350°F) mark 4 for 1 hour or until it pulls away from the sides of the tin and feels firm to the touch. Turn out on to a wire rack to cool completely.

WHOLEMEAL DATE AND BANANA BREAD

It may seem unusual to have a cake made entirely without sugar, but this is because of the high proportion of dates used in this recipe. Dates have the highest natural sugar content of all dried fruit and if used in cakes such as this one there is no need to add extra sugar.

—————— • ——————

M A K E S   1 0 – 1 2   S L I C E S

225 g (8 oz) stoned dates, roughly chopped

5 ml (1 level tsp) bicarbonate of soda

300 ml (½ pint) milk

275 g (10 oz) self-raising wholemeal flour

100 g (4 oz) butter or margarine

75 g (3 oz) shelled hazelnuts, chopped

2 medium ripe bananas

1 egg, beaten

30 ml (2 tbsp) clear honey

1   Grease a 1.3 litre (2¼ pint) loaf tin and line with greaseproof paper.
2   Put the dates in a pan with the soda and milk. Bring slowly to boiling point, stirring, then remove from the heat and leave until cold.
3   Put the flour in a large bowl and rub in the butter. Stir in the hazelnuts, reserving 30 ml (2 tbsp) for the decoration.
4   Peel and mash the bananas, then add to the flour mixture with the dates and the egg. Beat well to mix.
5   Spoon the mixture into the prepared tin and bake in the oven at 180°C (350°F) mark 4 for 1–1¼ hours until a skewer inserted in the centre comes out clean.
6   Leave the loaf to cool in the tin for about 5 minutes. Turn out, peel off the lining paper and place on a wire rack.
7   Heat the honey gently, then brush over the top of the loaf. Sprinkle with the reserved hazelnuts and leave until cold.

CIDER LOAF

This is a moist loaf that keeps well. Use wholemeal or white self-raising flour.

·

M A K E S   A B O U T   1 2   S L I C E S

150 ml (¼ pint) sweet cider

225 g (8 oz) mixed dried fruit

150 g (5 oz) self-raising flour

75 g (3 oz) light brown soft sugar

50 g (2 oz) blanched almonds, chopped

finely grated rind of 1 orange

finely grated rind of 1 lemon

1 medium eating apple, peeled, cored and grated

1 egg

1   Put the cider and the fruit in a saucepan and bring to the boil. Pour into a bowl and leave to soak for at least 8 hours or overnight.
2   Grease a 900 ml (1½ pint) loaf tin and line with greaseproof paper.
3   Add the remaining ingredients to the fruit mixture and beat together thoroughly. Turn into the prepared tin and bake in the oven at 180°C (350°F) mark 4 for 1 hour or until golden brown and firm to the touch. Turn out on to a wire rack to cool.

YOGURT FIG LOAF

This moist, fat-free loaf keeps well wrapped in foil.

·

M A K E S   A B O U T   1 2   S L I C E S

150 ml (¼ pint) orange juice

225 g (8 oz) no-soak dried figs, chopped

100 g (4 oz) dark brown soft sugar

250 g (9 oz) self-raising wholemeal flour

1 egg

150 ml (¼ pint) natural yogurt

45 ml (3 tbsp) milk

1   Grease a 1.7 litre (3 pint) loaf tin and line with greaseproof paper.

2   Put the orange juice, figs and sugar in a bowl and leave to soak for 1 hour.
3   Mix the remaining ingredients into the soaked figs and beat together thoroughly.
4   Spoon into the prepared tin and bake in the oven at 180°C (350°F) mark 4 for 1¼–1½ hours or until a warmed skewer inserted in the centre comes out clean. Leave to cool in the tin for 10 minutes, then turn out on to a wire rack to cool.

MALTED FRUIT LOAF

This loaf is cooked covered with a weighted lid to give the traditional malt bread texture and shape.

·

M A K E S   6 – 8   S L I C E S

350 g (12 oz) plain flour

2.5 ml (½ level tsp) bicarbonate of soda

5 ml (1 level tsp) baking powder

250 g (9 oz) sultanas

30 ml (2 level tbsp) demerara sugar

135 ml (9 tbsp) malt extract

2 eggs, beaten

200 ml (7 fl oz) strained cold black tea

1   Grease a 1.3 litre (2¼ pint) loaf tin and line with greaseproof paper. Grease the underside of a baking sheet.
2   Sift the flour, bicarbonate of soda and baking powder together in a bowl. Stir in the sultanas.
3   Slowly heat together the demerara sugar and malt extract. Do not boil. Pour on to the dry ingredients. Add the eggs and tea and beat well.
4   Turn the mixture into the prepared tin. Cover with the baking sheet, greased side down. Place a weight on top. Bake in the oven at 150°C (300°F) mark 2 for about 1½ hours. Turn out and cool on a wire rack. Wrap and keep for two days before eating.

FIG AND APPLE LOAF

Use a heavy-based pan with a tightly fitting lid to prevent the apple mixture from sticking and burning.

•

MAKES 12 SLICES

225 g (8 oz) cooking apples, peeled, cored and chopped

150 g (5 oz) dried figs, chopped

finely grated rind and juice of 1 lemon

125 g (4 oz) butter or margarine

125 g (4 oz) dark brown soft sugar

2 eggs

125 g (4 oz) self-raising flour

1   Grease a 1.7 litre (3 pint) loaf tin and line with greaseproof paper.
2   Put the apples, figs and 45 ml (3 tbsp) water in a saucepan with the lemon rind and juice. Cook over a gentle heat until a soft purée. Beat well and leave to cool.
3   Cream together the butter and sugar until light and fluffy. Gradually beat in the eggs then lightly beat in the flour.
4   Spoon one-third of the cake mixture into the prepared tin and spread it over the base. Spread half of the fig mixture on top. Repeat the layering, finishing with cake mixture.
5   Bake in the oven at 170°C (325°F) mark 3, for about 1 hour 10 minutes or until well risen and firm to the touch. Cover with foil half-way through cooking if the loaf browns too quickly. Turn out and cool on a wire rack.

PRUNE AND NUT LOAF

This fruity teabread improves as it matures, the flavour and moisture from the fruit penetrating the cake and mellowing it over a number of days.

•

MAKES 8 – 10 SLICES

275 g (10 oz) self-raising flour

pinch of salt

7.5 ml (1½ level tsp) ground cinnamon

75 g (3 oz) butter or margarine

75 g (3 oz) demerara sugar

1 egg

100 ml (4 fl oz) milk

50 g (2 oz) shelled walnuts, chopped

100 g (4 oz) no-soak prunes, chopped

15 ml (1 tbsp) clear honey

1   Grease a 2 litre (3½ pint) loaf tin, line with greaseproof paper and grease the paper.
2   Sift the flour and salt into a bowl and add the cinnamon. Rub in the fat until the mixture resembles fine breadcrumbs.
3   Stir in the sugar, and make a well in the centre. Add the egg and milk and gradually draw in the dry ingredients to form a smooth dough.
4   Using floured hands shape the mixture into sixteen even-sized rounds. Place eight in the base of the tin. Sprinkle over half of the nuts and all of the prunes.
5   Arrange the remaining dough rounds on top and sprinkle over the remaining chopped walnuts.
6   Bake in the oven at 190°C (375°F) mark 5 for about 50 minutes or until firm to the touch. Check near the end of cooking time and cover with greaseproof paper if it is overbrowning.
7   Turn out on to a wire rack and leave to cool for 1 hour. When cold brush with the honey to glaze. Wrap and store for 1–2 days in an airtight tin before slicing and buttering.

LARGE CAKES
AND SPONGES

A cake for all occasions, that's what you'll find in this chapter: a huge range from everyday cakes to more elaborate ones suitable for a special afternoon tea party. There is nothing to compare with the satisfaction of baking, serving and eating your own homemade cake. Cake making can never be a hit-and-miss affair and there are a few golden rules to success. If you read the information on ingredients and cake-making methods on pages 7–20 before you start you can be sure of a perfect result every time.

Left to right: BALMORAL ALMOND CAKE *(page 102),* CHOCOLATE AND HAZELNUT CAKE *(page 99),* FARMHOUSE SULTANA CAKE *(page 90),* VICTORIA SANDWICH CAKE *(page 94)*

STORING CAKES

·

When the cake is completely cold, store it in a tin with a tightly fitting lid.

Most types of cake are best eaten quite fresh, but rich fruit cakes and gingerbreads improve with keeping and should be stored for at least 24 hours before being cut – even longer if they are really rich. Fruit cakes which are to be kept for several months should be wrapped in grease-proof paper then foil before being put in the tin.

Un-iced cakes can be stored by wrapping them first in greaseproof paper and then in foil or cling film. This is especially useful for awkward-sized cakes. Iced cakes are best stored in a tin, but can be very loosely 'capped' with foil, so that the icing is not disturbed. Cream-filled or -decorated cakes should be stored in the refrigerator.

FREEZING CAKES

·

Most undecorated cakes – sponge, creamed Victoria, Madeira, light fruit cakes – freeze well: wrap them and seal, excluding as much air as possible. Frosted and iced cakes are only suitable for short-term storage. It is a good idea to freeze the parts for a filled cake separately, putting together, for example, the sandwich layers, cream rosettes and strawberries while they are still frozen and allowing the cake to thaw out before serving. It is not worth using valuable freezer space for rich fruit cakes as these keep so well anyway.

When freezing a glacé-iced or butter cream-frosted gâteau, put it in the freezer without wrapping and open freeze until firm, then wrap. To prevent crushing, the cake may be placed in a heavy cardboard box. Pack cup cakes in a single layer in a rigid cardboard box, then over-wrap with foil and freeze. See the chart opposite.

THAWING CAKES IN THE MICROWAVE

·

Large plain cakes can be thawed in the micro-wave. The time taken will depend upon the size and density of the cake. All cakes should be placed on a sheet of absorbent kitchen paper and then on a microwave roasting rack. Set the oven to LOW or DEFROST and cook for 1–1½ minutes, then turn over and leave to stand for 5 minutes. Repeat until the cake is thawed, being careful not to overheat or the cake will be dry.

Freezing and Thawing Instructions

Type	Freezer Storage Time	Preparation	Freezing	Thawing and Serving
Cake mixtures (uncooked)	2 months NB whisked sponge mixtures do not freeze well uncooked.	Put rich creamed mixtures into containers, or line the tin to be used later with greased foil and add the cake mixture.	Freeze uncovered. When frozen, remove from tin, package in foil and over-wrap. Return to freezer.	To thaw, leave at room temperature for 2–3 hours then fill tins to bake. Preformed cake mixtures can be returned to the original tin, without wrapping but still in foil lining. Place frozen in preheated oven and bake in usual way, but allow longer cooking time.
Cakes (cooked) Un-iced	6 months	Bake in usual way. Leave until cold on a wire rack.	Wrap and seal.	Leave in package and thaw at room temperature. Small cakes take 1–2 hours and large cakes 2–4 hours.
Layer cakes	5–6 months	Do not spread or layer cakes with jam before freezing.	Wrap plain cake layers separately or together with waxed paper between the layers.	Cream cakes may be sliced while frozen for a better shape and quick thawing. Un-iced layer cakes thaw in 1–2 hours at room temperature. Iced layer cakes take up to 4 hours.
Swiss roll	6 months	These are best rolled up in cornflour not sugar, if they are to be frozen without a filling.	Wrap and seal.	Unfilled Swiss rolls thaw in 1–2 hours.
Iced	2 months		Open freeze (whole or cut) until icing is frozen, then wrap, seal and pack in boxes to protect the icing.	Unwrap before thawing so that the wrapping will not stick to the icing.

Fruit Brazil Cake (below)

FRUIT BRAZIL CAKE

Nuts bought in their shells should feel heavy; if they feel light they are likely to be stale.

MAKES ABOUT 12 SLICES

175 g (6 oz) butter or margarine

175 g (6 oz) caster sugar

3 eggs, size 2, beaten

125 g (4 oz) plain white flour

125 g (4 oz) self-raising flour

125 g (4 oz) Brazil nuts, chopped

50 g (2 oz) candied lemon peel, chopped

125 g (4 oz) no-soak dried apricots, chopped

125 g (4 oz) sultanas

2 tablespoons apricot jam, sieved and melted

225 g (8 oz) marzipan

a few Brazil nuts, to decorate

1 Grease a deep 20.5 cm (8 inch) round cake tin or a 1.7 litre (3 pint) loaf tin and line with greaseproof paper.

2 Put the butter and sugar in a bowl and cream together until light and fluffy. Gradually beat in the eggs.

3 Sift the flours together and fold into the creamed mixture, followed by the nuts, peel and fruit.

4 Spoon into the prepared tin, level the surface and bake the cake in the oven at 180°C (350°F) mark 4 for about 1¼ hours or until a fine warmed skewer inserted in the centre comes out clean. Cool for 10 minutes in the tin, then turn out on to a wire rack to cool completely.

5 Brush the top of the cake with the apricot jam. Roll out the marzipan to fit the cake and press on top.

6 Crimp the edges and score the top in a diamond pattern. Decorate with the Brazil nuts. Grill the cake to brown the top.

DUNDEE CAKE

A rich, buttery fruit cake with blanched almonds on top.

M A K E S   A B O U T   1 2   S L I C E S

100 g (4 oz) currants

100 g (4 oz) seedless raisins

50 g (2 oz) blanched almonds, chopped

100 g (4 oz) chopped mixed peel

275 g (10 oz) plain white flour

225 g (8 oz) butter or margarine

225 g (8 oz) light brown soft sugar

finely grated rind of 1 lemon

4 eggs, beaten

25 g (1 oz) split almonds, to decorate

1 Grease a deep 20 cm (8 inch) round cake tin. Line with greased greaseproof paper.

2 Combine the fruit, chopped nuts and mixed peel in a bowl. Sift in a little flour and stir until the fruit is evenly coated.

3 Cream the butter and sugar together until pale and fluffy, then beat in the lemon rind.

4 Add the eggs to the creamed mixture a little at a time, beating well after each addition.

5 Sift the remaining flour over the mixture and fold in lightly with a metal spoon, then fold in the fruit and nut mixture.

6 Turn the mixture into the prepared tin and make a slight hollow in the centre with the back of a metal spoon. Arrange the almonds on top.

7 Bake in the oven at 170°C (325°F) mark 3 for 2–2½ hours until a fine warmed skewer inserted in the centre comes out clean. Check after 2 hours and cover with several layers of greaseproof paper if it is overbrowning.

8 Cool in the tin for 15 minutes, before turning out on to a wire rack to cool completely. Wrap in greaseproof paper and foil and store in an airtight tin for at least 1 week to mature.

DUNDEE CAKE (above)

EGGLESS FRUIT CAKE

This crumbly cake, packed with fruit, is useful for those who wish to reduce their saturated fat and cholesterol intake since it is made with polyunsaturated vegetable fat and without eggs.

·

M A K E S   A B O U T   1 2   S L I C E S

FOR THE CAKE

225 g (8 oz) white vegetable fat

450 g (1 lb) plain flour

7.5 ml (1½ level tsp) ground mixed spice

175 g (6 oz) caster sugar

225 g (8 oz) mixed dried fruit

50 g (2 oz) candied orange peel, chopped

10 ml (2 level tsp) bicarbonate of soda

300 ml (½ pint) milk

30 ml (2 tbsp) white wine vinegar

finely grated rind of 1 orange

FOR THE ICING AND DECORATION

100 g (4 oz) icing sugar, sifted

25 ml (1½ tbsp) orange juice

chopped candied orange peel, to decorate

1 Grease a deep 20.5 cm (8 inch) round cake tin and line the base with greaseproof paper.
2 Rub the fat into the flour until the mixture resembles fine breadcrumbs. Stir in the spice, sugar, fruit and orange peel.
3 Dissolve the bicarbonate of soda in the milk, add the vinegar and orange rind then mix quickly into the dry ingredients.
4 Turn into the tin and make a slight hollow in the centre. Bake in the oven at 190°C (375°F) mark 5 for about 1 hour 35 minutes or until risen and firm to the touch. Turn out and cool on a wire rack.
5 To make the icing, mix the icing sugar and the orange juice together and drizzle over the cake. Sprinkle with the orange peel.

FARMHOUSE SULTANA CAKE

A slightly spicy fruit cake, packed with sultanas.

·

M A K E S   A B O U T   1 6   S L I C E S

225 g (8 oz) plain white flour

10 ml (2 level tsp) mixed spice

5 ml (1 level tsp) bicarbonate of soda

225 g (8 oz) plain wholemeal flour

175 g (6 oz) butter or block margarine

225 g (8 oz) dark brown soft sugar

225 g (8 oz) sultanas

1 egg, beaten

about 300 ml (½ pint) milk

10 sugar cubes, to decorate

1 Grease and line a deep 20.5 cm (8 inch) square, loose-bottomed cake tin.
2 Sift the white flour, spice and bicarbonate of soda into a large bowl and stir in the wholemeal flour. Rub in the fat until the mixture resembles fine breadcrumbs and stir in the sugar and sultanas.
3 Make a well in the centre and gradually pour in the egg and milk. Beat gently until well mixed and of a soft dropping consistency, adding more milk if necessary.
4 Turn the mixture into the prepared tin and level the surface. Roughly crush the sugar cubes and scatter over the cake.
5 Bake in the oven at 170°C (325°F) mark 3 for about 1 hour 40 minutes or until a fine, warmed skewer inserted into the centre comes out clean. Turn out to cool on a wire rack.

GUINNESS CAKE

Soaking the fruit ensures a moist, well-flavoured cake.

•

M A K E S   A B O U T   1 6   S L I C E S

175 g (6 oz) glacé cherries, halved
225 g (8 oz) sultanas
225 g (8 oz) seedless raisins
225 g (8 oz) currants
finely grated rind of 1 lemon
7.5 ml (1½ level tsp) mixed spice
450 ml (15 fl oz) can Guinness
175 g (6 oz) butter or margarine
175 g (6 oz) dark brown soft sugar
3 large eggs, beaten
350 g (12 oz) plain flour

1   Put the cherries, sultanas, raisins, currants, lemon rind, spice and Guinness in a large bowl. Stir to mix, cover and leave to soak overnight.

2   Grease a deep 20.5 cm (8 inch) cake tin and line the base and sides with greaseproof paper.

3   Cream the butter and sugar together until light and fluffy. Gradually beat in the eggs, soaked fruit and flour and spoon into the prepared tin.

4   Bake in the oven at 170°C (325°F) mark 3 for about 2½ hours or until a fine warmed skewer inserted in the centre comes out clean. Cover with greaseproof paper if it browns too quickly. Cool for 10 minutes in the tin then turn out on to a wire rack to cool. Wrap in greaseproof paper and foil and store for 2–3 days in an airtight tin before eating.

GRANDMOTHER'S BOILED FRUIT CAKE

Bringing the fruits to the boil means that they absorb the tea and sugar mixture to make a deliciously moist cake.

•

M A K E S   8   S L I C E S

300 ml (½ pint) freshly made black tea, strained
100 g (4 oz) butter or margarine
150 g (5 oz) light brown soft sugar
175 g (6 oz) currants
175 g (6 oz) sultanas
15 ml (3 level tsp) ground mixed spice
275 g (10 oz) plain white flour
10 ml (2 level tsp) bicarbonate of soda
1 egg

1   Grease a deep 18 cm (7 inch) round cake tin.

2   Put the tea, margarine, sugar, currants, sultanas and spice in a saucepan and bring to the boil, reduce the heat and simmer for 20 minutes. Cool.

3   Beat in the sifted flour and bicarbonate of soda with the egg. Turn the mixture into the tin, level the surface and bake in the oven at 180°C (350°F) mark 4, for about 1 hour or until a fine warmed skewer inserted in the centre comes out clean. If the cake browns too quickly, cover with a piece of greaseproof paper. Turn out and cool on a wire rack.

HALF POUND CAKE

So named, because the main ingredients are added in 225 g (8 oz) or half pound quantities, making it an easy recipe to remember.

— • —

M A K E S   A B O U T   1 6   S L I C E S

225 g (8 oz) butter or margarine

225 g (8 oz) caster sugar

4 eggs, beaten

225 g (8 oz) plain white flour, sifted

225 g (8 oz) seedless raisins

225 g (8 oz) mixed currants and sultanas

100 g (4 oz) glacé cherries

pinch of salt

2.5 ml (½ level tsp) ground mixed spice

15 ml (1 tbsp) brandy

walnut halves, to decorate

1   Grease a deep 20.5 cm (8 inch) round cake tin and line with greaseproof paper.

2   Cream the butter and sugar together until pale and fluffy. Gradually add the eggs, beating well after each addition. Fold in the flour, fruit, salt and spice, then add the brandy to make a soft dropping consistency.

3   Turn into the prepared tin, level the top and decorate with the walnuts. Bake in the oven at 150°C (300°F) mark 2 for about 2½ hours. If the top gets too brown, cover with greaseproof paper. Leave to cool in the tin for 30 minutes, then turn out on to a wire rack to cool.

HALF POUND CAKE *(above)*

FRUIT-CRUSTED CIDER CAKE

If you don't own a tart frame, use a 20.5 cm (8 inch) square cake tin instead.

·

MAKES 8–10 SLICES

45 ml (3 tbsp) golden syrup

150 g (5 oz) butter or margarine

350 g (12 oz) cooking apples, peeled, cored and finely chopped

45 ml (3 tbsp) mincemeat

50 g (2 oz) cornflakes, crushed

125 g (4 oz) caster sugar

2 eggs, beaten

125 g (4 oz) self-raising flour

45 ml (3 tbsp) dry cider

1 Line a 35.5 × 11.5 cm (14 × 4½ inch) tart frame with foil. Grease the foil.

2 Put the syrup into a pan with 25 g (1 oz) butter and heat until melted. Add the apple, mincemeat and cornflakes and mix together.

3 Put the remaining butter and the sugar into a bowl and beat together until pale and fluffy. Gradually beat in the eggs. Fold in flour and cider.

4 Turn into the frame and level the surface. Spread the apple mixture on top.

5 Bake in the oven at 170°C (325°F) mark 3 for 45–50 minutes or until firm to the touch. Cool in the tin for 1 hour, then cut into bars.

FRUIT-CRUSTED CIDER CAKE (above)

VICTORIA SANDWICH CAKE

This versatile mixture is a basis for many cakes. Flavour with chocolate, coffee, orange or lemon.

———————— • ————————

MAKES ABOUT 8 SLICES

FOR THE CAKE

175 g (6 oz) butter or margarine, softened

175 g (6 oz) caster sugar

3 eggs, beaten

175 g (6 oz) self-raising flour

FOR THE FILLING

45–60 ml (3–4 level tbsp) jam

300 ml (10 fl oz) whipping cream, whipped (optional)

caster sugar, to dredge

1 Grease two 18 cm (7 inch) sandwich tins and line with greaseproof paper.
2 Beat the butter and sugar together until pale and fluffy. Add the eggs, a little at a time, beating well after each addition. Fold in half the flour using a metal spoon, then fold in the rest.
3 Divide the mixture evenly between the tins and level the surface. Bake in the oven at 190°C (375°F) mark 5 for about 20 minutes until they are well risen, firm to the touch and beginning to shrink away from the sides of the tins. Turn out and cool on a wire rack.
4 When the cakes are cool, sandwich them together with jam and cream, if using, and sprinkle the top with sugar.

VARIATIONS

Chocolate

Replace **45 ml (3 level tbsp)** flour with **45 ml (3 level tbsp) cocoa powder**. Sandwich the cakes with chocolate butter cream, made by dissolving **15 ml (1 level tbsp) cocoa powder** in a little hot water and beating with **75 g (3 oz) butter**, **175 g (6 oz) icing sugar** and **15–30 ml (1–2 tbsp) milk**.

Coffee

Add **10 ml (2 level tsp) instant coffee powder**, dissolved in a little warm water, to the creamed butter and sugar mixture with the eggs, *or* use **10 ml (2 tsp) coffee essence**. Sandwich the cakes with coffee butter cream, made by dissolving **10 ml (2 level tsp) instant coffee** in a little warm water and beating with **75 g (3 oz) butter** and **175 g (6 oz) icing sugar**.

Orange or Lemon

Add the **finely grated rind of an orange** *or* **lemon** to the mixture. Sandwich the cakes together with orange or lemon butter cream, made by beating **75 g (3 oz) butter** with **175 g (6 oz) icing sugar**, the **finely grated rind of 1 lemon** *or* **1 orange** and **15–30 ml (1–2 tbsp) juice**.

All-in-one Cake

Add **5 ml (1 level tsp) baking powder** to the ingredients for the basic recipe. Simply put all of the ingredients in a large bowl and beat until smooth and glossy.

WHISKED SPONGE

This classic fatless sponge does not keep well and should be eaten on the day of making.

———————— • ————————

MAKES ABOUT 8 SLICES

FOR THE SPONGE

3 eggs

100 g (4 oz) caster sugar

75 g (3 oz) plain flour

45–60 ml (3–4 tbsp) strawberry or apricot jam, to fill

caster sugar, to dredge

1 Grease two 18 cm (7 inch) sandwich tins, line with greaseproof paper, then dust with a mixture of flour and caster sugar.
2 Put the eggs and sugar in a large bowl and stand over a pan of hot water. Whisk the eggs and sugar until doubled in volume and thick enough to leave a thin trail on the surface of the batter when the whisk is lifted.
3 Remove the bowl from the heat and

continue whisking for a further 5 minutes, until the mixture is cool.

4 Sift half the flour over the mixture and fold it in very lightly, using a large metal spoon. Sift and fold in the remaining flour in the same way.

5 Pour the mixture into the tins, tilting the tins to spread the mixture evenly. Do not use a palette knife or spatula to smooth the mixture as this will crush out the air bubbles.

6 Bake in the oven at 190°C (375°F) mark 5 for 20–25 minutes, until well risen, firm to the touch and beginning to shrink away from the sides. Turn out and cool on a wire rack.

7 When the cakes are cold, sandwich them together with jam and dredge with caster sugar.

VARIATIONS

Swiss Roll

Make the sponge as above but use 100 g (4 oz) plain flour and fold in with 15 ml (1 tbsp) hot water. Pour into a lined 33 × 23 cm (13 × 9 inch) Swiss roll tin.

1 Tilt the tin backwards and forwards to spread the mixture in an even layer. Bake in the oven at 200°C (400°F) mark 6 for 10–12 minutes until golden brown, well risen and firm.

2 Meanwhile, place a sheet of greaseproof paper over a damp tea towel. Dredge the paper with caster sugar.

3 Quickly turn out the cake on to the paper, trim off the crusty edges and spread with jam. Roll up the cake with the aid of the paper. Make the first turn firmly so that the whole cake will roll evenly and have a good shape when finished, but roll more lightly after this turn.

4 Place seam-side down on a wire rack and dredge with sugar.

Chocolate Swiss Roll

Make the sponge as for Swiss roll, above, but replace 15 ml (1 level tbsp) flour with **15 ml (1 level tbsp) cocoa powder**. Turn out the cooked sponge and trim as above, then cover with a sheet of greaseproof paper and roll with the paper inside. When cold, unroll and remove the paper. Spread with **whipped cream** and re-roll. Dust with **icing sugar**.

GENOESE CAKE

It is important to add the butter slowly, carefully and lightly, in step 5, or the cake will have a heavy texture.

•

M A K E S   A B O U T   8   S L I C E S

FOR THE CAKE

40 g (1½ oz) butter

3 eggs, size 2

75 g (3 oz) caster sugar

65 g (2½ oz) plain flour

15 ml (1 level tbsp) cornflour

FOR THE FILLING AND DECORATION

300 ml (10 fl oz) double cream, whipped

icing sugar, for dredging

1 Grease two 18 cm (7 inch) sandwich tins or one 18 cm (7 inch) deep round cake tin and line with greaseproof paper.

2 Put the butter into a saucepan and heat gently until melted, then remove from the heat and leave for a few minutes to cool slightly.

3 Put the eggs and sugar in a bowl, place over a pan of hot water and whisk until pale and creamy and thick enough to leave a trail on the surface when the whisk is lifted. Remove from the heat and whisk until cool.

4 Sift the flours together into a bowl. Fold half the flour into the egg mixture with a metal spoon.

5 Pour half the cooled butter around the edge of the mixture. Gradually fold in the remaining butter and flour alternately. Fold in very lightly or the butter will sink and result in a heavy cake.

6 Pour the mixture into the tins. Bake sandwich cakes in the oven at 180°C (350°F) mark 4 for 25–30 minutes, or the deep cake for 35–40 minutes, until well risen, firm to the touch and beginning to shrink away from the sides of the tin. Turn out and cool on a wire rack.

7 Sandwich the cakes together with the cream and dredge the top with icing sugar. The large cake may be cut in half horizontally and sandwiched with cream or left plain and served simply dusted with icing sugar.

ORANGE MADEIRA CAKE

Madeira is a classic cake that can be recognized by the strip of citron peel on the top.

•

M A K E S   A B O U T   1 2   S L I C E S

175 g (6 oz) butter or margarine

175 g (6 oz) caster sugar

3 eggs, beaten

150 g (5 oz) self-raising flour

100 g (4 oz) plain flour

finely grated rind of 1 orange

30 ml (2 tbsp) orange juice

1 thin slice citron peel

1   Grease a 1.4 litre (2½ pint) loaf tin and line the base with greaseproof paper.

2   Cream together the butter and sugar until pale and fluffy. Gradually beat in the eggs. Sift together the flours and fold in to the mixture. Fold in the orange rind and juice.

3   Spoon into the tin and level the surface. Place the citron peel on top.

4   Bake in the oven at 170°C (325°F) mark 3 for about 1 hour 15 minutes or until firm to the touch. Turn out on to a wire rack to cool.

VARIATIONS

Plain Madeira Cake
Omit the orange rind and juice and replace with **30 ml (2 tbsp) milk.** Add **2.5 ml (½ tsp) vanilla essence,** *or* use **vanilla sugar** in place of caster.

Victorian Seed Cake
Make as Plain Madeira Cake, adding **10 ml (2 tsp) caraway seeds.** Omit the citron peel. The cake may also be baked in a deep 18 cm (7 inch) round cake tin.

VICTORIA SEED CAKE *(above)*

FROSTED COCONUT CAKE

An unusual cake with a coconut meringue topping.

•

MAKES 8 SLICES

50 g (2 oz) shelled hazelnuts
225 g (8 oz) butter or block margarine
225 g (8 oz) caster sugar
5 eggs
2.5 ml (½ tsp) vanilla flavouring
125 g (4 oz) plain flour
125 g (4 oz) self-raising flour
40 g (1½ oz) desiccated coconut
75 g (3 oz) icing sugar
shredded coconut, to decorate

1　Grease a 20 cm (8 inch) round spring-release tin. Base-line with greased greaseproof paper.

2　Spread the nuts out on a baking sheet and

FROSTED COCONUT CAKE (below)

brown in the oven at 200°C (400°F) mark 6 for 5–10 minutes. Put into a soft tea towel and rub off the skins. Chop the nuts finely.

3　Put the butter and sugar into a bowl and beat until pale and fluffy. Whisk 4 whole eggs and 1 yolk together and gradually beat into the creamed mixture with the vanilla flavouring.

4　Fold the flours into the mixture with 25 g (1 oz) desiccated coconut, and half the nuts.

5　Turn into the prepared tin and bake in the oven at 180°C (350°F) mark 4 for 45 minutes.

6　Meanwhile prepare a meringue topping: whisk the egg white until stiff and gradually sift and whisk in the icing sugar, keeping the mixture stiff. Fold in the remaining desiccated coconut and chopped hazelnuts.

7　Spoon the meringue topping on to the cake, after it has cooked for 45 minutes, and scatter with shredded coconut.

8　Return to the oven for 20–30 minutes or until a fine warmed skewer inserted in the centre comes out clean. Check after 15 minutes and cover with greaseproof paper if it is over-browning. Leave to cool completely for 1 hour.

BATTENBURG CAKE

To make a pink and white Battenburg, omit the cocoa and milk and colour half of the mixture with food colouring.

•

MAKES ABOUT 10 SLICES

175 g (6 oz) butter or margarine

175 g (6 oz) caster sugar

vanilla flavouring

3 eggs, beaten

175 g (6 oz) self-raising flour

15 g (½ oz) cocoa powder

milk

apricot jam

350 g (12 oz) white marzipan or almond paste (see pages 148–51)

icing sugar

1 Grease and line a Swiss roll tin measuring 30.5 × 20.5 × 2 cm (12 × 8 × ¾ inches) and divide it lengthwise with a 'wall' of greaseproof paper or kitchen foil.

2 Cream the butter and sugar together until light and fluffy. Add a few drops of vanilla flavouring then gradually add the eggs a little at a time, beating well after each addition. When all the egg has been added, lightly fold in the flour, using a metal spoon.

3 Turn half of the mixture into one side of the tin. Fold the sifted cocoa into the other half with a little milk and spoon this mixture into the second side of the tin.

4 Bake in the oven at 190°C (375°F) mark 5, for 40–45 minutes, until well risen and firm to the touch. Turn out and cool on a wire rack.

5 When the cake is cold, cut each half in half lengthwise. Spread all the sides of the strips with jam and stick each yellow strip to a brown strip. Then stick one double strip on top of the other, so that the colours alternate. Press the pieces well together.

6 Roll out the marzipan thinly on a work surface dusted with a little icing sugar, into a rectangle measuring about 35.5 × 25.5 cm (14 × 10 inches). Wrap completely around the cake. Press firmly against the sides and trim the edges. Crimp along the outer edges and score the top of the cake with a sharp knife to give a criss-cross pattern.

DEVIL'S FOOD CAKE

This classic recipe comes from the United States and makes a cake of huge proportions in true American style!

•

MAKES 16–18 SLICES

FOR THE CAKES

450 g (1 lb) plain flour

15 ml (1 level tbsp) bicarbonate of soda

pinch of salt

75 g (3 oz) cocoa powder

345 ml (½ pint + 3 tbsp) milk

10 ml (2 tsp) vanilla flavouring

150 g (5 oz) butter or margarine

400 g (14 oz) dark brown soft sugar

4 eggs

FOR THE AMERICAN FROSTING AND DECORATION

700 g (1½ lb) caster sugar

3 egg whites

50 g (2 oz) plain chocolate, optional

1 Grease three 22 cm (8½ inch) straight-sided sandwich tins and line with greaseproof paper.

2 Sift together the flour, bicarbonate of soda and salt. Mix together the cocoa, milk and vanilla flavouring until smooth.

3 Using an electric hand-held mixer, cream the butter until pale and fluffy, then gradually beat in the sugar. Add the eggs one at a time, beating very thoroughly after each addition. When all the eggs are added, beat in the flour and cocoa mixtures alternately until all is added.

4 Divide the mixture between the prepared tins and bake in the oven at 180°C (350°F) mark 4, for about 35 minutes, until firm to the touch. Turn out on to a wire rack and cool.

5 To make the American frosting, put the sugar and 180 ml (¼ pint plus 2 tbsp) water in a heavy-based saucepan and heat gently until the

98

sugar has dissolved. When completely dissolved, boil rapidly to 115°C (240°F) – use a sugar thermometer to check the temperature.

6 Meanwhile, whisk the egg whites in a large deep bowl until stiff. Allow the bubbles to settle, then slowly pour the hot syrup on to the egg whites, whisking constantly. When all the sugar syrup is added, continue whisking until the mixture stands in peaks and just starts to become matt around the edges. The icing sets quickly, so work rapidly.

7 Sandwich the three cakes together with a little of the frosting. Spread the remaining frosting over the top and sides of the cake with a palette knife. Pull the icing up into peaks all over, then leave the cake on a cooling rack for 30 minutes, to allow the icing to set slightly.

8 Place the chocolate in a small basin and stand it in a pan of simmering water, until melted. Spoon into a greaseproof paper piping bag and drizzle over the top of the cake. Leave to set completely.

CHOCOLATE BISCUIT CAKE

Vary this simple cake by using different biscuits.

•

MAKES ABOUT 8 SLICES

125 g (4 oz) plain chocolate

15 ml (1 tbsp) golden syrup

125 g (4 oz) butter or margarine

125 g (4 oz) digestive biscuits, crushed

25 g (1 oz) seedless raisins

25 g (1 oz) glacé cherries, halved

50 g (2 oz) flaked almonds, toasted

1 Grease a loose-bottomed 18 cm (7 inch) flan tin.

2 Break the chocolate into a bowl and place over a pan of simmering water. Add the syrup and butter and stir until the chocolate and butter have melted. Remove from the heat and cool slightly.

3 Mix in the biscuits, fruit and nuts. Turn into the tin, level the top, then chill until set.

CHOCOLATE AND HAZELNUT CAKE

Chocolate and hazelnuts are a winning combination in this delicious cake.

•

MAKES ABOUT 10 SLICES

FOR THE CAKE

225 g (8 oz) unsalted butter, softened

225 g (8 oz) light brown soft sugar

4 eggs, separated

100 g (4 oz) self-raising flour

pinch of salt

100 g (4 oz) ground hazelnuts

100 g (4 oz) plain chocolate, finely grated

FOR THE FUDGE ICING AND DECORATION

225 g (8 oz) icing sugar

50 g (2 oz) cocoa

50 g (2 oz) unsalted butter

30 ml (2 tbsp) milk

25 g (1 oz) hazelnuts, chopped

1 Grease a deep 23 cm (9 inch) round cake tin and line with greaseproof paper.

2 Put the butter and sugar into a bowl and beat together until pale and fluffy. Beat in the egg yolks one at a time, then fold in the flour and salt. Stir in the hazelnuts and chocolate.

3 Whisk the egg whites until stiff, then fold into the cake mixture. Pour into the prepared tin and bake in the oven at 170°C (325°F) mark 3 for 1 hour 15 minutes or until a fine warmed skewer inserted in the centre comes out clean. Leave to cool in the tin.

4 To make the fudge icing, sift the icing sugar and cocoa together, then put into a heavy-based pan with the butter and the milk. Heat gently until the butter has melted; beat until smooth. Remove from the heat.

5 Cut the cake in half horizontally. Spread a little icing over one half, then top with the other. Swirl the remaining icing on the top and sprinkle with the nuts.

MARBLED CHOCOLATE RING CAKE

To make a paper piping bag, see page 153.

M A K E S   A B O U T   8   S L I C E S

FOR THE CAKE

50 g (2 oz) plain chocolate
5 ml (1 tsp) vanilla flavouring
225 g (8 oz) butter
225 g (8 oz) caster sugar
4 eggs, size 2
225 g (8 oz) plain flour
10 ml (2 level tsp) baking powder
2.5 ml (½ level tsp) salt
50 g (2 oz) ground almonds
30 ml (2 tbsp) milk

FOR THE CHOCOLATE FROSTING

200 g (7 oz) plain chocolate
100 g (4 oz) butter

1 Grease a 1.7 litre (3 pint) ring mould.
2 To make the cake, break the chocolate into

Marbled Chocolate Ring Cake (below)

a heatproof bowl. Add the vanilla flavouring and 15 ml (1 tbsp) water and stand over a pan of simmering water. Stir until the chocolate is melted, remove from the heat and leave to cool.
3 Put the butter and the caster sugar into a bowl and beat together until pale and fluffy. Beat in the eggs one at a time.
4 Fold the flour, baking powder and salt into the creamed mixture with the ground almonds. Stir in the milk. Spoon half the mixture into the ring mould and level the surface.
5 Stir the cooled but still soft chocolate into the remaining cake mixture. Spoon into the tin. Draw a knife through the cake mixture in a spiral. Level the surface of the mixture again.
6 Bake in the oven at 180°C (350°F) mark 4 for about 55 minutes or until a fine warmed skewer inserted in the centre comes out clean. Turn out on to a wire rack and leave to cool.
7 To make the chocolate frosting, break 150 g (5 oz) of the chocolate into a heatproof bowl with 30 ml (2 tbsp) water and the butter. Stand over a pan of simmering water and stir until the chocolate is melted, then pour over the cake, working quickly. Leave to set for 1 hour.
8 Melt the remaining chocolate. Spoon into a greaseproof paper piping bag, snip off the tip and drizzle over the cake.

CHERRY AND COCONUT CAKE

Wash any excess syrup from glacé cherries before use and dry thoroughly, then toss in a little flour.

•

M A K E S   A B O U T   1 0   S L I C E S

250 g (9 oz) self-raising white flour

1.25 ml (¼ level tsp) salt

125 g (4 oz) butter or margarine

75 g (3 oz) desiccated coconut

125 g (4 oz) caster sugar

125 g (4 oz) glacé cherries, finely chopped

2 eggs, size 6, beaten

225 ml (8 fl oz) milk

25 g (1 oz) shredded coconut

1 Grease a 1.3 litre (2¼ pint) loaf tin. Line the base with greaseproof paper, grease the paper and dust with flour.

2 Put the flour and salt into a bowl and rub in the fat until the mixture resembles fine breadcrumbs. Stir in the desiccated coconut, sugar and cherries.

3 Whisk together the eggs and milk and beat into the dry ingredients. Turn the mixture into the tin, level the surface and scatter over the shredded coconut.

4 Bake in the oven at 180°C (350°F) mark 4 for 1½ hours until a fine warmed skewer inserted in the centre comes out clean. Check after 40 minutes and cover with greaseproof paper if overbrowning. Turn out on to a wire rack to cool.

CHERRY AND COCONUT CAKE (above)

BALMORAL ALMOND CAKE

A Balmoral cake tin is a ribbed loaf-shaped tin about 25.5 cm (10 inches) long, and is available from specialist kitchen shops. If you don't own one, use a 900 ml (1½ pint) loaf tin instead.

•

MAKES ABOUT 8 SLICES

FOR THE CAKE

125 g (4 oz) butter or margarine

125 g (4 oz) caster sugar

almond flavouring

2 eggs, beaten

50 g (2 oz) ground almonds

125 g (4 oz) self-raising flour

30 ml (2 tbsp) milk

FOR THE ICING AND DECORATION

50 g (2 oz) butter

125 g (4 oz) icing sugar

almond flavouring

toasted flaked almonds, to decorate

icing sugar, for dredging

1 Grease a 900 ml (1½ pint) Balmoral cake tin or use a 900 ml (1½ pint) loaf tin.
2 Cream together the butter and the caster sugar until light and fluffy. Add a few drops of almond flavouring. Beat in the eggs a little at a time. Fold in the ground almonds and flour with the milk. Spoon into the prepared tin and bake in the oven at 170°C (325°F) mark 3 for 45–50 minutes or until risen and firm to the touch. Turn out on to a wire rack to cool.
3 To make the icing, cream the butter and icing sugar together and flavour with one or two drops of almond flavouring. Pipe down the centre of the cake, decorate with the almonds and dust lightly with icing sugar.

CRUNCHY-TOP LOAF CAKE

If some of the topping falls off the cake when you turn it out, simply press it back into position with your fingertips.

•

MAKES 12 SLICES

FOR THE TOPPING

50 g (2 oz) plain flour

100 g (4 oz) caster sugar

20 ml (4 level tsp) ground cinnamon

50 g (2 oz) butter

FOR THE CAKE

350 g (12 oz) plain flour

225 g (8 oz) caster sugar

20 ml (4 level tsp) baking powder

pinch of salt

175 g (6 oz) butter or margarine

finely grated rind of 1 lemon

2 eggs

175 ml (6 fl oz) milk

2 large eating apples, peeled, cored and thinly sliced

1 Grease a 1.7 litre (3 pint) loaf tin.
2 To make the topping, put the flour, sugar and cinnamon in a bowl and rub in the butter until the mixture resembles fine breadcrumbs.
3 To make the cake, sift the flour, sugar, baking powder and salt together and rub in the butter until the mixture resembles fine breadcrumbs. Add the lemon rind. Beat the eggs and milk together, pour on to the dry ingredients and mix to a soft consistency. Turn into the prepared tin and arrange a layer of apples on top. Sprinkle with the topping and smooth with the back of a spoon.
4 Bake in the oven at 190°C (375°F) mark 5, for about 1½ hours. Cover with foil if it shows signs of overbrowning. Turn out carefully on to a wire rack lined with a clean towel, turn right way up and leave to cool.

MOIST LEMON SYRUP CAKE

Make sure that you complete step 4 while the cake is still warm or the syrup will not be absorbed.

·

MAKES ABOUT 8 SLICES

FOR THE CAKE
125 g (4 oz) butter or margarine
75 g (3 oz) light brown soft sugar
75 g (3 oz) caster sugar
finely grated rind of 2 lemons
2 eggs
175 g (6 oz) self-raising flour
1.25 ml (¼ level tsp) salt

FOR THE LEMON SYRUP AND DECORATION
juice of 2 lemons
125 g (4 oz) icing sugar
lemon slices, to decorate

1   Grease a deep 20.5 cm (8 inch) round cake tin.
2   Cream together the butter and sugars until pale and fluffy. Add the lemon rind then beat in the eggs one at a time. Fold in the flour and salt.
3   Turn the mixture into the prepared tin and bake in the oven at 180°C (350°F) mark 4 for 50–60 minutes, until well risen and firm to the touch. Turn out on to a wire rack.
4   To make the syrup, beat the lemon juice into the icing sugar. While the cake is still hot, prick all over with a fine skewer and brush evenly all over with the lemon mixture. Repeat until all the glaze is absorbed. Leave until cold.
5   Simmer the lemon slices in a little water until tender, use to decorate the top of the cake.

BUTTERSCOTCH CAKE

A rich cake for those with a sweet tooth.

·

MAKES 10 SLICES

FOR THE CAKE
100 g (4 oz) butter or margarine
175 g (6 oz) light brown soft sugar
2 eggs, separated
15 ml (1 tbsp) golden syrup
120 ml (8 tbsp) milk
2.5 ml (½ tsp) vanilla flavouring
225 g (8 oz) self-raising flour
pinch of salt

FOR THE CARAMEL ICING
225 g (8 oz) light brown soft sugar
30 ml (2 tbsp) milk
25 g (1 oz) butter

FOR THE DECORATION
whole nuts (brazils, walnuts, almonds)
clear honey

1   Grease a deep 18 cm (7 inch) square cake tin and line with greaseproof paper.
2   Cream together the butter and sugar until light and fluffy. Beat in the egg yolks. Stir in the syrup, milk and vanilla flavouring. Fold in the flour and salt. Whisk the egg whites until stiff then fold gently into the mixture.
3   Spoon into the prepared cake tin and level the surface. Bake in the oven at 180°C (350°F) mark 4, for about 1 hour. Remove from tin and cool on a wire rack.
4   To make the caramel icing, put all the ingredients into a saucepan. Bring slowly to the boil, stirring all the time, then boil gently for 7 minutes. Remove from the heat. Beat until thick and creamy then spread on top of the cake with a wet knife.
5   To decorate, place whole nuts around the top edge of the cake, and brush them with a little clear honey to glaze.

PEAR AND NUT CAKE

Choose dessert pears which are just ripe. Overripe fruit will give a soggy, watery cake.

·

MAKES ABOUT 8 SLICES

550 g (1¼ lb) pears, peeled and cored

75 g (3 oz) butter or margarine

45 ml (3 tbsp) clear honey

2 eggs, beaten

100 g (4 oz) self-raising wholemeal flour

100 g (4 oz) self-raising white flour

5 ml (1 level tsp) baking powder

2.5 ml (½ level tsp) ground mace

50 g (2 oz) shelled walnuts, chopped

1 Grease a deep 18 cm (7 inch) round cake tin and line with greaseproof paper.
2 Purée three-quarters of the pears in a blender or food processor until smooth. Thinly slice the remaining pears and reserve.
3 Cream the butter and honey together, then gradually add the eggs, flours, baking powder, mace and walnuts. Mix in the pear purée.
4 Put half the mixture in the prepared tin, lay the reserved pear slices on top and cover with the remaining mixture. Bake in the oven at 190°C (375°F) mark 5 for about 1 hour or until a fine warmed skewer inserted into the centre comes out clean. Cool in the tin before turning out. Leave until the next day before slicing.

CARROT CAKE (above right)

CARROT CAKE

Root vegetables were often used to lend sweetness to 18th-century cakes and puddings. Beetroots, parsnips and carrots were all common ingredients, but of these, only carrot is still favoured today. It makes a very pleasant, moist cake, without any hint of carrot in the taste.

·

MAKES ABOUT 10 SLICES

FOR THE CAKE

225 g (8 oz) butter

225 g (8 oz) light brown soft sugar

4 eggs, separated

finely grated rind of ½ orange

15 ml (1 tbsp) lemon juice

175 g (6 oz) self-raising flour

5 ml (1 level tsp) baking powder

50 g (2 oz) ground almonds

100 g (4 oz) walnut pieces, chopped

350 g (12 oz) young carrots, peeled and grated

FOR THE TOPPING

225 g (8 oz) cream cheese

10 ml (2 tsp) clear honey

5 ml (1 tsp) lemon juice

chopped walnuts, to decorate

1 Grease and line a deep 20.5 cm (8 inch) round cake tin.
2 Cream the butter and sugar together in a bowl until pale and fluffy. Beat in the egg yolks, then stir in the orange rind and the lemon juice.
3 Sift in the flour and baking powder, then stir in the ground almonds and chopped walnuts.
4 Whisk the egg whites until stiff, then fold into the cake mixture with the carrots. Pour into the prepared tin and hollow the centre slightly.
5 Bake at 180°C (350°F) mark 4 for about 1½ hours. Cover with foil after 1 hour if it looks too brown.
6 Leave to cool slightly, then turn out on to a wire rack and remove the lining paper. Leave to cool.
7 To make the topping, beat together the cheese, honey and lemon juice and swirl over the top of the cake. Sprinkle with the walnuts.

ORANGE-GLAZED GINGER CAKE

The flavours of orange and ginger go together perfectly. For a more intense flavour, add the finely grated rind of 1 orange to the cake mixture.

•

MAKES ABOUT 12 SLICES

FOR THE CAKE

125 g (4 oz) lard
125 g (4 oz) caster sugar
1 egg, beaten
275 g (10 oz) plain white flour
7.5 ml (1½ level tsp) bicarbonate of soda
2.5 ml (½ level tsp) salt
5 ml (1 level tsp) ground cinnamon
5 ml (1 level tsp) ground ginger
100 g (4 oz) golden syrup
100 g (4 oz) black treacle

FOR THE ORANGE GLACÉ ICING

100 g (4 oz) icing sugar
pared rind and juice of 1 orange

1 Grease a deep 23 cm (9 inch) round cake tin. Line with greaseproof paper and then grease the paper.
2 Put the lard and sugar into a bowl and beat together until pale and fluffy. Beat in the egg, then the flour, bicarbonate of soda, salt and spices.
3 Put the golden syrup, black treacle and 225 ml (8 fl oz) water in a pan and bring to the boil. Stir into the lard mixture, beating all the time until completely incorporated.
4 Turn the mixture into the prepared tin. Bake in the oven at 180°C (350°F) mark 4 for about 50 minutes or until a fine warmed skewer inserted in the centre comes out clean. Cool in the tin for about 10 minutes before turning out on to a wire rack to cool completely. Wrap and store in an airtight tin for 2 days.
5 Cut the orange rind into strips, put into a pan and cover with water. Boil until tender, about 10 minutes, and drain well.

6 Make an orange glacé icing by sifting the icing sugar into a basin, then beating in enough orange juice to make a smooth, fairly thick icing.
7 Evenly coat the top of the cake with the orange icing and leave to set for 1 hour. Sprinkle the orange strips around the top to decorate.

GINGERBREAD SLAB

Gingerbread should always be wrapped tightly in greaseproof paper and foil, then stored in an airtight tin for 2 days before eating. This allows the cake to mature and become moist and sticky.

•

MAKES 20 – 24 SLICES

125 g (4 oz) black treacle
125 g (4 oz) golden syrup
50 g (2 oz) butter or margarine
50 g (2 oz) lard
225 g (8 oz) plain white flour
1.25 ml (¼ level tsp) bicarbonate of soda
5 ml (1 level tsp) mixed spice
5 ml (1 level tsp) ground ginger
100 g (4 oz) dark brown soft sugar
150 ml (¼ pint) milk

1 Grease a deep 18 cm (7 inch) square cake tin. Line with greaseproof paper and then grease the paper.
2 Put the black treacle, golden syrup, butter and lard into a saucepan and heat gently until melted.
3 Sift the flour, bicarbonate of soda and spices into a bowl and stir in the sugar. Make a well in the centre and pour in the milk and treacle mixture. Beat well until smooth and of a thick pouring consistency.
4 Pour into the prepared tin and bake in the oven at 170°C (325°F) mark 3 for 1–1¼ hours or until a fine warmed skewer inserted in the centre of the cake comes out clean. Cool in the tin for 1 hour then turn out and cool completely on a wire rack.
5 Wrap in greaseproof paper and foil and store in an airtight tin for 2 days before eating.

PARKIN

The squares of Parkin should be served split and buttered.

——————— • ———————

MAKES 9 SQUARES

225 g (8 oz) plain flour

10 ml (2 level tsp) baking powder

10 ml (2 level tsp) ground ginger

50 g (2 oz) butter or margarine

50 g (2 oz) lard

225 g (8 oz) medium oatmeal

100 g (4 oz) caster sugar

175 g (6 oz) golden syrup

175 g (6 oz) black treacle

60 ml (4 tbsp) milk

1 egg, beaten

1   Grease a tin measuring 23 cm (9 inches) square and line with greaseproof paper.
2   Sift together the flour, baking powder and ginger and rub in the butter and lard until the mixture resembles fine breadcrumbs. Make a well in the centre. Add the oatmeal and sugar.
3   Put the syrup, treacle and milk in a small saucepan and heat gently until melted. Pour into the well with the egg. Mix until smooth, then pour into the tin.
4   Bake in the oven at 180°C (350°F) mark 4, for about 45 minutes–1 hour or until shrinking away from the edges. Don't worry if the cake dips slightly in the centre. Turn out and cool on a wire rack.
5   Wrap in greaseproof paper and foil and store for at least a week before eating.

APPLE CAKE

This wonderfully moist cake is bursting with apples and can be served cold at coffee time or warm with cream or thick yogurt as a dessert.

——————— • ———————

MAKES ABOUT 10 SLICES

4 eggs

150 g (5 oz) caster sugar

50 g (2 oz) plain white flour

100 g (4 oz) self-raising wholemeal flour

pinch of salt

5 ml (1 level tsp) baking powder

50 g (2 oz) fresh breadcrumbs

100 g (4 oz) butter, melted and cooled

90 ml (6 tbsp) milk

finely grated rind of ½ lemon

50 g (2 oz) sultanas

700 g (1½ lb) eating apples, peeled, cored and roughly chopped

icing sugar, for dredging

1   Grease a 24 cm (9½ inch) round spring-form cake tin.
2   Put the eggs and sugar in a large bowl and whisk until thick and creamy and the mixture leaves a trail when the whisk is lifted.
3   Sieve in the flours, salt and baking powder, adding any bran left in the sieve. Fold in lightly using a metal spoon. Add the remaining ingredients and fold in.
4   Turn the mixture into the prepared tin and bake in the oven at 180°C (350°F) mark 4 for about 1½ hours or until a fine warmed skewer inserted in the centre comes out clean. Cover with greaseproof paper if the cake browns too quickly.
5   Leave the cake to cool in the tin for 10 minutes then turn out on to a wire rack to cool. When cold, sift icing sugar over the top to decorate.

SMALL CAKES,
SCONES AND MUFFINS

In this chapter, you will find lots of quick recipes to keep the wolf from the door and to fill corners of sandwich boxes for school lunches or picnics. Children will find the recipes tempting and they might even like to try making some themselves – Chocolate Crackles and Banana Rock Cakes are especially easy for beginners.

Scones and muffins too are quick and easy to make and very popular whether hot or cold. You'll find most of the ingredients for all of these recipes in your store-cupboard, which is a great help if you unexpectedly find yourself with enough time on your hands to make a batch.

GRIDDLE SCONES (*page 122*)

RUBBED-IN CAKES

·

A lot of small cakes and scones are known as plain or rubbed-in cakes. All the rules about preparing ingredients are the same as when making large cakes.

Because they are low in fat, these cakes do not keep well and they are best eaten the day they are made.

SCONE MAKING

·

Self-raising flour is perfectly satisfactory for scones, although you get a slightly better rise with plain flour and a raising agent. If plain flour and baking powder are used instead of self-raising flour, allow 15 ml (1 level tbsp) baking powder to 225 g (8 oz) flour and sift them together twice before using. If you use cream of tartar and bicarbonate of soda in place of baking powder, allow 5 ml (1 level tsp) cream of tartar and 2.5 ml (½ level tsp) bicarbonate of soda to 225 g (8 oz) plain flour with ordinary milk, or 2.5 ml (½ level tsp) bicarbonate of soda and 2.5 ml (½ level tsp) cream of tartar with soured milk, as this contains an acid that will encourage the raising action.

Scones should be eaten the day they are made as they stale quickly.

Always pre-heat the oven or griddle and prepare baking sheets before you start to mix a scone dough as it must be baked immediately after mixing. Measure the ingredients accurately because the proportion of liquid to dry ingredients affects the texture of the finished product. Similarly, the correct amount of raising agent is important; the scones will be poorly risen and hard if there is not enough, but too much makes them rise quickly and then collapse and lose their shape, and gives them an unpleasant taste. Mix the raising agent thoroughly into the flour before adding the liquid, as uneven distribution causes irregular rising.

Adding liquid activates the raising agent, so work quickly from this stage onwards. Form the mixture quickly and lightly into a dough and then knead gently on a lightly floured surface. Too much flour on the surface will harden the dough, so add just enough to prevent it from sticking. Roll or press out the dough gently and cut quickly into scones with a floured cutter or a sharp knife. Press any trimmings together lightly and cut or shape them but do not knead again as this will make them tough. Put the shaped dough into the hot oven straight away before the raising agent stops working.

Heavy and badly risen scones
* Insufficient raising agent
* Heavy handling, especially during the kneading
* Insufficient liquid
* Oven too cool, or the position for baking too low in the oven.

Scones spread and lose their shape
* Slack dough, caused by too much liquid used to make the dough
* Too heavily greased tin. The fat melts on heating in the oven and 'pulls out' the soft dough before it has enough time to set
* Incorrect kneading (especially of the scraps for the second rolling) or twisting the cutter round as the scones were stamped out (such scones are oval instead of round when cooked).

Very rough surfaces
* Insufficient or unsatisfactory kneading
* Rough handling when transferring to the baking sheet

GRIDDLE SCONES

Scotch Pancakes or Drop Scones are made with a pouring batter. Like oven scones they can be made with baking powder or bicarbonate of soda and cream of tartar and the liquid can be either fresh or soured milk. Batters can be made in advance and stored overnight in the refrigerator. Stir thoroughly before using and add a little more milk if the mixture has thickened while standing.

The batter is cooked on a griddle – a thick round sheet of cast iron with a handle. It is one of the earliest cooking implements known to man and was originally used over hot coals. Nowadays it is heated on the hob. Before using a griddle for the first time it should be 'seasoned'. To do this, heat it well then rub with salt and absorbent kitchen paper. Remove the salt and reheat it slowly for about 15 minutes. Before cooking grease lightly with a little lard or oil. A non-stick griddle does not require this treatment and can be used straight away.

If you do not possess a griddle, you can use a heavy-based frying pan or the solid hotplate on an aga or electric cooker instead. If you use a hotplate make sure it has a smooth surface and is clean before you start.

Cooked Scotch Pancakes or Drop Scones should be soft and moist so try to contain the steam by stacking them and wrapping in a clean tea towel while you cook the rest of the batch.

MUFFINS

Muffins are cooked in a special muffin tray or a deep bun tray available from cook shops. Because muffins have a tendency to stick it's a good idea to place deep paper cake cases in the tins before adding the mixture.

Muffins should be turned out and preferably served at once or they will become soggy because of the steam produced. If they are to be served warm, but not immediately after cooking, lift them half out of their tins and leave them tilted to allow the steam to escape.

FREEZING

Small cakes, scones and muffins all freeze well for up to 6 months if plain, or 2 months if iced. Wrap tightly in large polythene bags or well-sealed freezer boxes. They will thaw at room temperature in about 1 hour. Scones, Scotch Pancakes or Drop Scones and Muffins can be reheated, wrapped in foil, in the oven at 200°C (400°F) mark 6 in about 10–15 minutes. Alternatively, thaw in the microwave, see below.

THAWING IN THE MICROWAVE

To absorb the moisture of thawing cakes, breads and pastry, place them on absorbent kitchen paper (remove as soon as thawed to prevent sticking). For greater crispness, place baked foods and the paper on a microwave rack to allow the air to circulate underneath.

QUEEN CAKES

These individual sponge cakes, enriched with sultanas, are very easy to prepare. Children enjoy piling the mixture into the paper cases – and licking the spoon!

•

MAKES 16

100 g (4 oz) butter

100 g (4 oz) caster sugar

2 eggs, beaten

100 g (4 oz) self-raising flour

50 g (2 oz) sultanas

1 Spread out 16 paper cases on baking sheets, or put them into patty tins.
2 Cream the butter and sugar together until pale and fluffy. Gradually beat in the egg, a little at a time, beating well after each addition. Fold in the flour, then the fruit.
3 Fill the paper cases half full. Bake at 190°C (375°F) mark 5 for 15–20 minutes, until golden brown. Transfer to a wire rack to cool.

VARIATIONS

Replace the sultanas with **one** of the following:
50 g (2 oz) chopped dates
50 g (2 oz) chopped glacé cherries
50 g (2 oz) chocolate chips

Fairy Cakes

Omit the sultanas and ice the cakes with glacé icing made from **350 g (12 oz) icing sugar** and **30–45 ml (2–3 tbsp) warm water, orange** *or* **lemon juice.**

ORANGE BUTTERFLY CAKES

Make lemon or lime butterfly cakes in the same way by substituting the orange with the appropriate fruit.

•

MAKES 12

75 g (3 oz) butter or margarine

75 g (3 oz) caster sugar

1 egg

150 g (5 oz) self-raising flour

finely grated rind and juice of ½ small orange

FOR THE BUTTER CREAM

finely grated rind of 1 small orange

15 ml (1 tbsp) orange juice

275 g (10 oz) icing sugar

50 g (2 oz) butter, softened

icing sugar, for dredging

orange shreds or small pieces of orange to decorate

1 Put twelve paper cake cases into twelve bun tins.
2 Put all of the cake ingredients into a bowl and beat together until smooth and glossy. Spoon the mixture into the paper cases.
3 Bake in the oven at 190°C (375°F) mark 5 for 15–20 minutes, until well risen and golden brown. Transfer to a wire rack to cool.
4 While the cakes are cooling, make the butter cream. Beat all of the ingredients together until pale and fluffy.
5 When the cakes are cold, cut a slice from the top of each and cut in half. Pipe or spoon a little butter cream on to each, then insert the slices of sponge at an angle to resemble the wings of a butterfly. Dust each cake with icing sugar and decorate with the orange.

ENGLISH MADELEINES *(opposite)*

ENGLISH MADELEINES

Not to be confused with French madeleines, which are baked in shallow, shell-shaped moulds, English madeleines are baked in dariole moulds then coated in jam and coconut.

•

MAKES 10

100 g (4 oz) butter or margarine

100 g (4 oz) caster sugar

2 eggs

100 g (4 oz) self-raising flour

30 ml (2 tbsp) red jam, sieved

50 g (2 oz) desiccated coconut

5 glacé cherries, halved and angelica pieces, to decorate

1 Grease ten dariole moulds and stand them on a baking sheet.

2 Put the butter and sugar into a bowl and beat together until pale and fluffy. Add the eggs a little at a time, beating well after each addition. Fold in the flour, using a tablespoon.

3 Turn the mixture into the moulds, filling them three-quarters full. Bake in the oven at 180°C (350°F) mark 4 for about 20 minutes until well risen and firm to the touch. Turn out on to a wire rack to cool for 20 minutes.

4 When the cakes are almost cold, trim the bases so they stand firmly and are all about the same height. Melt the jam in a saucepan.

5 Spread the coconut out on a large plate. Spear each cake on a skewer, brush with melted jam, then roll in the coconut to coat.

6 Top each madeleine with half a glacé cherry and small pieces of angelica.

SPONGE FINGERS

Serve sponge fingers with light fluffy mousses or for afternoon tea. Sponge drops are popular with children.

•

M A K E S   1 2

75 ml (5 level tbsp) plain flour

75 ml (5 level tbsp) caster sugar

1 egg

icing sugar, for dredging

1   Grease a sponge finger tray and dust with 15 ml (1 level tbsp) of the flour and 15 ml (1 level tbsp) of the sugar.

2   Put the egg and remaining sugar in a deep bowl and (unless you are using an electric mixer) stand this over a pan of hot water and whisk until light, creamy and stiff enough to retain the impression of the whisk for a few seconds. Remove from the heat and whisk until cool.

3   Sift half of the remaining flour over the mixture and fold in very lightly, using a metal spoon. Add the remaining flour in the same way.

4   Spoon just enough mixture into each hollow in the tray to reach the top. Bake in the oven at 200°C (400°F) mark 6, for about 10 minutes, until golden. Remove the sponge fingers carefully from the tray and cool on a wire rack. Dredge with icing sugar. Eat on day of making.

VARIATION

Sponge Drops

Complete the recipe for sponge fingers up to step 3. Spoon the mixture into a piping bag fitted with a 1 cm (½ inch) plain nozzle. Pipe twelve small rounds on to a greased baking tray. Bake as above. When cold, dust with icing sugar and sandwich together with **whipped cream** or **jam** and dip in **melted chocolate**, if liked. *Makes 6 pairs.*

LAMINGTONS

For a children's teaparty, cut the cake into stars, circles or even animal shapes.

•

M A K E S   1 2

FOR THE CAKES

40 g (1½ oz) butter or margarine

65 g (2½ oz) plain flour

15 ml (1 level tbsp) cornflour

3 eggs, size 2

75 g (3 oz) caster sugar

FOR THE ICING AND DECORATION

450 g (1 lb) icing sugar

75 g (3 oz) cocoa powder

15 g (½ oz) butter or margarine

100 ml (4 fl oz) milk

75 g (3 oz) desiccated coconut

1   Grease a 28 × 18 cm (11 × 7 inch) cake tin. Line with greased greaseproof paper.

2   To make the cakes, melt the butter and let it stand for a few minutes for the salt and any sediment to settle. Sift the flour and cornflour.

3   Put the eggs and sugar into a deep bowl and (unless you are using an electric mixer) place the bowl over a pan of simmering water and whisk until light and creamy – the mixture should leave a trail on the surface for a few seconds when the whisk is lifted. Remove from the heat and whisk for 5–10 minutes until cool.

4   Re-sift the flours and fold half into the egg mixture with a metal spoon.

5   Pour the cooled but still flowing butter round the edge of the mixture, taking care not to let the salt and sediment run in.

6   Fold the butter very lightly into the mixture, alternating with the rest of the flour.

7   Turn the mixture into the prepared tin. Bake in the oven at 190°C (375°F) mark 5 for 20–25 minutes until firm to the touch. Turn out on to a wire rack and leave to cool.

8   Meanwhile, make the icing. Sift the icing

sugar and cocoa into a heatproof bowl placed over a pan of simmering water.

9   Add the butter and the milk and stir over a gentle heat to a coating consistency.

10   Cut the cake into twelve even-sized pieces. Place on a wire cooling rack and stand the rack on a baking sheet. Spoon the icing over each cake to cover completely. Sprinkle the tops with coconut. Leave for 30 minutes until set.

ORANGE AND CARAWAY CASTLES

We used dariole moulds with a capacity of 75 ml (3 fl oz). If yours are slightly larger you can still use them but you will make fewer cakes.

MAKES 10

75 g (3 oz) butter or margarine

50 g (2 oz) caster sugar

120 ml (8 level tbsp) fine shred marmalade

finely grated rind of 1 orange

2 eggs, beaten

125 g (4 oz) self-raising flour

pinch of salt

2.5–5 ml (½–1 level tsp) caraway seeds

125 g (4 oz) toasted flaked almonds, roughly chopped

1   Grease 10 small dariole moulds and stand them on a baking sheet.

2   Cream together the butter and sugar until pale and fluffy. Beat in 30 ml (2 level tbsp) marmalade and the orange rind. Gradually beat in the eggs, then fold in the flour, salt and caraway seeds.

3   Divide the mixture between the prepared dariole moulds and bake at 170°C (325°F) mark 3 for 25 minutes or until well risen and firm to the touch. Turn out and cool on a wire rack.

4   Trim the bases of the cakes so that they stand level. Heat the remaining marmalade gently in a saucepan until melted. Spread the nuts out on a large plate. Spear each cake on a skewer, brush the tops and sides with marmalade, then roll in the nuts to coat.

BOSTON BROWNIES

Do not over-cook these Brownies.

MAKES ABOUT 16

50 g (2 oz) plain chocolate

65 g (2½ oz) butter or margarine, diced

175 g (6 oz) caster sugar

65 g (2½ oz) self-raising flour

1.25 ml (¼ level tsp) salt

2 eggs

2.5 ml (½ tsp) vanilla flavouring

50 g (2 oz) walnuts, roughly chopped

1   Grease a shallow 20.5 cm (8 inch) square cake tin and line with greaseproof paper.

2   Break up the chocolate and put it in a bowl with the butter. Stand the bowl over a pan of hot water and heat gently, stirring occasionally, until melted. Add the caster sugar.

3   Sift together the flour and salt into a bowl. Add the chocolate mixture, eggs, vanilla flavouring and walnuts. Mix thoroughly.

4   Pour the mixture into the prepared tin and bake in the oven at 180°C (350°F) mark 4 for 35–40 minutes until the mixture is risen and just beginning to leave the sides of the cake tin.

5   Cool in the tin, then cut into squares.

CHOCOLATE CRACKLES

Try adding dried fruit and nuts for a change.

MAKES 12

225 g (8 oz) chocolate polka dots

15 ml (1 tbsp) golden syrup

50 g (2 oz) butter or margarine

50 g (2 oz) cornflakes or Rice Crispies

1   Place 12 paper cases on a baking sheet. Melt the chocolate with the syrup and butter. Fold in the cornflakes, mix well, and divide between the cases.

GINGER WHIRLS

Instead of piping the cake mixture into the cases you can spoon it in. Make a hole in the centre of each, for the jam, with the end of a wooden spoon.

•

MAKES 12

225 g (8 oz) butter or margarine

75 g (3 oz) icing sugar

200 g (7 oz) plain flour

25 g (1 oz) cornflour

10 ml (2 level tsp) ground ginger

30 ml (2 tbsp) ginger marmalade

stem ginger (optional)

1 Arrange 12 paper cases in bun tins.
2 Cream the fat until soft, then sift in the icing sugar and cream together until pale and fluffy.
3 Sift together the flour, cornflour and ground ginger and fold into the creamed mixture.
4 Spoon the mixture into a piping bag fitted with a large star nozzle and pipe a whirl into each paper case.
5 Bake in the oven at 190°C (375°F) mark 5 for 15–20 minutes until golden brown. Leave to cool on a wire rack.
6 Fill the centre of each whirl with a little ginger marmalade and top with a sliver of stem ginger (if liked).

SWISS TARTS

These dainty tarts are made by piping a creamed mixture into paper cases and decorating with redcurrant jelly.

•

MAKES 12

225 g (8 oz) butter or margarine

50 g (2 oz) caster sugar

vanilla flavouring

225 g (8 oz) plain flour

icing sugar, for dredging

30 ml (2 tbsp) redcurrant jelly

1 Spread out 12 paper cake cases on a baking sheet, or put them into patty tins.

2 Cream the butter and sugar together until pale and fluffy. Add a few drops of vanilla flavouring, then gradually beat in the flour.
3 Transfer the mixture to a piping bag, fitted with a large star nozzle. Pipe the mixture into the paper cases: starting at the centre of each case, pipe in a spiral motion. Leave a small hole in the centre.
4 Bake in the oven at 180°C (350°F) mark 4 for 25–30 minutes or until pale golden brown.
5 Leave to cool in the cases. When the cakes are cold dredge with icing sugar. Spoon a little redcurrant jelly into the centre of each.

BANANA ROCK CAKES

Spoon the rock cake mixture on to the baking sheet – it may be too soft to shape.

•

MAKES ABOUT 10

200 g (7 oz) plain wholemeal flour

7.5 ml (1½ level tsp) baking powder

75 g (3 oz) butter or margarine

15 ml (1 level tbsp) light brown soft sugar

50 g (2 oz) sultanas

225 g (8 oz) bananas

5 ml (1 tsp) lemon juice

1 egg

1 Place the flour and baking powder in a bowl and rub in the butter until the mixture resembles fine breadcrumbs. Add the sugar and sultanas and mix well. Make a well in the centre.
2 Mash the bananas with the lemon juice and mix with the egg. Pour this mixture into the dry ingredients and beat until well mixed.
3 Spoon the mixture into about 10 'lumps' on a baking sheet, allowing room for spreading.
4 Bake at 200°C (400°F) mark 6 for about 15 minutes or until the cakes are well risen and golden brown. Cool on a wire rack.

ENGLISH MUFFINS

Serve English muffins for a traditional English tea.

•

MAKES ABOUT 14

5 ml (1 level tsp) caster sugar	
300 ml (½ pint) warm milk	
10 ml (2 level tsp) dried yeast	
450 g (1 lb) strong plain flour	
5 ml (1 level tsp) salt	
5 ml (1 level tsp) plain flour, for dusting	
5 ml (1 level tsp) fine semolina	

1   Dissolve the sugar in the milk, sprinkle the yeast over the surface and leave in a warm place for about 20 minutes or until frothy.

2   Sift the flour and salt together. Form a well in the centre. Pour the yeast liquid into the well, draw in the flour and mix to a smooth dough.

3   Knead the dough on a lightly floured surface for about 10 minutes until smooth and elastic. Place in a clean bowl, cover with a tea towel and leave in a warm place until doubled in size.

4   Roll out the dough on a lightly floured surface, using a lightly floured rolling pin, to about 0.5–1 cm (¼–½ inch) thick. Leave to rest, covered, for 5 minutes, then cut into rounds with a 7.5 cm (3 inch) plain cutter.

5   Place the muffins on a well-floured baking sheet. Mix together the flour and semolina and use to dust the tops. Cover with a tea towel and leave in a warm place until doubled in size.

6   Prepare a griddle or heavy-based frying pan as for Griddle Scones, see page 111. Cook the muffins on the griddle or frying pan for about 7 minutes each side. Cool on a wire rack.

ENGLISH MUFFINS (above)

ROCK BUNS

The title refers to the buns' shape not texture!

• ———— • ———— •

MAKES 12

225 g (8 oz) plain flour
pinch of salt
10 ml (2 level tsp) baking powder
100 g (4 oz) butter or margarine
75 g (3 oz) demerara sugar
75 g (3 oz) mixed dried fruit
finely grated rind of ½ lemon
1 egg
milk

1   Lightly grease two baking sheets.
2   Sift together the flour, salt and baking powder. Rub in the butter until it resembles fine breadcrumbs. Add the sugar, fruit and lemon rind and mix together thoroughly.
3   Using a fork mix to a moist but stiff dough with the beaten egg and a little milk.
4   Using two forks shape into really rocky heaps on the baking sheets. Bake at 200°C (400°F) mark 6, for about 20 minutes until golden brown. Cool on a wire rack. Rock buns are best eaten on the day of making.

UPSIDE DOWN CURRANT BUNS

Try other combinations of dried fruit and chopped nuts such as pistachios and apricots or pecans and raisins.

• ———— • ———— •

MAKES 15

30 ml (2 tbsp) currants
30 ml (2 tbsp) nibbed almonds
150 g (5 oz) butter or margarine
150 g (5 oz) caster sugar
2 eggs, beaten
2.5 ml (½ tsp) vanilla flavouring
finely grated rind of 1 lemon
100 g (4 oz) plain flour

1   Grease 15 fluted bun tins and divide the currants and almonds between the bases.
2   Cream together the butter and sugar until light and fluffy. Gradually beat in the eggs, vanilla flavouring and grated lemon rind. Sift over the flour and fold in.
3   Divide the mixture evenly between the tins and level with a knife.
4   Bake at 190°C (375°F) mark 5 for 25–30 minutes or until firm to the touch and golden brown. Ease out of the tins immediately and cool on a wire rack.

FLUTED CARAWAY BUNS

These buns can also be served topped with a spoonful of glacé icing and a halved glacé cherry.

• ———— • ———— •

MAKES 9

75 g (3 oz) butter or margarine
50 g (2 oz) caster sugar
2 eggs, beaten
30 ml (2 level tbsp) lemon cheese or curd
100 g (4 oz) self-raising flour
pinch of salt
2.5 ml (½ level tsp) caraway seeds
icing sugar, for dredging

1   Using lard, thoroughly grease 9 fluted patty tins measuring about 7 cm (2¾ inches) wide and 3 cm (1¼ inches) deep.
2   Cream the fat and sugar together until pale and fluffy. Add the egg, a little at a time, beating well after each addition. Fold in the lemon cheese.
3   Sift in the flour and salt and fold it in followed by the caraway seeds. Divide the mixture between the prepared tins and bake in the oven at 170°C (325°F) mark 3 for about 25 minutes.
4   Turn out and leave to cool on a wire rack.
5   Decorate each bun with a little sifted icing sugar.

CINNAMON CHERRY BARS

If you haven't got the right size tin use two small sandwich tins instead and cut the baked mixture into wedges.

MAKES 24

125 g (4 oz) ground almonds

1 egg

225 g (8 oz) plain flour

225 g (8 oz) caster sugar

175 g (6 oz) butter or margarine

5 ml (1 level tsp) ground cinnamon

finely grated rind of 1 lemon

125 g (4 oz) black cherry jam

icing sugar, for dredging

1 Lightly grease a 28 × 18 cm (11 × 7 inch) shallow tin.
2 Put the first seven ingredients into a large bowl and beat well.
3 Knead lightly. Cover and refrigerate for at least 30 minutes. Press half of the dough evenly into the prepared tin. Spread the jam over the surface.
4 On a lightly floured work surface, lightly knead the remaining dough. With well-floured hands, roll into pencil-thin strips. Arrange over the jam to form a close lattice pattern. Refrigerate for 30 minutes.
5 Bake at 180°C (350°F) mark 4 for 40 minutes or until golden brown and firm to the touch. Leave to cool then dredge with icing sugar. Cut into 24 bars and ease out of the tin.

COBURG BUNS

If you don't own the special bun tins, spoon the mixture into paper cake cases and place a blanched almond on top of each.

MAKES 12

6 blanched almonds, halved

150 g (5 oz) plain flour

5 ml (1 level tsp) bicarbonate of soda

2.5 ml (½ level tsp) ground allspice

2.5 ml (½ level tsp) ground ginger

2.5 ml (½ level tsp) ground cinnamon

50 g (2 oz) butter or margarine

50 g (2 oz) caster sugar

1 egg, beaten

15 ml (1 tbsp) golden syrup

60 ml (4 tbsp) milk

1 Grease twelve fluted bun tins and place half an almond in each.
2 Sift together the flour, bicarbonate of soda and spices. Cream together the fat and sugar until light and fluffy. Add the egg a little at a time, beating well after each addition.
3 Mix the syrup and milk and add to the creamed mixture alternately with the flour, folding in lightly until evenly mixed.
4 Divide the mixture between the tins and bake in the oven at 180°C (350°F) mark 4, for about 25 minutes, until firm to the touch. Turn out and cool on a wire rack. Coburg buns are best eaten on the day of making.

DOUBLE CHOCOLATE MUFFINS AND BLUEBERRY MUFFINS (opposite)

DOUBLE CHOCOLATE MUFFINS

Another classic from the United States, muffins are becoming increasingly popular here. And no wonder too, as they are quick to make and taste delicious, especially if served fresh from the oven.

•

MAKES 12

100 g (4 oz) plain chocolate, broken into pieces
50 g (2 oz) cocoa powder
225 g (8 oz) self-raising flour
5 ml (1 level tsp) baking powder
50 g (2 oz) dark brown soft sugar
pinch of salt
100 g (4 oz) plain chocolate polka dots
225 ml (8 fl oz) milk
60 ml (4 tbsp) vegetable oil
5 ml (1 tsp) vanilla flavouring
1 egg

1   Thoroughly grease 12 *deep* muffin or bun tins. Place a large paper cake case in each.
2   Put the chocolate into a large bowl and stand over a saucepan of simmering water. Heat gently until the chocolate melts.
3   Remove from the heat and stir in the remaining ingredients. Beat thoroughly together.
4   Spoon the mixture into the paper cases. Bake in the oven at 220°C (425°F) mark 7 for 15 minutes until well risen and firm to the touch. Serve warm.

MUESLI MUFFINS

Try serving these for breakfast for a change, with poached or scrambled eggs.

•

MAKES 4

75 g (3 oz) unsweetened muesli
75 g (3 oz) plain wholemeal flour
7.5 ml (1½ level tsp) baking powder
1 egg
150 ml (¼ pint) milk
30 ml (2 tbsp) clear honey

1   Grease 4 large shallow patty tins.
2   Put the muesli, flour and baking powder in a bowl and mix together.
3   Stir in the egg, milk and honey and beat until well mixed. Divide the batter between the prepared tins.
4   Bake in the oven at 190°C (375°F) mark 5 for 20 minutes, until risen and golden brown. Ease out of the tins. Serve warm, or cool on a wire rack. To serve, split each muffin and spread lightly with butter.

BLUEBERRY MUFFINS

It's important to use deep bun tins to make muffins.

•

MAKES 12

125 g (4 oz) plain wholemeal flour
225 g (8 oz) plain white flour
pinch salt
15 ml (1 level tbsp) baking powder
finely grated rind of 1 lemon
225 g (8 oz) blueberries
1 egg
175 g (6 oz) light brown soft sugar
about 200 ml (7 fl oz) milk
25 g (1 oz) butter or margarine, melted
milk, to glaze
caster sugar, for dusting

1   Thoroughly grease 12 *deep* muffin or bun tins. Place a large paper cake case in each.
2   Mix together the flours, salt and baking powder. Add the lemon rind and the blueberries.
3   Whisk the egg, brown sugar, milk and butter together and mix well with the dry ingredients. Spoon the mixture into the prepared paper cases. Do not fill more than two-thirds full.
4   Bake in the oven at 220°C (425°F) mark 7 for about 20 minutes or until well risen.
5   Brush the tops lightly with milk and sprinkle with caster sugar. Bake for a further 5 minutes until golden brown and firm to the touch. Serve warm and plain or split open and spread with butter.

GRIDDLE SCONES

If you do not possess a 'griddle' or 'girdle', use a thick-bottomed frying pan or the solid hot-plate of an electric cooker. See page 111 for how to prepare a griddle.

•

MAKES 12

225 g (8 oz) plain flour

5 ml (1 level tsp) bicarbonate of soda

10 ml (2 level tsp) cream of tartar

5 ml (1 level tsp) salt

small knob of lard, butter or margarine

25 g (1 oz) sugar

about 150 ml (¼ pint) milk

1 Sift together the flour, bicarbonate of soda, cream of tartar and salt. Rub in the lard and add the sugar. Mix to a soft dough with the milk.
2 Divide the dough into two portions. Lightly knead and roll each piece into a round about 0.5 cm (¼ inch) thick. Cut each round into six even triangles.
3 Cook on the griddle for about 5 minutes until evenly brown on one side, then turn over and cook on the second side for a further 5 minutes.
4 Wrap in a clean tea towel as they cook. Serve warm or place the tea towel on a wire rack and leave to cool. Eat Griddle Scones while fresh, buttering them lavishly.

SCOTCH PANCAKES OR DROP SCONES

For richer scones, add about 25 g (1 oz) butter or margarine, rubbing it into the flour.

•

MAKES ABOUT 8 – 10 PANCAKES

100 g (4 oz) self-raising flour

30 ml (2 level tbsp) caster sugar

1 egg, beaten

150 ml (¼ pint) milk

1 Prepare a griddle or heavy-based frying pan as for Griddle Scones, see page 111.
2 Mix the flour and sugar. Make a well in the centre and stir in the egg, with enough of the milk to make a batter of the consistency of thick cream. The mixing should be done as quickly and lightly as possible.
3 Drop the mixture in spoonfuls on to the hot griddle. For round pancakes, drop it from the point of the spoon, for oval ones, drop from the side.
4 Keep the griddle at a steady heat and when bubbles rise to the surface of the pancakes and burst – after 2–3 minutes – turn the pancake over, using a palette knife. Continue cooking for a further 2–3 minutes, until golden brown on the other side.
5 Place the cooked pancakes on a clean tea towel, cover with another towel and place on a rack to cool. (This keeps in the steam and the pancakes do not become dry.) Serve with butter or with whipped cream and jam.

POTATO SCONES

If using leftover mashed potato, warm it in the microwave for 2 minutes on HIGH, or in a saucepan, before adding the remaining ingredients.

•

MAKES 8 – 12

450 g (1 lb) potatoes, peeled and freshly boiled

salt

50 g (2 oz) butter

100 g (4 oz) plain flour

1 Prepare a griddle or heavy-based frying pan as for Griddle Scones, see page 111.
2 Pass the cooked potatoes through a sieve, season well with salt, beat in the butter and gradually work in all of the flour.
3 Place the dough on a floured surface and knead to a manageable consistency. Roll out to 0.5 cm (¼ inch) thickness and cut into 6.5 cm (2½ inch) rounds. Cook on the preheated greased griddle or frying pan for about 5 minutes, turning once, until golden brown on both sides.

ALMOND DROP SCONES WITH CINNAMON BUTTER

The batter may be made the evening before it is required, but stir in the grated apple just before cooking the scones.

———————— • ————————

M A K E S   1 0 – 1 2   S C O N E S

FOR THE CINNAMON BUTTER

100 g (4 oz) unsalted butter
50 g (2 oz) caster sugar
50 g (2 oz) demerara sugar
20 ml (4 level tsp) ground cinnamon

FOR THE SCONES

100 g (4 oz) plain flour
pinch of salt
7.5 ml (1½ level tsp) baking powder
25 g (1 oz) demerara sugar
25 g (1 oz) butter or margarine, melted
1 egg
120 ml (4½ fl oz) milk
5 ml (1 tsp) lemon juice
1 small crisp dessert apple

1 To make the butter, beat all the ingredients together. Spoon into a small pot, level the surface, cover and refrigerate. Remove from the refrigerator at least 30 minutes before serving.
2 Prepare a griddle or heavy-based frying pan as for Griddle Scones, see page 111.
3 Mix the flour, salt, baking powder and sugar together in a bowl. Make a well in the centre. Mix the butter, egg, milk and lemon juice together and pour into the well in the dry ingredients. Gradually draw the dry ingredients into the liquid to make a smooth thick batter. Grate in the apple.
4 Drop 3 or 4 small spoonfuls of the batter on to the griddle or frying pan, keeping the blobs spaced well apart, and spread each one out slightly with the back of the spoon. Cook for 2–3 minutes until bubbles appear on the surface, then turn each one over with a palette knife and cook on the other side for about 2 minutes.
5 Keep the scones warm between 2 tea towels whilst cooking the remaining scones in the same way. Serve warm, with the cinnamon butter.

WELSH CAKES

Welsh cakes are traditionally served warm, sprinkled with sugar and topped with a knob of butter.

———————— • ————————

M A K E S   A B O U T   1 6

225 g (8 oz) plain flour
5 ml (1 level tsp) baking powder
pinch of salt
50 g (2 oz) butter or margarine
50 g (2 oz) lard
75 g (3 oz) sugar
50 g (2 oz) currants
1 egg, beaten
about 30 ml (2 tbsp) milk

1 Prepare a griddle or heavy-based frying pan as for Griddle Scones, see page 111.
2 Sift together the flour, baking powder and salt. Rub in the fats until the mixture resembles fine breadcrumbs. Add the sugar and currants.
3 Make a well in the centre then add the egg and enough milk to make them a stiff paste similar to shortcrust pastry.
4 Roll out on a lightly floured surface until 0.5 cm (¼ inch) thick and cut into rounds with a 7.5 cm (3 inch) cutter.
5 Cook the cakes slowly on the griddle for about 3 minutes on each side, until golden brown. Cool on a wire rack. Eat on the day of making.

OVEN SCONES

Read the information on pages 110–111 and you will make perfect scones every time.

•

MAKES 10-12

225 g (8 oz) self-raising flour

2.5 ml (½ level tsp) salt

5 ml (1 level tsp) baking powder

25–50 g (1–2 oz) butter or margarine

150 ml (¼ pint) milk

beaten egg or milk, to glaze (optional)

1 Sift the flour, salt and baking powder together into a bowl, then rub in the fat until the mixture resembles fine breadcrumbs.

2 Make a well in the centre and stir in enough milk to give a fairly soft dough. Turn it on to a lightly floured surface, knead very lightly if necessary to remove any cracks, then roll out lightly to about 2 cm (¾ inch) thick, or pat it out with the hand.

3 Cut into 10 to 12 rounds with a floured 5 cm (2 inch) cutter or cut into triangles with a sharp knife. Place on a baking sheet, brush if wished with beaten egg or milk and bake at 230°C (450°F) mark 8 for 8–10 minutes, until brown and well risen. Transfer to a wire rack to cool.

VARIATIONS

If plain flour and baking powder are used instead of self-raising flour, allow 15 ml (1 level tbsp) baking powder to 225 g (8 oz) flour and sift them together twice before using.

If you use cream of tartar and bicarbonate of soda in place of baking powder, allow 5 ml (1 level tsp) cream of tartar and 2.5 ml (½ level tsp) bicarbonate of soda to 225 g (8 oz) plain flour with ordinary milk or 2.5 ml (½ level tsp) bicarbonate of soda and 2.5 ml (½ level tsp) cream of tartar with buttermilk.

Everyday Fruit Scones
Add **50 g (2 oz) currants, sultanas, seedless raisins** *or* **chopped dates** (or a mixture of fruit) to the dry ingredients in the basic recipe.

Rich Afternoon Tea Scones
Follow the basic recipe, adding **15–30 ml (1–2 level tbsp) caster sugar** to the dry ingredients and using **1 beaten egg** with **75 ml (5 tbsp) water or milk** in place of 150 ml (¼ pint) milk; **50 g (2 oz) dried fruit** may also be included.

CHEESE AND HERB SCONE WHIRLS

Scones are best served freshly baked, so if you have a freezer, make double the quantity and freeze them, uncooked.

•

MAKES 10

100 g (4 oz) self-raising wholemeal flour

100 g (4 oz) white self-raising flour

salt, to taste

50 g (2 oz) butter or margarine

100 g (4 oz) full-fat soft cheese

about 105 ml (7 tbsp) milk

5 ml (1 tsp) Dijon mustard

45 ml (3 tbsp) chopped fresh mixed herbs, such as rosemary, parsley, chives, basil

30 ml (2 level tbsp) freshly grated Parmesan cheese

1 Lightly grease a baking sheet and set aside.

2 Mix the flours and salt in a bowl. Add the butter and rub in until the mixture resembles fine breadcrumbs.

3 Mix together the cheese, about 75 ml (5 tbsp) of the milk and the mustard, then add to the dry ingredients and mix lightly to form a soft dough.

4 Knead briefly on a lightly floured surface, then roll out to a 12 × 25 cm (5 × 10 inch) oblong. Brush with the remaining milk and sprinkle evenly with the herbs.

5 Roll up from one long edge and cut into ten slices about 2.5 cm (1 inch) thick.

6 Place on the baking sheet. Brush the tops with milk and sprinkle with the Parmesan cheese. Bake in the oven at 220°C (425°F) mark 7 for 12–15 minutes, until risen and golden brown. Serve warm.

EMMENTAL PUFF ROLLS (page 42), CHEESE AND HERB SCONE WHIRLS (opposite)

CHEESE SCONES

For the best flavour, use a strong-flavoured Cheddar, or Cheddar with herbs and garlic.

•

MAKES ABOUT 16

225 g (8 oz) self-raising flour

pinch of salt

5 ml (1 level tsp) baking powder

40 g (1½ oz) butter or margarine

75–100 g (3–4 oz) Cheddar cheese, finely grated

5 ml (1 level tsp) mustard powder

about 150 ml (¼ pint) milk

1 Grease a baking sheet and set aside.
2 Sift the flour, salt and baking powder together and rub in the fat until the mixture resembles fine breadcrumbs.
3 Stir in half of the cheese, the mustard and enough milk to give a fairly soft, light dough.
4 On a lightly floured surface, roll out to about 2 cm (¾ inch) thick and cut into rounds with a 5 cm (2 inch) plain cutter. Put on the baking sheet, brush the tops with milk and sprinkle with the remaining cheese.
5 Bake in the oven at 220°C (425°F) mark 7 for about 10 minutes. Cool on a wire rack.

SPICED WALNUT SCONES

Serve these savoury scones with cheese.

•

MAKES 16

75 g (3 oz) walnut pieces

125 g (4 oz) plain wholemeal flour

125 g (4 oz) plain white flour

15 ml (3 level tsp) baking powder

2.5 ml (½ level tsp) chilli powder

pinch salt

50 g (2 oz) butter or margarine

10 ml (2 tsp) lemon juice

about 170 ml (6 fl oz) milk

1 Roughly chop the walnut pieces. Mix two-thirds of the walnuts with the flours, baking powder, chilli powder and salt. Rub in the butter.
2 Mix the lemon juice with the milk and stir into the dry ingredients. Knead lightly until just smooth and a soft dough is formed.
3 Roll out the dough to a 20.5 cm (8 inch) square, place on a baking sheet and mark into 16 squares.
4 Lightly brush the dough with milk and sprinkle with the remaining walnuts.
5 Bake in the oven at 220°C (425°F) mark 7 for about 18 minutes, or until well risen, golden brown and firm to the touch.
6 Serve warm, divided into squares.

BUTTERMILK SCONES

Buttermilk is the low-fat liquid remaining after butter has been made. It is ideal for making scones, drop scones or soda bread because it helps in the rising.

· ·

MAKES 8

100 g (4 oz) self-raising wholemeal flour

100 g (4 oz) self-raising flour

50 g (2 oz) butter or margarine

finely grated rind of 1 lemon

15 g (½ oz) light brown soft sugar

90 ml (3½ fl oz) buttermilk

5 ml (1 tsp) sesame seeds

1   Grease a baking sheet and set aside.
2   Put the flours into a mixing bowl, then rub in the butter until the mixture resembles fine breadcrumbs.
3   Stir in the lemon rind and sugar and mix to a soft dough with all but 5 ml (1 tsp) of the buttermilk. Knead gently on a lightly floured surface until smooth.
4   Roll out to a thickness of 2 cm (¾ inch) and, using a 5 cm (2 inch) fluted cutter, cut into 8 rounds.
5   Place on the baking sheet, brush with the remaining buttermilk and sprinkle with the sesame seeds. Bake in the oven at 230°C (450°F) mark 8 for 8–10 minutes or until well risen and golden brown. Cool on a wire rack.

DATE AND YOGURT SCONES

If you are counting calories, serve these scones split and spread with low-fat cheese and sugar-reduced jam.

· ·

MAKES 8

50 g (2 oz) stoned dates

75 g (3 oz) plain white flour

150 g (5 oz) plain wholemeal flour

15 ml (1 level tbsp) baking powder

pinch nutmeg

50 g (2 oz) butter or margarine

50 g (2 oz) light brown soft sugar

150 g (5 oz) natural yogurt

about 45 ml (3 tbsp) milk

1   Finely chop the dates, then coat in 25 g (1 oz) white flour. Place the remaining white and wholemeal flour in a bowl with the baking powder and nutmeg. Stir until well mixed.
2   Add the butter and rub in until the mixture resembles fine breadcrumbs. Stir in the sugar and chopped dates, then make a well in the centre of the mixture.
3   Place the yogurt in a small bowl, add 30 ml (2 tbsp) of the milk and whisk lightly until smooth. Pour into the well and mix with a palette knife to a soft dough. Leave to stand for about 5 minutes to allow the bran in the flour time to absorb the liquid.
4   Knead the dough lightly on a floured surface until just smooth. Roll out the dough until 2 cm (¾ inch) thick, then using a 5 cm (2 inch) round cutter, cut out 8 scones, re-rolling the dough as necessary. Place on a baking sheet, then carefully brush the tops with a little milk.
5   Bake in the oven at 230°C (450°F) mark 8 for about 10 minutes or until well risen and golden brown. Cool on a wire rack.

GÂTEAUX

All over Western Europe one can see patisseries displaying torte or gâteaux.

Austria and Germany are particularly famous for their torte, the most famous being Vienna's Sachertorte, which was invented by Franz Sacher to satisfy the sweet tooth of Prince Klemens von Metternich, a famous statesman. From its Black Forest, Germany has given us Schwarzwälder Kirschtorte – a rich chocolate cake made with morello cherries and cherry liqueur, that is more commonly known as Black Forest Gâteaux. France is famous for its gâteaux, meringues and roulades, while the larger, elaborate sponge gâteaux with mousse-like fillings are peculiar to Austria and Germany. The famous-named gâteaux are just the tip of the iceberg; all over Europe there are thousands more.

For perfect results, read the information on cake making methods on pages 15–21, before you start.

Left to right: CHOCOLATE AND CHESTNUT GÂTEAU *(page 135),* CHOCOLATE ROULADE WITH CRUSHED STRAWBERRY CREAM *(page 143),* GÂTEAU SAINT-HONORÉ *(page 130),* GÂTEAÙ ARMANDINE *(page 134)*

GÂTEAU SAINT-HONORÉ

This Parisian speciality is named in honour of an early French bishop, honoured as the patron saint of bakers. Don't be put off by the length of the recipe; the components can all be made in advance and the cake assembled 1–2 hours before serving.

·

M A K E S   6   S L I C E S

FOR THE PÂTE SUCRÉE

100 g (4 oz) plain flour

pinch of salt

50 g (2 oz) caster sugar

50 g (2 oz) butter, at room temperature

2 egg yolks

beaten egg, to glaze

FOR THE CHOUX BUNS

1 quantity choux pastry (see Profiteroles, page 185)

FOR THE CRÈME PÂTISSIÈRE

2 eggs

50 g (2 oz) caster sugar

30 ml (2 tbsp) plain flour

30 ml (2 tbsp) cornflour

300 ml (½ pint) milk

a few drops of vanilla flavouring

TO ASSEMBLE

300 ml (½ pint) double cream

45 ml (3 tbsp) caster sugar

glacé fruit or crystallized flowers, to decorate

1 To make the pâte sucrée, sift the flour and salt together on to a work surface or, preferably, a marble slab. Make a well in the centre of the mixture and add the sugar, butter and egg yolks.
2 Using the fingertips of one hand, pinch and work the sugar, butter and egg yolks together until well blended. Gradually work in all the flour, adding a little water if necessary to bind the mixture together. Knead lightly until

smooth. Wrap and chill for 30 minutes.
3 While the pastry is chilling, make the choux pastry.
4 Roll out the pâte sucrée on a lightly floured work surface to an 18 cm (7 inch) round. Place on a baking sheet and prick all over with a fork. Brush a 1 cm (½ inch) band of beaten egg round the edge.
5 Put the choux pastry into a piping bag fitted with a medium-sized plain nozzle and pipe a circle round the edge of the pâte sucrée. Brush with beaten egg.
6 Dampen a baking sheet and pipe about twenty walnut-sized choux balls on to it. Brush with beaten egg.
7 Bake both the flan and the choux balls in the oven at 190°C (375°F) mark 5 for about 15 minutes or until well risen and golden brown. When the choux buns are cooked, make a slit in the side of each to release the steam, then transfer with the flan to a wire rack and leave for 15–20 minutes to cool.
8 While the pastry is cooking, make the crème pâtissière. Cream the eggs and sugar together until really pale and thick. Sift the flour and cornflour into the bowl and beat in with a little cold milk until smooth.
9 Heat the rest of the milk until almost boiling and pour on to the egg mixture, stirring well all the time. Return the custard to the saucepan and stir over a low heat until the mixture boils. Add vanilla flavouring to taste and cook for a further 2–3 minutes. Cover and leave to cool.
10 Whip the cream until stiff. Reserving a little whipped cream for the top of the gâteau, put the rest into a piping bag fitted with a medium-sized nozzle and pipe some into each of the cold choux buns.
11 Put the sugar and 45 ml (3 tbsp) water into a heavy-based saucepan and boil until it just begins to turn straw-coloured around the edge. Dip the tops of the choux buns in the syrup.
12 Use the remainder of the syrup to stick the buns on to the choux pastry border to form a wall. Fill the centre of the gâteau with the crème pâtissière.
13 Pipe the reserved cream around the edge, in between the choux balls. Decorate with glacé fruit or crystallized flowers.

BLACK FOREST GÂTEAU

This famous and much loved cake from Germany is perfect for any grand occasion, or as a dessert for a dinner party. The cherries should really be fresh morello cherries, but as these are not always easy to come by, canned cherries are used instead. When fresh morello cherries are available, poach them in a sugar syrup and remove their stones.

— • —

MAKES 10 SLICES

FOR THE CAKE

100 g (4 oz) butter

6 eggs

225 g (8 oz) caster sugar

75 g (3 oz) plain flour

50 g (2 oz) cocoa

2.5 ml (½ tsp) vanilla flavouring

FOR THE FILLING AND DECORATION

two 425 g (15 oz) cans stoned black cherries, drained and syrup reserved

60 ml (4 tbsp) kirsch

600 ml (1 pint) whipping cream

100 g (4 oz) chocolate caraque (see pages 30–1)

5 ml (1 level tsp) arrowroot

1 Grease a deep 23 cm (9 inch) round cake tin and line the base with greaseproof paper.

2 Put the butter into a bowl, place over a pan of warm water and beat it until really soft but not melted.

3 Put the eggs and sugar into a large bowl, place over a pan of hot water and whisk until pale and creamy, and thick enough to leave a trail on the surface when the whisk is lifted. Remove from the heat and whisk until cool.

4 Sift the flour and cocoa together, then lightly fold into the mixture with a metal spoon. Fold in the vanilla flavouring and softened butter.

5 Turn the mixture into the prepared tin and tilt the tin to spread the mixture evenly. Bake at 180°C (350°F) mark 4 for about 40 minutes, until well risen, firm to the touch and beginning to shrink away from the sides of the tin.

6 Turn out of the tin on to a wire rack, covered with greaseproof paper, and leave to cool for 30 minutes.

7 Cut the cake into three horizontally. Place one layer on a flat plate. Mix together 75 ml (5 tbsp) cherry syrup and the kirsch. Spoon 45 ml (3 tbsp) over the cake layer.

8 Whip the cream until it just holds its shape, then spread a little thinly over the soaked sponge. Reserve a quarter of the cherries for decoration and scatter half the remainder over the cream.

9 Repeat the layers of sponge, syrup, cream and cherries. Top with the third cake round and spoon over the remaining kirsch-flavoured syrup.

10 Spread a thin layer of the remaining cream around the sides of the cake, reserving a third to decorate. Press on the chocolate caraque, reserving a few to decorate the top.

11 Spoon the remaining cream into a piping bag, fitted with a large star nozzle and pipe whirls of cream around the edge of the cake. Top each whirl with a chocolate curl.

12 Fill the centre with the reserved cherries. Blend the arrowroot with 45 ml (3 tbsp) cherry syrup, place in a small saucepan, bring to the boil and boil, stirring, for a few minutes until the mixture is clear. Brush the glaze over the cherries.

CARAMEL BANANA TORTE

In stage 6, work quickly, so that the caramel doesn't set before you have a chance to spread it over the top of the gâteau.

•

M A K E S   8   S L I C E S

FOR THE CAKE

175 g (6 oz) self-raising flour

1.25 ml (¼ level tsp) baking powder

1.25 ml (¼ level tsp) bicarbonate of soda

50 g (2 oz) butter or margarine, cut into pieces

150 g (5 oz) caster sugar

175 g (6 oz) ripe bananas

2.5 ml (½ level tsp) freshly ground nutmeg

45 ml (3 tbsp) milk

1 egg, beaten

FOR THE CARAMEL

75 g (3 oz) sugar

Caramel Banana Torte (below)

FOR THE FILLING AND DECORATION

175 g (6 oz) full fat soft cheese

30 ml (2 tbsp) lemon juice

30 ml (2 level tbsp) icing sugar

175 g (6 oz) ripe bananas

50 g (2 oz) flaked almonds, toasted

1   Grease a 20.5 cm (8 inch) round cake tin, line the base with greaseproof paper and grease the paper.

2   Sift the flour, baking powder and bicarbonate of soda into a bowl. Rub in the butter until the mixture resembles fine breadcrumbs, then stir in the caster sugar.

3   Peel the bananas and mash them in a bowl, then beat in the nutmeg, milk and egg. Stir the banana mixture into the dry ingredients.

4   Turn into the prepared tin and level the surface. Bake in the oven at 180°C (350°F) mark 4 for about 40 minutes. Cool in the tin for 5 minutes before turning out on to a wire rack to cool completely. Cut the cake in half horizontally.

5   To make the caramel, put the sugar into a small saucepan. Dissolve, without stirring, over gentle heat, then boil until a rich brown colour.

6   When the caramel is ready, immediately pour it on to the cake and use an oiled knife to spread the caramel so that it completely covers the top. Mark into eight portions with the point of a knife.

7   Put the soft cheese, lemon juice and icing sugar into a bowl and beat together. Peel and chop the bananas and add to half of the cheese mixture. Use this mixture to sandwich the cakes together.

8   Spread a little of the remaining cheese mixture around the sides of the cake and cover with most of the almonds. Decorate the top with the remaining cheese mixture and the remaining almonds.

CHOCOLATE AND CHESTNUT MERINGUE GÂTEAU

The meringues can be made in advance and stored in an airtight container. Do not sandwich them with the filling more than 2 hours before serving.

•

MAKES 10–12 SLICES

FOR THE CAKE

175 g (6 oz) shelled hazelnuts

6 egg whites

350 g (12 oz) caster sugar

FOR THE FILLING AND DECORATION

225 g (8 oz) dark or bitter chocolate

60 ml (4 tbsp) dark rum

350 g (12 oz) sweetened chestnut purée

300 ml (½ pint) double or whipping cream

chocolate caraque (see pages 30–1) or grated chocolate, to decorate

*Chocolate and Chestnut Meringue Gâteau
(below)*

1   Grease three 20.5 cm (8 inch) round sandwich tins and line the bases with grease-proof paper.

2   Toast the hazelnuts lightly under the grill, shaking the pan frequently. Transfer the nuts to a clean tea towel and rub gently while still hot to remove the skins. Grind until very fine.

3   Put the egg whites in a large bowl and whisk until very stiff and standing in peaks. Whisk in half of the sugar until the meringue is glossy. Fold in the remaining sugar with the hazelnuts.

4   Spoon the meringue into the prepared sandwich tins. Level the tops and bake in the oven at 180°C (350°F) mark 4 for 35–40 minutes until crisp.

5   Invert the tins on to a wire rack and turn out the meringues. Peel off the lining papers carefully. (Don't worry if the meringues are cracked.) Leave to cool.

6   To make the filling, break the chocolate in pieces into a heatproof bowl standing over a saucepan of gently simmering water. Add the rum and heat gently until the chocolate has melted, stirring only once or twice after the chocolate has started to melt. Remove from the heat and gradually blend in 225 g (8 oz) of the chestnut purée.

7   Put 1 meringue round, soft side uppermost, on a serving plate. Spread with half of the chocolate and chestnut mixture, then top with the second meringue round, crisp side uppermost. Spread with the remaining mixture then top with the last round.

8   Whip the cream until it holds its shape. Reserve 30 ml (2 tbsp) of the cream and swirl the remainder all over the gâteau to cover the top and sides completely. Blend the remaining chestnut purée into the reserved cream, then pipe around the edge. Decorate with chocolate caraque or grated chocolate. Chill in the refrigerator before serving.

CHOCOLATE FUDGE CAKE

This gooey, triple-layered chocolate cake is best cut with a large, sharp, wetted knife.

———————— • ————————

MAKES 12 – 14 SLICES

FOR THE CAKE

275 g (10 oz) plain flour

45 ml (3 tbsp) cocoa powder

6.25 ml (1¼ level tsp) baking powder

2.5 ml (½ tsp) bicarbonate of soda

large pinch of salt

100 g (4 oz) plain chocolate

150 g (5 oz) butter

225 g (8 oz) light brown soft sugar

2 eggs, size 2, beaten

150 ml (¼ pint) natural yogurt

2.5 ml (½ tsp) vanilla flavouring

FOR THE FUDGE ICING

450 g (1 lb) icing sugar

100 g (4 oz) cocoa powder

100 g (4 oz) butter

90 ml (6 tbsp) milk

1 Grease three 18 cm (7 inch) sandwich tins, line with greaseproof paper and grease the paper.

2 Sift together the flour, cocoa powder, baking powder, bicarbonate of soda and salt.

3 Break the chocolate into a bowl. Place over a saucepan of simmering water and heat gently, stirring, until the chocolate has melted. Leave to cool for 30 minutes.

4 Cream the butter and the brown sugar together until light and fluffy. Beat in the eggs, then fold in the chocolate, the sifted ingredients, the yogurt and the vanilla flavouring.

5 Turn the mixture into the prepared tins and level the surface. Bake in the oven at 190°C (375°F) mark 5 for 25–30 minutes until risen and firm to the touch. Turn out and leave to cool on a wire rack.

6 To make the fudge icing, sift the icing sugar and cocoa powder together, then put into a heavy-based saucepan with the butter and the milk. Heat gently until the butter has melted, then beat until smooth. Remove from the heat.

7 Use some of the fudge icing to sandwich the three cakes together. Cover the sides and top of the cake with the remaining icing.

GÂTEAU AMANDINE

A moule à manqué tin is a deep sandwich tin with sloping sides.

———————— • ————————

MAKES ABOUT 8 SLICES

FOR THE CAKE

3 large eggs

125 g (4 oz) caster sugar

75 g (3 oz) plain flour

FOR THE FILLING AND DECORATION

300 ml (½ pint) double cream

30 ml (2 tbsp) almond liqueur

30 ml (2 level tbsp) icing sugar

100 g (4 oz) flaked and toasted almonds

1 Grease a moule à manqué cake tin measuring 24 cm (9½ inches) across the top. Line the base with greaseproof paper.

2 Put the eggs and sugar in a bowl, stand it over a pan of hot water and whisk until thick, creamy and pale in colour. The mixture should be stiff enough to leave a trail when the whisk is lifted. Remove from the heat and continue whisking until cool.

3 Sift the flour over the surface and lightly fold in with a metal spoon.

4 Turn the mixture into the prepared tin and bake in the oven at 190°C (375°F) mark 5 for about 30 minutes, until well risen and golden brown. Turn out and cool on a wire rack.

5 Whip the cream with the liqueur and icing sugar, until it stands in soft peaks. Spread the cream all over the cake so that it is completely covered. Sprinkle over the nuts. Dust lightly with icing sugar and chill.

CHOCOLATE AND CHESTNUT GÂTEAU

Thin layers of chocolate sponge are sandwiched together with a rich, gooey chestnut cream. The easiest way to halve the cakes is to use a large knife with a long, sharp blade. Lay the cakes flat on a board, then slice through horizontally. When you sandwich the cakes back together, make sure that you replace them in their original position, or you may end up with a lop-sided cake.

—————————— • ——————————

MAKES 12 SLICES

FOR THE CAKE

50 g (2 oz) butter

4 eggs

100 g (4 oz) caster sugar

75 g (3 oz) plain flour

25 g (1 oz) cocoa powder

FOR THE FILLING AND DECORATION

100 g (4 oz) plain chocolate

425 g (15 oz) can natural chestnut purée

300 ml (½ pint) double cream

30 ml (2 tbsp) brandy

canned whole chestnuts, drained

grated chocolate

icing sugar, for dusting

1 Grease two 23 cm (9 inch) sandwich tins and line the bases with greaseproof paper.
2 Put the butter into a saucepan and heat gently until melted, then remove from the heat and leave to stand for a few minutes to cool slightly.
3 Put the eggs and sugar in a bowl, place over a pan of hot water and whisk until pale and creamy and thick enough to leave a trail on the surface when the whisk is lifted. Remove from the heat and whisk until cool.
4 Sift the flour and cocoa together into a bowl. Fold half of it into the egg mixture with a metal spoon. Pour half the cooled butter around the edge of the mixture. Gradually fold in the remaining butter and flour mixture alternately. Fold in very lightly or the butter will sink and result in a heavy cake.

5 Pour into the prepared tins and bake in the oven at 180°C (350°F) mark 4 for 25–30 minutes until well risen, firm to the touch and beginning to shrink away from the sides of the tin. Turn out and cool on a wire rack.
6 To make the filling, break the chocolate into a small bowl, stand over a pan of simmering water and heat until melted. Pour into a food processor with the chestnut purée and the cream and blend until smooth. Leave to cool and thicken slightly.
7 Carefully slice each cake in half horizontally and sandwich together with a little of the cream. Cover the top and sides with the remaining cream and mark in a decorative pattern with a palette knife. Decorate with chestnuts dipped in grated chocolate and dust lightly with a little icing sugar.

CHOCOLATE-WRAPPED ORANGE LIQUEUR GÂTEAU

A spectacular gâteau to make when you have some spare time. The sponge is soaked in a liqueur syrup, and coated in an intriguing chocolate frill that is easy to make but never fails to impress.

————————— • —————————

MAKES ABOUT 12 SLICES

FOR THE SPONGE

200 g (7 oz) self-raising flour
50 g (2 oz) cornflour
7.5 ml (1½ level tsp) baking powder
175 g (6 oz) caster sugar
3 eggs, separated
finely grated rind and juice of 1 small orange
105 ml (7 tbsp) bland vegetable oil
45 ml (3 tbsp) milk

FOR THE LIQUEUR SYRUP

100 g (4 oz) granulated sugar
finely grated rind and juice of 1 orange
45 ml (3 tbsp) orange liqueur

FOR THE DECORATION

2 large oranges
300 ml (½ pint) double cream
225 g (8 oz) plain chocolate
cocoa powder, for dredging

1 Grease a deep 22 cm (8½ inch) spring-form cake tin and line the base with greaseproof paper.

2 To make the sponge, mix together the flours, baking powder and sugar. Blend the egg yolks with the orange rind and juice, oil and milk, and mix into the dry ingredients. Beat thoroughly with a wooden spoon to make a smooth batter.

3 Whisk the egg whites until stiff then fold into the cake batter. Pour into the prepared tin and bake in the oven at 180°C (350°F) mark 4 for about 55 minutes or until well risen and firm to the touch.

4 Meanwhile, make the syrup. Put the sugar, orange rind and juice and 60 ml (4 tbsp) water in a heavy-based saucepan and heat gently until the sugar dissolves. Bring to the boil and boil rapidly for 2 minutes. Stir in the liqueur.

5 Prick the hot cake all over with a fork, then spoon over the hot syrup. Leave to cool.

6 When the cake is cold, peel the oranges, discarding all of the white pith. Roughly chop the flesh. Whip the cream until it forms soft peaks.

7 Remove the cake from the tin and place on a serving plate. Arrange the chopped orange on top. Spread the cream over the top and sides to cover completely.

8 Break the chocolate into a small bowl and stand over a saucepan of simmering water until melted. Meanwhile cut a strip of greaseproof paper long enough to go round the sides of the cake and wide enough to come 4 cm (1½ inches) above the cake. When the chocolate is melted, spread it evenly all over the paper with a palette knife. Leave to cool until no longer runny but still sticky when pressed with a finger.

9 Wrap the chocolate around the gâteau, pressing it gently on to the cream so that it sticks. Carefully pinch the chocolate and paper into pleats where it extends above the cake. Leave until set then carefully peel away the paper. Dust the top with a little cocoa powder.

CHOCOLATE-WRAPPED ORANGE LIQUEUR GÂTEAU (above)

WHITE CHOCOLATE GÂTEAU (*overleaf*)

WHITE CHOCOLATE GÂTEAU

This rich gâteau, covered in a mass of white chocolate curls, is delicious enough to be served as an alternative wedding cake. If doing so, place the cake on a large cake stand and surround with fresh flowers.

•

MAKES ABOUT 18 – 20 SLICES

FOR THE CAKE

75 g (3 oz) butter

6 eggs

175 g (6 oz) caster sugar

150 g (5 oz) plain flour

30 g (2 level tbsp) cornflour

FOR THE DARK CHOCOLATE MOUSSE FILLING

175 g (6 oz) plain chocolate

30 ml (2 tbsp) brandy

2 eggs, separated

300 ml (½ pint) double cream

5 ml (1 level tsp) powdered gelatine

FOR THE DECORATION

150 ml (¼ pint) double cream

275 g (10 oz) white chocolate

icing sugar, for dusting

1   For the cake, grease a 23 cm (9 inch) round spring-form tin, line with greaseproof paper and grease the paper.

2   Put the butter into a saucepan and heat gently until melted, then remove from the heat and leave to stand for a few minutes to cool slightly.

3   Put the eggs and sugar in a bowl, place over a pan of hot water and whisk until pale and creamy and thick enough to leave a trail on the surface when the whisk is lifted. Remove from the heat and whisk until cool.

4   Sift the flours together into a bowl. Fold half the flour into the egg mixture with a metal spoon. Pour half the cooled butter around the

edge of the mixture. Gradually fold in the remaining butter and flour alternately. Fold in very lightly or the butter will sink and result in a heavy cake.

5   Pour into the prepared tin. Bake in the oven at 180°C (350°F) mark 4 for 35–40 minutes, until well risen, firm to the touch and beginning to shrink away from the sides of the tin. Turn out and cool on a wire rack.

6   When the cakes are cold, make the mousse filling. Break the chocolate into a bowl and stand over a pan of simmering water until the chocolate melts. Remove from the heat and stir in the brandy and egg yolks. Whip the cream until it just stands in soft peaks, then fold into the chocolate mixture.

7   In a small bowl sprinkle the gelatine on to 15 ml (1 tbsp) water. Stand over a pan of simmering water and stir until dissolved. Cool, then stir into the chocolate mixture. Whisk the egg whites until stiff then fold in.

8   Cut the cake in half. Put one piece of sponge back in the tin. Pour the mousse on top. Put the second piece of sponge on top. Leave to set.

9   While the mousse is setting, make the decoration. Melt the white chocolate as in step 6. Spread out thinly on a marble slab or a clean, smooth work surface. Leave until set. When the chocolate is set, push a clean stripping knife (see note, below) across the chocolate at an angle of about 25° to roll off large fat chocolate curls. Chill until ready for decorating.

10   When the mousse is set, whip the cream until it holds its shape. Ease the cake out of the tin and cover with the cream. Cover completely with the chocolate curls and dust lightly with a little icing sugar.

Note A stripping knife is a decorator's tool used for scraping off wallpaper! It has a sharp flexible blade and is ideal for making large chocolate curls. We suggest that you buy one and keep it specifically for this purpose. A large sharp knife can be used instead (see pages 30–1) but does not make such large fat curls.

CHOCOLATE ROULADE WITH CRUSHED STRAWBERRY CREAM

This is best made in the height of summer with glorious ruby red English strawberries bursting with flavour. Whatever the variety of strawberry you use make sure they are ripe.

•

MAKES 8–10 SLICES

FOR THE ROULADE

100 g (4 oz) dark chocolate

4 eggs, separated

100 g (4 oz) caster sugar

FOR THE CRUSHED STRAWBERRY CREAM

150 ml (¼ pint) double cream

225 g (8 oz) ripe strawberries

15 ml (1 tbsp) icing sugar

150 g (¼ pint) Greek yogurt

few drops rose water (optional)

FOR THE DECORATION

caster sugar, for sprinkling

150 ml (¼ pint) double cream

icing sugar, for dusting

100 g (4 oz) ripe strawberries

few small rose, geranium or mint leaves

1 Grease a 23 × 33 cm (9 × 13 inch) Swiss roll tin, line with greaseproof paper and grease the paper. To make the roulade, break the chocolate into small pieces into a bowl and stand over a pan of simmering water. Heat gently until the chocolate melts.

2 Whisk the egg yolks with the sugar until very thick and pale in colour. Beat in the chocolate. Whisk the egg whites until stiff then fold carefully into the chocolate mixture.

3 Pour into the prepared tin and spread out evenly. Bake in the oven at 180°C (350°F) mark 4 for 20–25 minutes until well risen and firm to the touch.

4 While the roulade is cooking, lay a piece of greaseproof paper on a flat work surface and sprinkle generously with caster sugar.

5 When the roulade is cooked, turn it out on to the paper. Carefully peel off the lining paper. Cover the roulade with a warm, damp tea towel and leave to cool.

6 To make the crushed strawberry cream, whip the cream until it forms soft peaks. Hull and slice the strawberries. Mash half of the strawberries with the icing sugar until the juice starts to run. Fold into the cream with a few drops of rose water and the yogurt. Fold in the remaining sliced strawberries.

7 Spread the cream over the roulade. Starting from one of the narrow ends, carefully roll it up, using the paper to help. Do not worry if it cracks – this is quite usual and indeed adds to the appearance of the finished roulade.

8 Transfer the roulade to a serving plate and dust generously with icing sugar. To decorate, whip the remaining cream until it forms soft peaks and spoon into a piping bag fitted with a star nozzle. Pipe the cream down the centre of the roulade and the sides. Decorate with strawberries and rose, geranium or mint leaves.

CELEBRATION AND SPECIAL OCCASION BAKING

There is bound to be an occasion in your life when you will have to turn your hand to making and decorating an extra special celebration cake. Whether it's a birthday, christening, anniversary or even a wedding don't be daunted – if you follow our step-by-step instructions in this chapter you won't go wrong, and your family and friends will much appreciate the effort you have put into making and decorating the cake as well as the special taste of home baking. Read through all the instructions before beginning.

Also in this chapter you will find cakes and pastries which are baked only at certain times of the year. They are often surrounded by history and legend. Simnel Cake, for example, used to be associated with Mothering Sunday in England when girls in service were given a holiday and a cake to take home with them. Here too are Black Bun, a rich fruit mixture enclosed in a shortcrust pastry case and baked in Scotland for Hogmanay; Bûche de Noël from France; Lebkuchen from Germany and Panettone from Italy.

RICH FRUIT CELEBRATION CAKE

A rich fruit cake is the traditional cake for family celebrations. At weddings, christenings, anniversaries and Christmas, the centrepiece will most often be a beautiful cake decorated with royal icing; beneath the sugar coating will be a dark, glossy cake loaded with fruit, candied peel, nuts and spices and soaked with brandy.

Like other rich cakes, fruit cakes are made by the creaming method (see page 18), but the mixture has to be slightly stiffer than usual to support the weight of the fruit; if the mixture is too wet the fruit is inclined to sink to the bottom. Remember that all dried fruit should be thoroughly cleaned and dried before use, and glacé cherries should be rinsed to remove any excess syrup, then dried. Toss all fruit in a little of the measured flour before using.

You will find that creaming and mixing a rich fruit cake is quite hard work – especially if you are making a large cake – and that the baking time is long. It is useful, therefore, to know that you can mix the ingredients one day and bake the cake the next, if that is more convenient: when you have prepared the cake mixture, put it in the cake tin, cover loosely with a clean cloth and leave it in a cool place until you are ready to bake it.

Protect the outside of a rich fruit cake from overbrowning during the long cooking by wrapping a double thickness of brown paper around the outside of the tin. Stand the tin on several thicknesses of brown paper or newspaper, on a baking sheet, in the oven and cover the top of the cake towards the end of cooking, if necessary.

All fruit cakes keep well, but the richest actually improve if kept for 2 or 3 months before you cut them.

INGREDIENTS

The following table indicates the quantities of ingredients required to make rich fruit cakes in the standard range of square and round tins. If you are using an irregular or unusual shaped tin, you will need to calculate how much mixture is required to fill it. To do this, simply fill your chosen tin with water, and measure the water. Then look on the chart to find the cake with the same or nearest liquid capacity and use the quantities of ingredients given for that size cake.

Having decided on the size, shape and number of cakes required, check the quantities of ingredients on the chart. Don't attempt to make the bigger sizes of cake unless you have a really large oven, as you should allow at least 2.5 cm (1 inch) space between the oven walls and the tin. For a three-tier cake, bake the two smaller ones together and the largest one separately.

METHOD

1 Pick over dried fruit to remove any stalks, etc.

2 Halve or quarter glacé cherries, chop the flaked almonds.

3 Sift together the flour and spices. Add the grated lemon rind.

4 Cream the butter and gradually beat in the sugar. (A large Kenwood mixer is ideal. Divide in half and cream in two lots if making very large quantities.)

5 Beat in the eggs a little at a time. If the mixture shows signs of curdling, beat in 15–30 ml (1–2 tbsp) of the measured flour.

6 Fold in the remaining flour followed by the fruit, nuts and brandy. (When making very large quantities it is easier to use a clean washing-up bowl and mix with the hands.)

7 Spoon the mixture into the prepared tin(s) (see pages 21–2). Level the surface using the back of a spoon. Hollow out the centre of the cake slightly so that the top will be level when cooked.

8 The mixture can be left over night at this stage: cover the tin with a clean, dry cloth and put it in a cool place but not in the refrigerator.

9 Bake in the oven on the lowest shelf at 150°C (300°F) mark 2 for the time stated on the chart. Look at the cake half-way through cooking. If it seems to be browning too quickly, reduce the heat to 130°C (250°F) mark ½. Do this automatically when baking large cakes.

10 Allow the cake to cool in the tin.

11 When cold store as below.

RICH FRUIT CAKE

Note: when baking large cakes 20 cm (10 in) and upwards, it is advisable to reduce the oven heat to 130°C (250°F) mark ½ after two-thirds of the cooking time.

Square tin (side)	12.5 cm (5 in)	15 cm (6 in)	18 cm (7 in)	20.5 cm (8 in)	23 cm (9 in)	25.5 cm (10 in)	28 cm (11 in)	30.5 cm (12 in)	33 cm (13 in)
Round tin (diameter)	15 cm (6 in)	18 cm (7 in)	20.5 cm (8 in)	23 cm (9 in)	25.5 cm (10 in)	28 cm (11 in)	30.5 cm (12 in)	33 cm (13 in)	35.5 cm (14 in)
Approximate liquid capacity of mixture	600 ml (1 pint)	1 litre (1¾ pints)	1.4 litres (2.5 pints)	1.8 litres (3¼ pints)	3.7 litres (6½ pints)	4.1 litres (7¼ pints)	4.5 litres (8 pints)	6 litres (10½ pints)	6.6 litres (11½ pints)
Portions	16	20	28	36	48	72	92	120	136
Approximate cooked weight	900 g (2 lb)	1.1 kg (2½ lb)	1.6 kg (3½lb)	2.2 kg (4½lb)	2.7 kg (6lb)	4 kg (9 lb)	5.2 kg (11½ lb)	6.7 kg (15 lb)	7.7 kg (17 lb)
Ingredients Currants	200 g (7 oz)	225 g (8 oz)	350 g (12 oz)	400 g (14 oz)	625 g (1 lb 6 oz)	775 g (1 lb 12 oz)	1.1 kg (2 lb 8 oz)	1.5 kg (3 lb 4 oz)	1.7 kg (3 lb 12 oz)
Sultanas	75 g (3 oz)	100 g (4 oz)	125 g (4½ oz)	175 g (6 oz)	225 g (8 oz)	375 g (13 oz)	400 g (14 oz)	525 g (1 lb 3 oz)	625 g (1 lb 6 oz)
Seedless raisins	75 g (3 oz)	100 g (4 oz)	125 g (4½ oz)	175 g (6 oz)	225 g (8 oz)	375 g (13 oz)	400 g (14 oz)	525 g (1 lb 3 oz)	625 g (1 lb 6 oz)
Glacé cherries	50 g (2 oz)	50 g (2 oz)	75 g (3 oz)	125 g (4½ oz)	175 g (6 oz)	250 g (9 oz)	275 g (10 oz)	350 g (12 oz)	425 g (15 oz)
Mixed peel	25 g (1 oz)	25 g (1 oz)	50 g (2 oz)	75 g (3 oz)	100 g (4 oz)	150 g (5 oz)	200 g (7 oz)	250 g (9 oz)	275 g (10 oz)
Flaked almonds	25 g (1 oz)	25 g (1 oz)	50 g (2 oz)	50 g (2 oz)	100 g (4 oz)	150 g (5 oz)	200 g (7 oz)	250 g (9 oz)	275 g (10 oz)
Lemon rind (as a fraction of lemons)	a little	a little	a little	a little	¼ lemon	¼ lemon	½ lemon	½ lemon	1 lemon
Plain flour	150 g (5 oz)	175 g (6 oz)	200 g (7 oz)	300 g (11 oz)	400 g (14 oz)	600 g (1 lb 5 oz)	700 g (1 lb 8 oz)	825 g (1 lb 13 oz)	1 kg (2 lb 6 oz)
Mixed spice	1.25 ml (¼ level tsp)	1.25 ml (¼ level tsp)	2.5 ml (½ level tsp)	2.5 ml (½ level tsp)	5 ml (1 level tsp)	5 ml (1 level tsp)	10 ml (2 level tsp)	12.5 ml (2½ level tsp)	12.5 ml (2½ level tsp)
Cinnamon	1.25 ml (¼ level tsp)	1.25 ml (½ level tsp)	2.5 ml (½ level tsp)	2.5 ml (½ level tsp)	5 ml (1 level tsp)	5 ml (2 level tsp)	10 ml (2 level tsp)	12.5 ml (2½ level tsp)	12.5 ml (2½ level tsp)
Butter	125 g (4½ oz)	150 g (5 oz)	175 g (6 oz)	250 g (9 oz)	350 g (12 oz)	500 g (1 lb 2 oz)	600 g (1 lb 5 oz)	800 g (1 lb 12 oz)	950 g (2 lb 2 oz)
Dark brown soft sugar	125 g (4½ oz)	150 g (5 oz)	175 g (6 oz)	250 g (9 oz)	350 g (12 oz)	500 g (1 lb 2 oz)	600 g (1 lb 5 oz)	800 g (1 lb 12 oz)	950 g (2 lb 2 oz)
Eggs, beaten	2	2½	3	4	6	9	11	14	17
Brandy	15 ml (1 tbsp)	15 ml (1 tbsp)	15 ml (1 tbsp)	15–30 ml (1–2 tbsp)	30 ml (2 tbsp)	30–45 ml (2–3 tbsp)	45 ml (3 tbsp)	60 ml (4 tbsp)	90 ml (6 tbsp)
Approximate cooking time	2½ hrs	2½–3 hrs	3 hrs	3½ hrs	4 hrs	5½ hrs	7 hrs	8 hrs	8½ hrs

STORING THE CAKE

When the cake is cold wrap it in greaseproof paper and then in foil, making sure that it is completely covered. Store in a cool, dry place until you need to ice it. This cake is best left for about 3 months to mature before using. Note that you will need to start almond pasting the cake 3–4 weeks before icing. If liked, unwrap the cake every 2–3 weeks, prick the surface with a fine skewer and spoon over a little brandy or other spirit.

NOTES FOR COOKING CAKES

The cooking times and temperatures given on the charts are intended only as a guide – ovens vary widely. If you know that your oven is hot then cook for less than the stated time; if it is slow, then cook for longer. For fan ovens adjust the cooking times and temperatures in line with the manufacturers' instructions. Always test the cake before removing from the oven, by inserting a fine warmed skewer into the centre. It should come out clean when the cake is done.

TIERED CAKES

·

Traditionally a wedding cake has 2 or 3 tiers, which make for an impressive centrepiece. Second weddings or smaller occasions may, however, only warrant a single tier.

When making a tiered cake it is essential to get the proportions of the tiers correct, to give the desired triangular effect. Overleaf are examples of well-balanced cakes, the choice being dependent on the number of guests the cake is to serve.

THREE TIERS

Use a 30.5 cm (12 inch) cake with a 20.5 cm (8 inch) and a 15 cm (6 inch) cake. This will serve about 130.

Use a 28 cm (11 inch) cake with an 18 cm (7 inch) and a 12.5 cm (5 inch) cake. This will serve about 100.

The smallest base you should use is 28 cm (11 inches).

TWO TIERS

Use a 30.5 cm (12 inch) cake with an 18 cm (7 inch) cake. This will serve about 110.

Use a 25.5 cm (10 inch) cake with a 15 cm (6 inch) cake. This will serve about 60.

The smallest base you should use is 25.5 cm (10 inches).

SUPPORTING THE TIERS

The tiers of a royal iced cake are supported on pillars. Pillars between the base cake and the next tier are usually 9 cm (3½ inches) high and those between the middle tier and top tier 7.5 cm (3 inches) high. They are available in white or silver polythene or white plaster.

Fondant icing, unlike royal icing, does not have the strength to support tiers. Specially adapted drilled pillars, which support the weight of the tiers on wooden skewers, should be used. Alternatively, special 'swan-necked' stands can be hired from specialist shops. These offer 3 positions at which the cake can be placed.

COUNTDOWN TO THE DAY

When making and decorating a celebration cake it is important that sufficient time is allowed between the various stages for the almond paste and royal icing layers to dry thoroughly. You should aim to complete the cake about a week before it is required, no earlier. You can, however, almond paste and fondant ice a cake on the same day.

19–30 days before Apply the almond paste.

Loosely cover the cake and store in a cool, dry place for 7–14 days.

12–16 days before Apply the first coat of royal icing and leave to dry for 1–2 days, then apply the second coat.

10–14 days before Apply the third coat of royal icing and leave to dry for 1–2 days.

8–12 days before Assemble or make all the decorations required for the cake.

7 days before Complete all further decorating a week before the cake is to be served. Do not assemble a tiered cake, however, until the very last possible moment.

CAKE BOARDS

Cake boards, known in the trade as drums, should be of good quality. They are available in silver or gold. Choose a board that measures 5 cm (2 inches) larger than the cake. For a very large cake use a board 4 cm (1½ inches) larger than the cake.

ALMOND PASTE

Almond paste or marzipan is usually only applied to fruit cakes. Here it performs two important functions: it creates a smooth foundation for the icing, and protects the cake from discolouring the decoration. For both these reasons it is important to apply the marzipan as neatly as possible.

You can either make your own almond paste, following the recipes below, or buy it ready made. When buying ready-made, choose the white variety not the yellow. Check that it is fresh, as old stock may have hardened at the edges. Ready-made is the best choice as it is less likely to discolour the icing.

If royal icing a cake, cover the cake with almond paste 1–2 weeks before the first coat of icing, to allow the almond paste to dry. Home-made almond paste takes longer to dry out than the shop-bought variety.

QUANTITY GUIDE

Square tin (side)	12.5 cm (5 inches)	15 cm (6 inches)	18 cm (7 inches)	20.5 cm (8 inches)	23 cm (9 inches)	25.5 cm (10 inches)	28 cm (11 inches)	30.5 cm (12 inches)	33 cm (13 inches)
Round tin (diameter)	15 cm (6 inches)	18 cm (7 inches)	20.5 cm (8 inches)	23 cm (9 inches)	25.5 cm (10 inches)	28 cm (11 inches)	30.5 cm (12 inches)	33 cm (13 inches)	35.5 cm (14 inches)
Almond paste	350 g (12 oz)	450 g (1 lb)	550 g (1 lb 4 oz)	800 g (1 lb 12 oz)	900 g (2 lb)	1 kg (2 lb 4 oz)	1.1 kg (2 lb 8 oz)	1.4 kg (3 lb)	1.6 kg (3 lb 8 oz)

The above table indicates the amount of almond paste needed to cover various sizes of square and round cakes. Purchase accordingly or multiply the recipes as appropriate.

UNCOOKED METHOD
M A K E S   4 5 0 g   (1 l b)

225 g (8 oz) ground almonds

125 g (4 oz) caster sugar

125 g (4 oz) icing sugar

1 egg

5 ml (1 tsp) lemon juice

5 ml (1 tsp) sherry

1–2 drops vanilla essence

1   Place the almonds and sugars in a bowl and mix together. Whisk the egg with the remaining ingredients and add to the dry mixture.
2   Stir well to mix. Knead with your hands until the paste is smooth. Wrap in cling film.

BOILED METHOD
M A K E S   4 5 0 g   (1 l b)

225 g (8 oz) preserving or granulated sugar

pinch of cream of tartar

175 g (6 oz) ground almonds

1 egg white

50 g (2 oz) icing sugar

1   Put the sugar and 75 ml (5 tbsp) water in a heavy-based saucepan and dissolve over a low heat. When the syrup reaches boiling point, add the cream of tartar and boil to 116°C (240°F).
2   Remove the pan from the heat and stir rapidly until the syrup begins to 'grain'.
3   Stir in the almonds and egg white. Cook for a few minutes over a low heat, stirring.

4   Pour on to an oiled marble slab or wooden chopping board, add icing sugar and work well with a palette knife, lifting the edges of the mixture and turning them into the centre.
5   As soon as the mixture is sufficiently cool, knead it until smooth. Additional icing sugar may be kneaded in if the mixture is too wet. Wrap in cling film until ready to use.

COVERING THE CAKE WITH ALMOND PASTE

1   If the cake has a very uneven top, cut it level or roll out a sausage shape of almond paste and stick it on to the edges with hot apricot glaze (see recipe on page 150), then turn the cake over so that the flat bottom becomes the top.
2   Sift some icing sugar on to a clean work surface. Roll out half the almond paste slightly larger than the top of the cake. Using the tin as a guide, cut the almond paste to fit. Brush the top of the cake with hot apricot glaze. Carefully lift the almond paste on to the cake and smooth over, neatening the edges if necessary. Place on a board, which should be 5 cm (2 inches) larger than the cake size.
3   Cut two pieces of string – one the height of the cake plus almond paste, and one the length around the cake. Roll out the remaining almond paste and, using the string as a guide, trim the almond paste neatly to size. Brush the sides of the cake and the almond paste rim with apricot glaze. Roll up the almond paste strip loosely. Place on end on to the side of the cake and carefully unroll to cover the sides of the cake. Follow the same method to cover the sides of a square cake, but cut four oblong strips to fit each side. Unroll them carefully around the sides so that they cover them evenly. Use a small palette knife to smooth the joins. Roll a rolling pin lightly over the top to flatten.

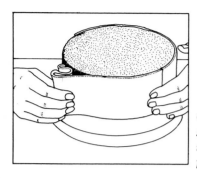

Covering the sides of a cake with almond paste

4 Place the cake on a cake board (see page 148) and leave in a warm, dry room to dry out for at least a week before icing. An almond pasted cake should *never* be tightly covered as this prevents it drying out. If liked, simply lay a piece of greaseproof paper over the top to protect the cake from dust.

APRICOT GLAZE

MAKES ABOUT 150 ml (^{1}/$_4$ pint)

---
125 g (4 oz) apricot jam
---

1 Place the jam and 30 ml (2 tbsp) water in a small pan. Heat gently, stirring, until the jam begins to melt. Bring to the boil and simmer for 1 minute.
2 Using a nylon sieve, strain the jam into another small pan. Use whilst hot.

FONDANT (MOULDING) ICING

·

Fondant is also known as sugar paste. It is a very versatile icing and it provides an easy-to-apply covering as well as a means to mould your own decorations. As with almond paste, fondant can be made at home or purchased ready made from supermarkets.

MAKES 450g (1lb)

---
400 g (14 oz) icing sugar
---
1 egg white
---
50 g (2 oz) liquid glucose or glucose syrup
---

1 Sift the icing sugar into a large bowl. Make a well in the centre and add the egg white and glucose. Beat these ingredients with a clean, wooden spoon, gradually pulling the icing sugar in from the sides of the bowl.
2 When the mixture becomes stiff, turn on to a surface sprinkled with icing sugar. Knead thoroughly to give a smooth and manageable paste.
3 Store tightly wrapped in polythene.

QUANTITY GUIDE
The table below indicates the amount of fondant needed to cover various-sized square or round cakes. Either purchase accordingly or multiply the recipe as appropriate.

COVERING CAKES WITH FONDANT ICING
1 Make or buy the quantity of fondant according to the chart.
2 Sprinkle a clean work surface with icing sugar and dredge your rolling pin. Roll out the icing until it is approximately 12.5–15 cm (5–6 inches) larger than the cake top.
3 Supporting the icing on a rolling pin, place the icing centrally over the top of the cake, allowing the icing to drape over the sides. For a round cake, trim away the excess icing that forms folds with a pair of scissors. For a square cake trim away the excess icing at the four corners. Press the icing on to the sides of the cake. Work it with your hands, sprinkled with cornflour, from the centre of the cake, gently easing the icing down the sides to give an even covering. Trim excess icing from the bottom of the cake using a sharp knife. Smooth over, using

Square tin (side)	12.5 cm (5 inches)	15 cm (6 inches)	18 cm (7 inches)	20.5 cm (8 inches)	23 cm (9 inches)	25.5 cm (10 inches)	28 cm (11 inches)	30.5 cm (12 inches)	33 cm (13 inches)
Round tin (diameter)	15 cm (6 inches)	18 cm (7 inches)	20.5 cm (8 inches)	23 cm (9 inches)	25.5 cm (10 inches)	28 cm (11 inches)	30.5 cm (12 inches)	33 cm (13 inches)	35.5 cm (14 inches)
Fondant (moulding icing)	350 g (12 oz)	450 g (1 lb)	700 g (1 lb 4 oz)	800 g (1 lb 12 oz)	900 g (2 lb)	1 kg (2 lb 4 oz)	1.1 kg (2 lb 8 oz)	1.4 kg (3 lb)	1.6 kg (3 lb 8 oz)

a circular movement with the fingers. Take care if you have long fingernails or wear rings as these will mark the icing.

4 Leave for about 2 days to dry before decorating.

COLOURING FONDANT ICING

Edible liquid, paste and powder colours can quickly be kneaded into prepared fondant. Add in the same way as for royal icing (see pages 152–3).

Hardened fondant icing can be painted in the same way as royal icing (see page 153).

ROYAL ICING

·

Royal icing is the traditional icing for covering and decorating special occasion cakes.

Omit the glycerine from the recipe if the icing is to cover a tiered cake, as a very hard surface is required to support the tiers.

Once prepared royal icing should be kept tightly covered.

M A K E S   4 5 0 g   (1 l b)

2 egg whites or albumen powder

10 ml (2 level tsp) liquid glycerine

450 g (1 lb) icing sugar

1 If you are using the egg whites with the glycerine, place them in a bowl and stir just enough to break up the egg whites. If using albumen powder, mix it according to the manufacturer's instructions.

2 Using a clean wooden spoon (it is wise to keep a spoon specifically for making royal icing), add a little sieved icing sugar and start gently mixing. The less air you incorporate the better, so mix slowly.

3 Add a little more icing sugar as the mixture becomes lighter. Continue to add the sugar,

stirring gently but thoroughly until the mixture is stiff and is standing in a soft peak. If the icing is required for coating, it should form soft peaks, for piping it should be a little stiffer. Transfer to a bowl with a close-fitting lid and cover the icing closely with cling film to exclude the air and prevent the surface of the icing drying out. Then seal. When required, stir the icing slowly to regain a usable consistency.

Note If using an electric mixer, add ¼–⅓ of the icing sugar to begin with and start mixing on a medium speed. As the volume increases, gradually add the rest of the sugar. It is the initial beating which makes the icing light and easy to handle. The addition of too much icing sugar without sufficient beating can result in a heavy icing which is difficult to handle for coating or piping. If the icing is made in an electric mixer it must be left for at least 24 hours covered as above. Stir before using.

QUANTITY GUIDE

The table below indicates the amount of royal icing needed to cover various-sized square and round, almond-pasted cakes. Multiply the recipe as appropriate. Remember that it is better not to make up more than 900 g (2 lb) at a time as smaller quantities of icing keep better. The chart below will give you enough icing for 2–3 coats (depending on how skilful you are). It is difficult to give an accurate guide as to the amount of icing needed for piping work – allow approximately 450 g (1 lb) royal icing to elaborately pipe a 30.5 cm (12 inch) cake.

FLAT ICING A CAKE WITH ROYAL ICING

·

Always apply royal icing over a layer of almond paste rather than directly on to the cake.

Square tin (side)	12.5 cm (5 inches)	15 cm (6 inches)	18 cm (7 inches)	20.5 cm (8 inches)	23 cm (9 inches)	25.5 cm (10 inches)	28 cm (11 inches)	30.5 cm (12 inches)	33 cm (13 inches)
Round tin (diameter)	15 cm (6 inches)	18 cm (7 inches)	20.5 cm (8 inches)	23 cm (9 inches)	25.5 cm (10 inches)	28 cm (11 inches)	30.5 cm (12 inches)	33 cm (13 inches)	35.5 cm (14 inches)
Royal icing sugar weight	450 g (1 lb)	550 g (1 lb 4 oz)	700 g (1 lb 8 oz)	900 g (2 lb)	1 kg (2 lb 4 oz)	1.1 kg (2 lb 8 oz)	1.4 kg (3 lb)	1.6 kg (3 lb 8 oz)	1.8 kg (4 lb)

It is easier to apply royal icing in separate stages. The sides or top can be iced first, then left to dry for 24 hours before the next surface is iced. Two or 3 coats give the smoothest finish.

BASIC EQUIPMENT

An icing turntable about 15–20 cm (6–8 inches) high. Those that are precision made are the easiest to use.

A steel icing ruler for the top of the cake.

A serrated icing comb and plain scraper.

Small palette knife about 15 cm (6 inches) long.

TO COVER THE TOP

1 Put a large spoonful of icing on to the centre of the cake and smooth out, using a palette knife in a paddling motion. This helps to eliminate air bubbles.

2 Draw an icing ruler across the top of the cake towards you, maintaining an even pressure and keeping the ruler at an angle of about 30°. Repeat, backwards and forwards, until the icing is smooth.

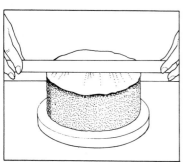

Icing the top of a cake

3 Remove surplus icing by running a palette knife around the edge of the cake, holding it at right angles to the cake. Don't worry if you don't achieve a very flat surface straight away. If necessary, scoop up excess icing from the sides on to the top of the cake and start again. Work quickly, though, as the icing will set quickly in a warm room. Leave to dry for at least 24 hours. Tightly cover the surface of the remaining icing with cling film and store in a cool place (not the refrigerator).

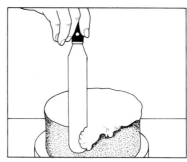

Removing surplus icing

TO COVER THE SIDES

1 For best results place the cake on an icing turntable. Spread a layer of icing on to the sides using the same paddling motion as for the top. Smooth the surface roughly.

2 Hold the side scraper at an angle of about 45° to the sides of the cake. Keeping the scraper still, revolve the turntable with the other hand, making just over one revolution. To achieve this, start with both hands at the back of the cake, the turning hand across the one holding the scraper. Move the hands in opposite directions. Draw the scraper off quickly to leave only a slight mark.

3 With a palette knife, carefully clean off excess icing at the top of the cake and base. Leave to dry for 24 hours. Store the remaining icing as above.

FURTHER COATS

1 Trim off any rough icing with a sharp knife. Clean fine sandpaper can be used to achieve a very smooth finish. Brush off loose icing with a clean pastry brush.

2 Repeat the layers of icing as before. Three coats should be sufficient, but a fourth layer can be added to the top surface to strengthen it and to ensure an ultra-smooth finish. Leave to dry for 24 hours before attempting to apply any decorations.

COLOURING ROYAL ICING

Royal icing can be easily coloured with paste liquid and powder colours.

Food colours are very concentrated so add them a little at a time. The best method is to dip a cocktail stick into the colour and then into the icing. Mix well. Continue adding colour and mixing until the correct shade is achieved. If the correct colour is not available try mixing 2 or 3 colours together to achieve the required result. If you want to use coloured icing to flat ice a cake, make up sufficient to carry out all coats otherwise shading will result, as it is extremely difficult to match a shade exactly.

PAINTING ROYAL ICING
Hardened royal icing can be painted to create designs, by using a thin paintbrush dipped in colouring. If you find the colour runs, add a touch of royal icing or icing sugar to thicken the colour before applying it.

Gold and Silver Metallic colours are often called for on formal celebration cakes. These should be used in small quantities and painted on to finished decorations, *not* mixed with the icing. Don't paint large areas as the colour should not be consumed in large quantities.

TIPS FOR SUCCESSFUL ICING
Royal icing attracts both grease and water, which can cause flat icing to discolour. The following tips should avoid this happening.

* Ensure that the marzipan covers the cake well – it acts as a protective coating between the cake and icing.

* Avoid getting *any* apricot glaze or cake crumbs on to the surface of the icing.

* Don't overwork the marzipan. This draws out the oils naturally present in the almonds.

* Shop-bought marzipan is more stable than homemade and less likely to cause problems.

* Allow at least a week for the marzipan to dry before applying the icing.

* Use icing that is of the correct consistency ('soft peak').

* Store the iced cake in a *dry* cool place away from direct sunlight.

* Never finish a royal iced cake more than one week before the occasion.

DECORATING FLAT-ICED SPECIAL OCCASION CAKES
·

The icing on the cake is the finishing touch that turns an ordinary cake into a loving creation. Decorations for formal cakes should be something spectacular or eye-catching, so you will need to master piping techniques (see pages 154–6). You should aim to complete the cake about a week before it is required – no earlier.

EQUIPMENT
Simple decorations need no special equipment, but the right tools do help when you start to attempt more elaborate work.

An icing turntable gives you clearance from the working surface and enables you to turn the cake freely. If you do not have a turntable, place the cake board on an upturned plate to give it a little lift from the working surface.

An icing nail is a small metal or polythene nail with a large head that is designed to hold decorations, such as icing roses, while you make them. It enables you to hold the decoration securely, and turn it without damaging it. A cork fixed to a skewer can be used instead.

Piping bags can be made from greaseproof paper (see below), or bought ready-made in fabric. Special icing pumps are also available.

Nozzles can be used with paper or fabric piping bags. A fine plain nozzle (for writing and piping straight lines and simple designs), plus a star or shell nozzle, are the basics; more advanced piping work demands a whole range of different shapes and sizes. For use with paper piping bags, choose nozzles without a screw band.

TO MAKE AND FILL A GREASEPROOF PAPER ICING BAG
1 Fold a 25.5 cm (10 inch) square of greaseproof paper in half diagonally, to form a triangle.

2 Take one point from the long side, fold up to meet the middle point and twist under to form a cone.

3 Holding the middle points with one hand, take the second point from the other long side and twist over the cone to meet the middle points being held together. Secure all 3 together with a staple to form a firm cone.

4 Cut off the very tip of the bag with a pair of scissors and drop in the required nozzle.

5 Spoon in royal icing to little more than half full. Don't overfill the bag. Fold the bag over to trap in the icing.

HOLDING A GREASEPROOF ICING BAG

Open the hand and place the icing bag across the palm of the hand. Place the thumb on the cushion of folded paper at the top of the bag. Fold over the four fingers and apply a steady, even pressure until the icing begins to come out of the nozzle.

HOLDING A NYLON ICING BAG

Place the thumb and forefinger around the icing in a nylon icing bag and twist tightly 2 or 3 times. This stops the icing squeezing out of the top of the bag when pressure is applied.

Open the hand and place the icing bag across the palm of the hand. Clasp the bag where it is twisted with the thumb and forefinger and maintain an even grip. Fold over the other 3 fingers and apply a steady but even pressure until the icing begins to come out of the nozzle. Wipe the icing away from the nozzle and you are ready to start piping.

HOW TO USE A PLAIN NOZZLE

The consistency of the icing should be a little slacker than that for stars but at the same time able to hold its shape. Select a suitable nozzle: a very fine aperture requires considerable practice, a medium aperture is the most generally useful, a wide aperture is on the broad side for lines and writing. Place the nozzle in a bag and fill it with icing.

To pipe a straight line Place the top of the nozzle at the place where the straight line is to begin, holding it at an angle of about 45°. Apply slight pressure to the icing bag and as the icing starts to flow from the nozzle, lift the icing bag about 2.5 cm (1 inch) above the flat icing. Move the hand in the direction of the line allowing the icing to fall evenly. Do not pull the line taut, allow a little flexibility to keep a sagging line.

About 1 cm (½ inch) before the line is to finish, stop squeezing the icing bag and gently lower the tip of the nozzle to the surface. This action will end the line neatly. If you continue to squeeze the icing bag, the line will end with an ugly knob. Don't attempt to pipe a line with the nozzle touching the cake, as this results in an uneven line.

Trellis is a series of straight lines piped in one direction the same width apart. Repeat piping a second layer either at an angle to give diamond shapes or straight resulting in squares. Repeat piping further layers if wished over those already piped.

To pipe curved lines Once you have control of the icing flowing from the nozzle, you can progress to curved lines and loops. Make a template, draw a series of even-sized scallops on a piece of greaseproof paper or thin card and use for practising. Place the top of the nozzle at the start of the line, lift the nozzle and allow the line to drape along the curve of the scallop. Lower the nozzle back to the surface as the join between each scallop is reached. This is a development from trellis.

Writing Use the method for straight and curved lines, letting the icing drop nearer the surface. Practise simple capitals to start with, then go on to script. The letters can be drawn on grease-proof paper and pricked out on to the icing surface with a pin, or piped freehand.

To pipe dots Hold the top of the nozzle with the bag almost upright on the surface. Squeeze the icing bag slightly and at the same time lift the nozzle enough to form a dot. Almost at the same time break off the piping in a hardly visible down and up movement. Different sized dots can be formed by varying the nozzle size and the pressure on the bag.

HOW TO USE A PETAL NOZZLE

Cut small squares of non-stick or waxed paper and attach each one with a dot of icing to the top of an icing nail or a cork fixed to a skewer.

To pipe a rose place the nozzle in an icing bag with the tip cut away a little more than when using a star nozzle. Half fill with icing. Hold the nozzle with the thin part uppermost. Pipe a cone of icing, twisting the nail between the thumb and forefinger to form the rosebud.

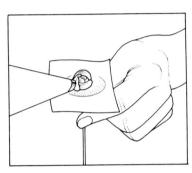

Piping a rose

Pipe petals – vary the shape of the roses by adding as many or as few as you wish. Overlap each one slightly and as the petal is piped open up and curl the edge by twisting the nozzle slightly away from the bud keeping the wide end against the nail. Leave the rose on the paper for at least 12 hours to dry. These roses keep for a week or so in an airtight container but any colour used may alter during long storage. Leaves can be piped directly on to the cake to represent sprays.

To pipe a daisy work with the thick edge of the nozzle to the centre and pipe 5 even-sized 'leaf' petals so that they meet in the middle. Keep the nozzle upright and use slight pressure to form a daisy head.

HOW TO USE A STAR NOZZLE

Star nozzles vary in the number of points and size of the piped star, rosette, scroll, etc.

For a star place the selected nozzle in the icing bag and add the icing. Hold the nozzle almost upright to the iced surface. Pipe out sufficient icing to form the star and withdraw the nozzle with a quick but hardly noticeable down-and-up action to release the icing neatly.

For a rosette use the same nozzle but move the piped icing in a circular motion – a nest-like formation – enclosing the centre. Pull the nozzle sharply away from the rosette to finish without forming a point or tail.

For a shell hold the nozzle at an angle to the surface and just above it. Squeeze the icing out until a 'head' is formed then gradually release the pressure and pull away the icing to leave a neat point and well-formed shell.

A shell border is achieved by piping a series of well-formed shells together each having its own identity with the head of one shell touching and fractionally overlapping the top of the next. In place of a straight shell edge the shells can be piped at an angle to one another.

For a scroll This is, in its simplest form, an elongated shell. A double scroll is piped in an S shape with two shell heads, one at each end.

RUN OUTS

A run out is a shaped piece of icing made to look like a letter, figure, flower, leaf, animal, etc. It is piped on to non-stick or waxed paper and fixed on to the cake when it is completely dry. Alternatively the run out can be piped directly on to the cake. In this case keep the royal icing of a flowing consistency.

1 Draw the outline distinctly on a piece of white card. Cut non-stick or waxed paper squares to amply cover it. Fix a piece over the outline with a spot of icing in each corner or hold with fingers of free hand.

2 Using an icing bag fitted with a plain no. 1 (fine) or no. 2 (medium) nozzle, trace a continuous line of piped icing on the waxed paper around the outline.

3 Using the same nozzle (or a forcing bag with the very tip cut off) pipe slightly softer icing into the centre of the shape. Using a skewer or tip of a pointed knife ease the icing to fill the shape with just enough icing to give a slightly domed finish. Small shapes can be gently tapped on the work surface. For large areas it may be easier to spoon the slacker icing into the shape. Repeat to give the number of shapes needed for the cake design with a few extras to cover breakages.

4 Leave for 1–2 days until completely dry.

5 Pipe in lines, dots or other details to complete the run out.

6 Lightly 'paste' the back of run out with icing and place in position within the overall design.

WEDDING CAKES

PLANNING THE DESIGN

It has become increasingly popular for some colour to be included in the design of wedding cakes. Only a small amount should be used, however, which ideally should pick up the colour of the bridesmaids' dresses.

When planning a design for a tiered wedding cake, you should aim to have the darkest colours, largest flowers and heaviest piping on the base tier and get progressively lighter as you move up the cake.

When you have decided on your design, draw out the pattern on a piece of greaseproof paper the same size as the top of the bottom tier of the cake. Do the same for the sides, if required. Scale the pattern down for the smaller tiers.

Place each paper pattern on its respective tier and prick out the key points on to the icing with a fine pin. You can then use these as a guide when applying the decorations.

When planning the design, don't forget to allow for the placing of the pillars that will support the tiers. Mark their position with pin pricks, but fix them only after the decoration is finished (see below).

ASSEMBLING THE CAKE

Don't assemble the cake, except as a practice run, until as near to the time of the reception as possible. This is essential for a royal iced cake as icing that has not hardened completely will crack if stacked too early.

Arrange for the cake to be stacked *just* before the guests arrive at the reception – never leave it assembled for hours before.

Fixing pillars to royal iced cakes Place a blob of icing on the base of the pillars and fix in position on the bottom tier of the cake. Carefully position the next tier on top of the pillars. Repeat with the remaining pillars and tiers.

Fixing pillars to fondant iced cakes Special drilled pillars with wooden skewers should be used (see page 148). Place the pillars in position on the bottom 2 tiers of the cake and insert the skewers through the holes in the pillars and into the cake, until the point of each skewer reaches the cake drum. Mark each skewer with a pencil 3 mm (⅛ inch) *above the top of its pillar.* Remove the skewers, leaving the pillars in position, and cut off the ends of the skewers at the pencil marks. Replace the trimmed skewers and assemble the cake. The weight of the tiers will now be supported by the skewers, rather than the pillars, which are for decoration.

STORING THE TOP TIER

If you want to store the iced top tier after the wedding, or a wedge from the lower tiers, wrap in greaseproof paper and then foil but do not keep it for longer than 2 months as mould can develop between the almond paste and the cake, and the icing may also start to yellow.

For long-term storage, remove the almond paste and royal icing then wrap the cake and store as above. Put on new almond paste and icing shortly before the cake is required.

DECORATING CAKES FOR CHILDREN'S BIRTHDAY PARTIES

Small children are always delighted with a novelty birthday cake, particularly if the cake depicts a favourite toy or story character. Not only is it a thrill for the children, but if you are preparing a birthday spread, the cake immediately becomes the centrepiece.

Fruit cakes are not always popular with children, so follow the Madeira cake recipe on page 159 and bake the cake in the shape you require. Number- and alphabet-shaped cake tins can be bought from specialist cookware shops. Alternatively, bake the cake in a large roasting tin, make a greaseproof paper template of the child's favourite cartoon character, etc, and use a guide for cutting the cooked cake.

Children's cakes can be covered with fondant

icing (see pages 150–1), butter cream or glacé icing (see page 27) and then decorated with favourite sweets or chocolate biscuits.

Remember that cakes look fresher if iced on the day of the party, although you may prefer to do this the night or day before. Store cakes overnight in an airtight container, not in the refrigerator as this will dry them out. Bear in mind that the colour from some sweets will 'bleed' into the icing if it is iced and decorated too soon and that biscuits will absorb moisture from the icing then lose their crispness.

ROSEBUD WEDDING CAKE (*overleaf*)

ROSEBUD WEDDING CAKE

Practice makes perfect when it comes to piping the decoration on a wedding cake, so try out your skills first on a board or a piece of paper before you tackle piping on the actual cake. Read the notes on pages 154–6 before starting. Traditionally the top tier is kept for the christening of the first child – if you intend to do this, then there will be enough cake left to serve about 140 people

·

one 30.5 cm (12 inch) round Rich Fruit Celebration Cake, covered in almond paste (see pages 146–7)

one 23 cm (9 inch) round Rich Fruit Celebration Cake, covered in almond paste (see pages 148–51)

one 15 cm (6 inch) round Rich Fruit Celebration Cake, covered in almond paste (see pages 148–51)

one 40.5 cm (16 inch) round cake board

one 28 cm (11 inch) round cake board

one 20.5 cm (8 inch) round cake board

pink royal icing made with 225 g (8 oz) icing sugar (see page 151)

white royal icing made with 2.7 kg (6 lb) icing sugar (see page 151)

four 9 cm (3½ inch) and four 7.5 cm (3 inch) round pillars

pink ribbon

fresh pink roses, optional

1   To make the icing roses, place a little royal icing on the top of an icing nail and stick a small square of non-stick or waxed paper on top. Place a petal nozzle in an icing bag and half-fill with pink royal icing. Pipe a cone of icing, twisting the nail between the thumb and forefinger, to form the centre of the icing rose.

2   Pipe five or six petals around the centre of the rose, overlapping each and piping the outer petals so they are more open and lie flatter. Repeat with more roses to make at least 22. Make a few more than this, if you have enough icing, to allow for breakages. Dry for 24 hours on the paper.

3   Place the cakes on the cake boards, then flat ice with two coats of royal icing (see pages 151–2). Leave to dry for 2 days between coats, and for a further 2 days after the final coat.

4   Place the pillars in position on the base and middle cakes and prick round each with a pin, for positioning later.

5   Cut a circle of greaseproof paper to the size of the top of each cake. Fold the largest 2 into 8 segments, the smallest into 6 segments. Using a compass or the bottom of a glass with the right diameter, pencil a scallop on the rounded edge between the folds about 5 cm (2 inches) deep for big cakes, and about 2.5 cm (1 inch) deep for the top tier. Cut out the scallops.

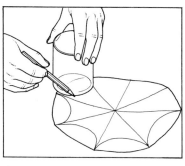

Marking the pattern on paper

6   Open out the paper and place the smallest piece in the centre of the smallest cake and the 2 larger pieces in the centre of the 2 largest cakes. Place on cake and hold the paper with one hand while pricking the scalloped outline on to the icing.

7   Remove the paper and, using an icing bag fitted with a plain no. 2 icing nozzle and filled with white icing, pipe a line of icing along the inner edge of the scallops. Pipe a trellis inside each scallop.

8   Using an icing bag fitted with a plain (no. 1) nozzle and filled with white icing, pipe a line 0.5 cm (¼ inch) outside the scalloped edge. Pipe two Vs and three dots at the join of each scallop.

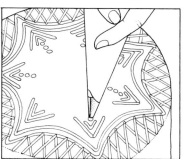

Decorating the top of the cake

9 Secure a piece of ribbon around each cake using headed pins.

10 Using an icing bag fitted with a three-point star nozzle and filled with white icing, pipe a star or shell border around the base of the cakes.

11 Carefully position the four 9 cm (3½ inch) pillars on top of the bottom (largest) cake layer using the pin pricks as a guide and secure them with icing. Place the second cake layer on top, then the remaining pillars. Secure the pillars with icing and place the remaining cake layer on top.

12 Complete the decoration by placing an icing rose at each of the points where the scallops meet. Add fresh pink roses, if liked.

MADEIRA CAKE

INGREDIENTS

The following table indicates the quantities of ingredients required to make Madeira cakes to fit the standard range of square and round tins. If you want to make a shaped cake, such as a number or heart, you need to know how much mixture is required to fill the special tin. This is quite simple to calculate. Simply fill the tin with water, to the depth you require the cake to be, and measure the water. Then look on the chart to find the cake with the same or nearest liquid capacity and use the quantities of ingredients given for that size cake. Remember to fill the tin only as deep as you want the finished cake to be – not necessarily to the very top.

The quantities given on the chart produce an intentionally shallow cake with depths ranging from 2.5–4 cm (1–1½ inches). This is the ideal depth of cake for cutting into novelty shapes, etc.

Having decided on the shape and size of the cake, check off the quantities of ingredients on the chart.

METHOD

1 Grease and line the tin(s) as directed on pages 21–2.

2 Soften the butter, add the sugar. Cream together until pale and fluffy.

3 Sift together the flours.

4 Beat the eggs – one at a time – into the creamed mixture. If it looks near to curdling add 15–30 ml (1–2 tbsp) flour.

5 Fold in the remaining flour with the grated lemon rind and juice. Turn into the prepared tin and level the top.

6 Bake at 170°C (325°F) mark 3 for the time given on the chart.

7 Allow to cool in the tin for 5–10 minutes then turn out on a wire rack to cool completely.

Square tin (side)	12.5 cm (5 in)	15 cm (6 in)	18 cm (7 in)	20.5 cm (8 in)	23 cm (9 in)	25.5 cm (10 in)	28 cm (11 in)	30.5 cm (12 in)	33 cm (13 in)
Round tin (diameter)	15 cm (6 in)	18 cm (7 in)	20.5 cm (8 in)	23 cm (9 in)	25.5 cm (10 in)	28 cm (11 in)	30.5 cm (12 in)	33 cm (13 in)	35.5 cm (14 in)
Approximate liquid capacity of finished cake	300 ml (½ pint)	750 ml (1¼ pints)	1 litre (1¾ pints)	1.1 litres (2½ pints)	1.8 litres (3¼ pints)	2.1 litres (3¾ pints)	2.6 litres (4½ pints)	3 litres (5¼ pints)	3.4 litres (6 pints)
Portions	5	10	12	16	24	26	34	36	44
Approximate cooked weight	265 g (9½ oz)	550 g (1¼ lb)	680 g (1½ lb)	900 g (2 lb)	1.1 kg (2½ lb)	1.6 kg (3½ lb)	1.9 kg (4¼ lb)	2 kg (4½ lb)	2.5 kg (5½ lb)
Ingredients Butter	50 g (2 oz)	100 g (4 oz)	175 g (6 oz)	225 g (8 oz)	275 g (10 oz)	350 g (12 oz)	400 g (14 oz)	450 g (1 lb)	500 g (1 lb 2 oz)
Caster sugar	50 g (2 oz)	100 g (4 oz)	175 g (6 oz)	225 g (8 oz)	275 g (10 oz)	350 g (12 oz)	400 g (14 oz)	450 g (1 lb)	500 g (1 lb 2 oz)
Self-raising flour	50 g (2 oz)	100 g (4 oz)	175 g (6 oz)	225 g (8 oz)	275 g (10 oz)	350 g (12 oz)	400 g (14 oz)	450 g (1 lb)	500 g (1 lb 2 oz)
Plain flour	25 g (1 oz)	50 g (2 oz)	75 g (3 oz)	100 g (4 oz)	150 g (5 oz)	175 g (6 oz)	200 g (7 oz)	225 g (8 oz)	250 g (9 oz)
Eggs	1	2	3	4	5	6	7	8	9
Grated lemon rind and juice	¼ lemon	½ lemon	1 lemon	1 lemon	1½ lemons	1½ lemons	2 lemons	2 lemons	2½ lemons
Cooking time	45 min	1 hr–1¼ hr	1 hr and 15–30 min	1 hr and 15–30 min	1 hr and 15–30 min	1 hr and 20–30 min	1 hr and 20–30 min	1 hr and 20–30 min	1 hr and 30–40 min

CHRISTMAS CAKE

A simpler way of decorating this cake is to simply spoon the icing on to the cake and roughly smooth it with a palette knife. Using the palette knife, pull the icing into rough peaks to give a snow effect.

———————— • ————————

M A K E S   A B O U T   2 5   S L I C E S

FOR THE CAKE

225 g (8 oz) currants

225 g (8 oz) sultanas

225 g (8 oz) seedless raisins, chopped

100 g (4 oz) chopped mixed peel

100 g (4 oz) glacé cherries, halved

50 g (2 oz) nibbed almonds

225 g (8 oz) plain white flour

pinch of salt

2.5 ml (½ level tsp) ground mace

2.5 ml (½ level tsp) ground cinnamon

225 g (8 oz) butter

225 g (8 oz) dark brown soft sugar

finely grated rind of 1 lemon

4 eggs, beaten

30 ml (2 tbsp) brandy

FOR THE GLAZE

60 ml (4 tbsp) apricot jam

15 ml (1 tbsp) lemon juice

FOR THE DECORATION

900 g (2 lb) almond paste (see pages 148–51)

900 g (2 lb) royal icing (see page 151)

narrow red and green ribbons, a red candle and wide red ribbon, to finish

CHRISTMAS CAKE (above)

1   Grease a 20.5 cm (8 inch) round or an 18 cm (7 inch) square cake tin. Line with a double thickness of greaseproof paper, and tie a double band of brown paper round the outside.

2   Mix together the fruit, peel and almonds. Sift the flour, salt and spices into a separate bowl.

3   Cream the butter, sugar and grated lemon rind together until the mixture is pale and fluffy. Add the eggs, a little at a time, beating well after each addition to prevent curdling.

4   Fold half the flour lightly into the mixture with a metal spoon, then fold in the rest and add the brandy. Finally, fold in the fruit.

5   Turn the mixture into the prepared tin, spreading it evenly and making sure there are no air pockets. Make a hollow in the centre with the back of a spoon. Stand the tin on a layer of newspaper or brown paper in the oven and bake at 150°C (300°F) mark 2 for about 3¾ hours. Cover the top with several layers of greaseproof paper after 1½ hours to avoid overbrowning.

6   When the cake is cooked, leave to cool in the tin and then turn out. Wrap in several layers of greaseproof paper, then in foil and store in an airtight tin for at least 1 month.

7   About 14–20 days before required, place the cake upside down on a 23 cm (9 inch) cake board. To make the apricot glaze, heat the jam with the lemon juice until melted. Sieve then cool before brushing all over the cake.

8   Measure and cover the cake with almond paste as described on pages 149–50. Cover loosely and leave to dry in a cool, dry place for 4–5 days.

9   To flat ice the cake, see the instructions on pages 151–2. You will be left with a small amount of icing for the decoration.

10   Using a piping bag fitted with an eight-point star nozzle, pipe a shell border round the top edge using the leftover icing. Pipe a shell border around the bottom edge.

11   Make a ribbon rosette with the narrow ribbons. Cut 3 longer pieces of green ribbon and 3 of red and arrange on top of the cake to form a star shape. Fix the ribbons and rosette in place with a little icing. Stand the candle firmly in the centre of the rosette. Place the wide red ribbon round the cake and secure with a pin. Lay a piece of narrow green ribbon over the wide ribbon, making sure it is central, then secure.

SWEDISH GINGER CAKE

Swedish Ginger Cake is moist, dark and spicy. Serve it with coffee and sherry when visitors call during the festive season.

•

MAKES ABOUT 10 SLICES

100 g (4 oz) butter or margarine
175 g (6 oz) caster sugar
3 eggs, beaten
200 g (7 oz) plain flour
5 ml (1 level tsp) bicarbonate of soda
7.5 ml (1½ level tsp) ground ginger
5 ml (1 level tsp) ground mixed spice
150 ml (¼ pint) soured cream
25 g (1 oz) stem ginger, chopped
15 ml (1 tbsp) stem ginger syrup
15 ml (1 tbsp) black treacle

1   Grease an 18 cm (7 inch) square cake tin, line with greaseproof paper and grease the paper.

2   Put the butter in a bowl and beat until soft. Gradually add the sugar and beat until fluffy. Add the eggs, a little at a time, beating well after each addition until thoroughly incorporated.

3   Sift together the flour, bicarbonate of soda, ground ginger and mixed spice. Fold half into the creamed mixture. Add the soured cream, stem ginger and syrup, black treacle and remaining flour. Fold in until well mixed.

4   Spoon the mixture into the prepared tin. Bake in the oven at 170°C (325°F) mark 3 for about 1¼ hours until the centre is firm to the touch.

5   Leave the cake to cool in the tin for about 15 minutes, then turn out on to a wire rack and leave to cool completely. Store in an airtight container for up to 2 weeks. Serve with butter.

SIMNEL CAKE

Simnel Cake is traditionally served on Easter Sunday. The balls of marzipan represent the 11 faithful disciples.

·

M A K E S   A B O U T   2 0   S L I C E S

175 g (6 oz) butter or block margarine, softened

175 g (6 oz) caster sugar

3 eggs

225 g (8 oz) plain flour

pinch of salt

2.5 ml (½ level tsp) ground cinnamon

2.5 ml (½ level tsp) grated nutmeg

100 g (4 oz) glacé cherries, washed, dried and cut into quarters

50 g (2 oz) cut mixed peel, chopped

250 g (9 oz) currants

100 g (4 oz) sultanas

finely grated rind of 1 lemon

milk, if necessary

one quantity of almond paste (see pages 148–51)

1 egg white, to fix and glaze

ribbon

fresh or crystallized flowers, to decorate

1   Grease an 18 cm (7 inch) round cake tin. Line with greaseproof paper and grease the paper.
2   Cream the butter and sugar until pale and fluffy. Gradually beat in the eggs.
3   Sift in the flour, salt and spices and fold into the mixture with a metal spoon. Add all the fruit and the lemon rind, folding together to give a smooth dropping consistency. If a little too firm add 15–30 ml (1–2 tbsp) milk.
4   Divide the Almond Paste in half. Lightly dust a surface with icing sugar and roll out one half to a 16 cm (6½ inch) circle.
5   Spoon half the cake mixture into the prepared tin. Place the round of almond paste on top and cover with the remaining cake mixture. Press down gently with the back of a spoon to level the surface.
6   Tie a double thickness of brown paper round the outside of the bin. Bake in the oven at 150°C (300°F) mark 2 for about 2½ hours. When

cooked the cake should be a rich brown colour, and firm to the touch.
7   Cool in the tin for about 1 hour, then turn out. Ease off the greaseproof paper and leave to cool completely on a wire rack.
8   Divide the remaining Almond Paste in two. Roll out one half to a 17 cm (7½ inch) circle and the rest into eleven small balls. Lightly beat the egg white and brush over the top of the cake. Place the circle of Almond Paste on top, crimp the edges, and with a little of the egg white fix the balls around the top edge of the cake.
9   Brush the Almond Paste with the remaining egg white and cook under a hot grill for 1–2 minutes until the paste is well browned. Tie a ribbon around the cake and decorate with fresh or crystallized flowers.

MINCE PIES

A pretty idea to make mince pies look more attractive for the Christmas season is to decorate the top of each pie with a festive shape made from the pastry trimmings.

·

M A K E S   A B O U T   2 0

225 g (8 oz) plain flour

pinch of salt

100 g (4 oz) butter or margarine

30 ml (2 tbsp) caster sugar

2 egg yolks

350–450 g (12 oz–1 lb) mincemeat

icing or caster sugar, for dusting

1   To make the pastry, put the flour and salt in a bowl and rub in the butter until the mixture resembles fine breadcrumbs. Stir in the sugar. Work in the egg yolks and enough water to make a smooth dough. Knead lightly.
2   Roll out the pastry on a floured surface until about 0.3 cm (⅛ inch) thick. Cut out about 20 rounds with a 7.5 cm (3 inch) fluted cutter, plus 20 smaller rounds with a 5.5 cm (2¼ inch) fluted cutter.
3   Line 6.5 cm (2½ inch) patty tins with the larger rounds and fill with mincemeat. Dampen the edges of the small rounds with water and place on top. Press the edges together to seal.

Make a small slit in each top.

4 Bake in the oven at 220°C (425°F) mark 7 for 15–20 minutes, until a light golden brown. Leave to cool on a wire rack. Serve dusted with sugar.

BÛCHE DE NOËL

Bûche de Noël is traditionally eaten in France at Christmas time. This and the English Yule Log date back to the days when a huge log used to be burnt on Christmas Eve.

· ·

MAKES ABOUT 8 SLICES

FOR THE MERINGUE MUSHROOMS
1 egg white

50 g (2 oz) caster sugar

FOR THE SWISS ROLL
100 g (4 oz) caster sugar, plus extra for dredging

75 g (3 oz) plain flour, plus a little extra for dredging

3 eggs

30 ml (2 tbsp) cocoa powder

FOR THE BUTTER CREAM
225 g (8 oz) unsalted butter

50 g (2 oz) plain chocolate

500 g (1 lb) icing sugar

440 g (15½ oz) can sweetened chestnut purée

FOR THE DECORATION
icing sugar, for sifting holly sprigs

1 For the meringue mushrooms, line a baking sheet with non-stick paper. Whisk the egg white until stiff, add half of the sugar and whisk again until stiff. Fold in the remaining sugar.

2 Spoon the meringue into a piping bag fitted with a plain nozzle. Pipe the meringue on to the prepared baking sheet to resemble small mushroom caps and, separately, stalks. Bake in the oven at 110°C (225°F) mark ¼ for about 1½ hours until dry. Leave to cool for at least 15 minutes.

3 For the Swiss roll, grease a 33 × 23 cm (13 × 9 inch) Swiss roll tin. Line with greaseproof paper and grease the paper. Dredge with the extra caster sugar then the extra flour, knocking out any excess.

4 Put the eggs and sugar in a deep bowl and stand it over a saucepan of simmering water. Whisk until thick enough to leave a trail on the surface when the whisk is lifted. Do not overheat the bowl by letting it come into contact with simmering water or by having the heat under the saucepan too high.

5 Take the bowl off the saucepan and whisk the mixture for 5 minutes until cool. Sift in the flour and cocoa and gently fold through the mixture. Fold in 15 ml (1 tbsp) hot water.

6 Pour the mixture gently into the prepared tin and lightly level the surface. Bake in the oven at 200°C (400°F) mark 6 for about 12 minutes until slightly shrunk away from the tin.

7 Meanwhile, place a sheet of greaseproof paper over a tea towel. Dredge the paper with caster sugar and turn the cake out on to it. Trim off the crusty edges with a sharp knife. Roll up with the paper inside. Transfer to a wire rack, seam side down and leave to cool for 20 minutes.

8 To make the butter cream, put the butter in a bowl and beat until soft. Put the chocolate and 15 ml (1 tbsp) water in a bowl over a pan of hot water. Melt, then leave to cool slightly. Gradually sift and beat the icing sugar into the softened butter, then add the cool chocolate.

9 Unroll the cold Swiss roll and spread the chestnut purée over the surface. Roll up again without the paper inside. Place on a cake board or plate.

10 Cut a thick diagonal slice off one end of the Swiss roll and attach with butter cream to the side of the roll.

11 Using a piping bag and a large star nozzle, pipe thin lines of butter cream over the log. Pipe 1 or 2 swirls of butter cream to represent knots in the wood. Sandwich the meringue caps and stalks together with a little butter cream to form mushrooms. Decorate the log with the mushrooms and sprigs of holly. Dust lightly with sifted icing sugar. Store in an airtight container for up to 2–3 days.

Bûche de Noël (page 163)

PANETTONE

PANETTONE (*below*)

Panettone comes from Milan in northern Italy. The cakes are exported in attractive tall boxes, which can be seen at Christmas hanging in Italian delicatessens all over the world. Panettone made at home is not so tall as the commercial varieties, and its texture is not so open, but it makes a light alternative to Christmas fruit cakes.

•

MAKES ABOUT 10 SLICES

350 g (12 oz) plain white flour
20 g (¾ oz) fresh yeast or 15 g (2¼ tsp) dried
225 ml (8 fl oz) tepid milk
100 g (4 oz) butter, softened
2 egg yolks
50 g (2 oz) caster sugar
75 g (3 oz) candied peel, chopped
50 g (2 oz) sultanas
pinch of grated nutmeg
egg yolk, to glaze

1   Sift the flour into a large bowl and make a well in the centre. Blend the fresh yeast with the milk. If using dried yeast, sprinkle it on to the milk and leave in a warm place for 15 minutes or until frothy. Add the yeast liquid to the flour and mix well together, gradually drawing in the flour from the sides of the bowl. Leave to stand in a warm place for 45 minutes or until doubled.

2   Add the softened butter to the dough with 2 of the egg yolks, the sugar, candied peel, sultanas and nutmeg. Mix well together. Leave to stand again in a warm place for a further 45 minutes or until doubled in bulk.

3   Meanwhile, cut 3 strips of baking parchment, each one measuring 56 × 25.5 cm (22 × 10 inches). Fold each piece over lengthways.

4   Stand the 3 pieces of parchment together on a greased baking sheet to make a 17 cm (6½ inch) circle and secure with staples. Place the dough inside the paper and leave in a warm place for about 1 hour or until risen to the top of the paper.

5   Cut the top of the dough in the shape of a cross, then brush with egg yolk, to glaze. Bake on the lowest shelf of the oven at 200°C (400°F) mark 6 for 20 minutes, then lower the temperature to 180°C (350°F) mark 4 for a further 40 minutes or until a fine warmed skewer inserted in the centre comes out clean. Leave to cool in the paper. Panettone may be stored in an airtight tin for a maximum of 1 week.

LEBKUCHEN

These German biscuits are spicy and crisp – they are part of Weinachtsbäckerei, *the famous collection of biscuits and small cakes that are traditional around Christmas time. They were originally baked in monasteries 700 years ago, when honey was used, because sugar was unknown in Europe at the time. The bakers who made these biscuits in 17th-century Germany took their profession so seriously that they even formed a guild, calling themselves* Lebküchner.

•

MAKES ABOUT 40

175 g (6 oz) clear honey

50 g (2 oz) caster sugar

30 ml (2 tbsp) vegetable oil

1 egg yolk

5 ml (1 level tsp) cocoa powder

6 drops of lemon oil

2.5 ml (½ level tsp) ground cardamom

2.5 ml (½ level tsp) ground cinnamon

1.25 ml (¼ level tsp) ground cloves

good pinch of cayenne pepper

250 g (8 oz) plain flour

15 ml (3 level tsp) baking powder

75 g (3 oz) ground almonds

75 g (3 oz) ground hazelnuts

75 g (3 oz) dried apricots, finely chopped

50 g (2 oz) chopped mixed peel

FOR THE ICING AND DECORATION

175 g (6 oz) icing sugar

1 egg white

coloured ribbon

1 Put the honey, sugar, vegetable oil and 30 ml (2 tbsp) water in a heavy-based saucepan and heat gently until melted. Leave until cold, then stir in the egg yolk, cocoa powder, lemon oil and spices.

2 Sift the flour and baking powder together. Add two-thirds of the flour to the spice mixture and stir well to mix.

3 Mix the remaining flour with the nuts, apricots and peel. Add to the spice mixture and mix well until combined.

4 Turn the dough out on to a floured surface and knead lightly until it comes together. Roll out until very thin (about 5 mm (¼ inch)) thick.

5 Stamp into about 40 shapes using fancy biscuit cutters. Re-roll any odd bits of pastry, if necessary.

6 Stamp out a small hole in some of the biscuits with an apple corer, drinking straw or skewer. Leave the rest of the biscuits plain.

7 Place the biscuit shapes on greased baking sheets and bake in batches in the oven at 170°C (325°F) mark 3 for 12–15 minutes until just beginning to colour. Transfer to a wire rack until cold and crisp.

8 To make the icing, sift the icing sugar into a bowl, then beat in the egg white and 1–2 drops of warm water to make a thick spreading consistency.

9 Spread or pipe the icing immediately over the biscuits and leave on the wire rack to set for 2–3 hours.

10 Thread coloured ribbon through the holes in the biscuits and tie to secure.

HOT CROSS BUNS

Hot cross buns were traditionally eaten for breakfast on Good Friday in the 18th century. They are still widely sold and enjoyed at Easter time.

•

MAKES 12

FOR THE DOUGH

25 g (1 oz) fresh yeast or 15 ml (1 level tbsp) dried

50 g (2 oz), plus 5 ml (1 level tsp) caster sugar

150 ml (¼ pint) tepid milk

450 g (1 lb) strong white flour

5 ml (1 level tsp) salt

5 ml (1 level tsp) mixed spice

5 ml (1 level tsp) ground cinnamon

2.5 ml (½ level tsp) ground nutmeg

50 g (2 oz) butter, melted and cooled

1 egg, beaten

75 g (3 oz) currants

30 ml (2 level tbsp) chopped mixed peel

FOR THE PASTRY

50 g (2 oz) plain flour

25 g (1 oz) butter or margarine

FOR THE GLAZE

60 ml (4 tbsp) milk and water, mixed

45 ml (3 level tbsp) caster sugar

1 Blend the yeast, 5 ml (1 level tsp) caster sugar, milk, 75 ml (5 tbsp) tepid water and 100 g (4 oz) of the flour together and leave in a warm place for about 20 minutes or until frothy.

2 Sift the remaining flour, salt, spices and the remaining sugar into a bowl. Stir in the butter, egg, yeast liquid, currants and peel and mix to a soft dough.

3 Turn on to a lightly floured surface and knead for about 10 minutes, until smooth and elastic and no longer sticky. Cover with a clean tea towel and leave to rise in a warm place until doubled in size. Turn the dough out on to a floured surface and knead for 2–3 minutes. Divide the dough into twelve pieces and shape into round buns.

4 Place on a greased baking sheet, cover and leave in a warm place until doubled in size.

5 Meanwhile, make the pastry. Rub the fat into the flour and bind together with water. Roll out thinly on a floured surface and cut into thin strips about 9 cm (3½ inches) long. Dampen the pastry strips and lay two on each bun to make a cross.

6 Bake in the oven at 190°C (375°F) mark 5 for 15–20 minutes, until golden brown. For the glaze, heat the milk, water and sugar together. Brush the hot buns twice with glaze, then cool.

BARM BRACK

In Ireland Barm Brack is traditionally eaten at Hallowe'en.

•

MAKES 1 LARGE LOAF

15 g (½ oz) fresh yeast or 7.5 ml (1½ level tsp) dried and a pinch of sugar

25 g (1 oz) butter or margarine

450 g (1 lb) strong white flour

60 ml (4 level tbsp) caster sugar

2.5 ml (½ level tsp) ground ginger

freshly grated nutmeg

175 g (6 oz) sultanas

175 g (6 oz) currants

50 g (2 oz) chopped candied peel

1 Blend the fresh yeast with 300 ml (½ pint) tepid water. If using dried yeast, sprinkle it on to the water with the pinch of sugar and leave in a warm place for 15 minutes or until frothy.

2 Rub the butter into the flour, then stir in half of the sugar, the ginger and nutmeg to taste. Stir in the fruit and peel and mix well together. Make a well in the centre and stir in the yeast liquid.

3 Beat well together until the dough leaves the sides of the bowl clean. Turn on to a lightly floured surface and knead well for about 10 minutes, until smooth and elastic. Place in a clean bowl. Cover with oiled cling film and leave in a warm place for about 1 hour, until doubled in size.

4 Turn the dough on to a floured surface and knead lightly. Shape the dough into a large round or oval and place on a greased baking sheet. Cover and leave in a warm place for about 30 minutes, until doubled in size.

5 Bake at 230°C (450°F) mark 8 for 15 minutes, then reduce the oven temperature to 200°C (400°F) mark 6 and bake for a further 20–30 minutes, until the bread sounds hollow when tapped on the bottom.

6 Dissolve the remaining sugar in 15 ml (1 tbsp) hot water and brush over the loaf to glaze. Return to the oven for 2–3 minutes, then transfer to a wire rack to cool.

BLACK BUN

*Black Bun, or Yule Cake, is traditionally baked in
Scotland at the year's end for Hogmanay.*

•

M A K E S   A B O U T   1 2   S L I C E S

FOR THE PASTRY

225 g (8 oz) plain flour

pinch of salt

100 g (4 oz) butter or margarine

FOR THE FILLING

225 g (8 oz) plain flour

5 ml (1 level tsp) ground cinnamon

5 ml (1 level tsp) ground ginger

5 ml (1 level tsp) ground allspice

5 ml (1 level tsp) cream of tartar

5 ml (1 level tsp) bicarbonate of soda

450 g (1 lb) seedless raisins

450 g (1 lb) currants

50 g (2 oz) chopped mixed peel

100 g (4 oz) chopped almonds

100 g (4 oz) dark brown soft sugar

1 egg, beaten

150 ml (¼ pint) whisky

about 60 ml (4 tbsp) milk

beaten egg, to glaze

BLACK BUN (below)

1   Grease a deep 20 cm (8 inch) round cake tin.

2   To make the pastry, put the flour and salt in
a bowl and rub in the butter until the mixture
resembles fine breadcrumbs. Add enough water
to bind to a dough. Knead lightly, then roll out
two-thirds on a lightly floured working surface
into a round about 35 cm (14 inches) in
diameter. Line the prepared tin with the pastry,
making sure it overhangs the sides.

3   Sift together the flour, spices, cream of tartar
and bicarbonate of soda. Mix in the raisins,
currants, peel, almonds and sugar.

4   Add the egg, whisky and milk and stir until
the mixture is evenly moistened. Pack the filling
into the pastry case and fold the top of the
pastry over the filling.

5   On a lightly floured surface, roll out the
remaining dough to a 20 cm (8 inch) round.
Moisten the edges of the pastry case, put the
pastry round on top and seal firmly together.

6   With a skewer, make four or five holes right
down to the bottom of the cake, then prick all
over the top with a fork and brush with egg.

7   Bake in the oven at 180°C (350°F) mark 4 for
2½–3 hours or until a fine warmed skewer inserted in the centre comes out clean. Check near
the end of cooking time and cover with several
layers of greaseproof paper if it is becoming too
brown. Turn out on to a wire rack to cool.

STOLLEN (*page 171*)

GINGERBREAD HOUSE (*overleaf*)

169

GINGERBREAD HOUSE

Make this delightful house as an alternative Christmas Cake or for a child's birthday party.

·

450 g (1 lb) plain flour

7.5 ml (1½ level tsp) bicarbonate of soda

30 ml (2 level tbsp) ground ginger

15 ml (1 level tbsp) ground cinnamon

2.5 ml (½ level tsp) ground cloves

175 g (6 oz) butter or margarine

225 g (8 oz) light brown soft sugar

90 ml (6 tbsp) golden syrup

1 egg, beaten

½ quantity royal icing (page 151)

assorted sweets and little biscuits, to decorate

1 Cut out templates for the house according to the diagram, using greaseproof paper or cardboard. Line 2 baking sheets with non-stick baking parchment.

2 Sift the flour, bicarbonate of soda and spices into a bowl. Rub in the butter with your fingertips until the mixture resembles fine breadcrumbs. Add the sugar and mix well.

3 Put the syrup in a warm basin and beat in the egg. Stir this mixture into the flour. Mix together to form a soft dough and knead until smooth. Cut in half and wrap one half in cling film.

4 On a lightly floured surface, roll out the other half of the dough to 0.5 cm (¼ inch) thickness. Using the templates, cut out one of each shape with a sharp knife, and carefully transfer to the prepared baking sheets. Cut out windows and a front door, if liked. Straighten the edges and chill in the refrigerator for 15 minutes.

5 Bake in the oven at 190°C (375°F) mark 5 for 8–10 minutes until golden brown. Leave to cool on the baking sheet for 5 minutes, then transfer to a wire rack and cool completely.

6 Knead the trimmings together with the remaining gingerbread dough and roll out as before. Cut out one of each of the shapes, transfer to the lined baking sheet and bake as before.

7 Using the royal icing, sweets and biscuits, decorate the flat walls, windows and doors. Allow to dry for about 4–6 hours.

8 Assemble the house by cementing the four walls together with royal icing and securing to a 25.5 cm (10 inch) square cake board. Allow to dry for 4–6 hours. Stick the chimney pieces together and allow to dry.

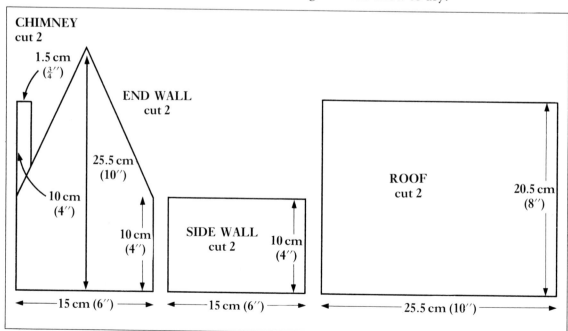

9 If liked, fill the inside of the house with sweets. Using more royal icing, cement the roof pieces to the house and add the chimney. Allow to dry for 4–6 hours.

10 Cover the roof and chimney with royal icing, forking up to resemble snow and icicles, adding extra to the windows, if liked. Press sweets lightly into the icing to decorate the roof and walls. Spread more icing over the cake board and decorate with more sweets, or dust with icing sugar to resemble snow. Dry for at least 8 hours. Eat within 2 days.

STOLLEN

In Germany, Stollen is eaten throughout the Christmas period with afternoon coffee.

•

MAKES 12 SLICES

15 g (½ oz) fresh yeast or 7.5 ml (1½ tsp) dried plus a pinch of sugar

100 ml (4 fl oz) tepid milk

225 g (8 oz) strong plain flour

1.25 ml (¼ level tsp) salt

25 g (1 oz) butter or margarine

grated rind of 1 small lemon

50 g (2 oz) chopped mixed peel

50 g (2 oz) currants

50 g (2 oz) sultanas

25 g (1 oz) blanched almonds, chopped

½ a beaten egg

icing sugar, to dredge

1 Grease a large baking sheet.

2 Crumble the fresh yeast into a bowl and cream with the milk until smooth. If using dried yeast, sprinkle on to the milk with the sugar and leave in a warm place for 15 minutes or until the surface is frothy.

3 Put the flour and salt into a bowl and rub in the butter. Add the lemon rind, fruit and nuts. Add the yeast mixture and the egg and mix thoroughly to a soft dough.

4 Turn on to a lightly floured working surface and knead for about 10 minutes until smooth. Cover with a clean cloth and leave to rise in a warm place for about 1 hour until doubled in size.

5 Knead the dough for 2–3 minutes, then roll into an oval shape measuring about 23 × 18 cm (9 × 7 inches). Mark a line lengthways with the rolling pin.

6 Carefully fold the dough in half along the marked line. Place on the baking sheet, cover with a clean cloth and leave in a warm place for about 40 minutes until doubled in size.

7 Bake in the oven at 200°C (400°F) mark 6 for about 30 minutes until well risen and golden brown. Transfer to a wire rack to cool. When cold, dredge all over with icing sugar.

PASTRIES, PIES AND FLANS

Pastry of various kinds provides the base for many luscious confections, such as flaky Mille Feuilles, mouthwatering cream puffs and rich cheesecakes, as well as pies, turnovers and flans.

Despite the mystique attached to making pastry, the only secrets to success are patience, practice and care. Unless you are making choux or phyllo (strudel) pastry, the golden rule is keep everything cool – kitchen, work surface, utensils, ingredients and yourself. Handle the pastry as little as possible and use just your fingertips for rubbing in the fat. If the mixture shows signs of becoming the least bit sticky and unmanageable, chill it briefly in the refrigerator.

Each kind of pastry has its own particular texture and flavour and is suited to a certain range of recipes.

Left to right: GLAZED FRUIT TARTS *(page 190),* PANADE *(page 187)* AND CHOCOLATE ECLAIRS *(page 185)*

INGREDIENTS FOR MAKING PASTRY

FLOUR

For most pastries plain flour is the best flour to use. Wholemeal flour can be used for shortcrust or suetcrust pastry – it produces a dough which is more difficult to roll out but has a distinctive flavour and texture when cooked. Shortcrust can also be made with self-raising flour, which gives a softer more crumbly texture.

Suetcrust, unlike other pastries, needs a flour *and* a raising agent to lighten the dough. Puff pastry and phyllo (strudel) pastry need to be made with strong plain flour, as this contains extra gluten which strengthens the dough for the rolling and folding of puff pastry and allows phyllo pastry to be stretched out very thinly. Strong plain flour can be used for choux pastry, making it rise more, but it may also slightly toughen the resulting pastry.

RAISING AGENT

Suetcrust pastry needs a raising agent; either plain flour sifted with 12.5 ml (2½ level tsp) baking powder to each 225 g (8 oz), or self-raising flour can be used. Do not add baking powder to self-raising flour as this produces an unpleasant flavour. Steam acts as the raising agent in flaked pastries in combination with the air enclosed in the layers of dough. In choux pastry the raising agents are eggs and steam.

SALT

The quantity of salt varies according to the type of pastry. Only a pinch of salt is added to shortcrust pastry for flavour, while a measured quantity is added to hot-water crust to strengthen the gluten in the flour and allow for the amount of handling during shaping. Salt is also needed to strengthen the gluten in the flour with flaked pastries.

FAT

Butter, margarine and lard are the most commonly used fats, but proprietary vegetable shortenings (both blended and whipped) and pure vegetable oils can give excellent results.

Generally, the firmer block margarine should be used rather than soft tub margarine.

For shortcrust pastry, butter, margarine, lard or vegetable fat can be used alone, though margarine tends to give a firmer pastry which is rather yellow in colour. Good results are achieved with an equal mixture of fats – butter or margarine for flavour with lard for shortness. For the richer pastries, it is better to keep to the amount of fat specified in the recipies.

For suetcrust pastry, suet is used. This is the fat around the kidneys, heart and liver of beef and mutton. It is available ready shredded.

LIQUID

Use chilled water to make pastry dough and add just enough to make the dough bind. It is important to add the liquid carefully, as too much will make the cooked pastry tough and too little will produce a crumbly baked pastry. Egg yolks are often used as the binding liquid to enrich shortcrust pastry. Lemon juice is added to flaked pastries to soften the gluten in the flour and make the dough more elastic.

SUGAR

Caster sugar may be added to rich shortcrust or flan pastries if the pastry is to be used for a sweet dish.

TYPES OF PASTRY

SHORT PASTRIES

Shortcrust pastry This, which is probably the most widely used pastry, is made by the rubbing-in method. It is quick and simple to produce and forms the basis of a wide range of pastry cakes. The recipe is on page 186.

Flan pastry A slightly richer pastry, made by the same method as shortcrust. It is usually sweetened and is ideal for flan cases, small tartlets and other sweet pastries. The recipe is on page 194.

Pâte sucrée (sugar pastry) The French equivalent to enriched shortcrust, this is thin, crisp yet melting in texture and keeps its shape well. It is the best choice for continental patisserie. The recipe is on page 190.

FLAKED PASTRIES

Puff pastry The richest of all the pastries, puff gives the most even rising, the most flaky effect and the crispest texture, but because of the time it takes, most people make it only occasionally. It requires very careful handling and whenever possible should be made the day before it is to be used, so that it has time to become firm and cool before it is shaped and baked. If you have a freezer, it is well worthwhile making up a bulk batch and packing it in amounts that are practical to thaw and use. Bought puff pastry, either chilled or frozen, is very satisfactory, but remember to only roll it out to a maximum thickness of 0.3 cm (⅛ inch), as it rises very well.

'First rollings' are used where appearance is important. 'Second rollings' (usually the trimmings) can be used where appearance is not so important.

The recipe for puff pastry is on page 182.

Flaky pastry This can be used instead of puff pastry if a great rise is not needed. The instructions may seem rather complicated at first reading, but are less difficult than they appear, and if you follow them carefully you should be able to obtain really good results. The recipe is on page 181.

Rough puff pastry This is similar in appearance and texture to flaky pastry, though perhaps not so even, but it is quicker and easier to make and can be used instead of flaky except when even rising and appearance are particularly important, e.g. when making Mille Feuilles. Today, bought ready-made puff pastry is frequently used to replace homemade rough puff pastry. Use a 215 g (7½ oz) packet to replace homemade pastry made with 100 g (4 oz) flour and a 370 g (13 oz) packet to replace homemade pastry made with 225 g (8 oz) flour. Bought pastry should be rolled out slightly thinner than homemade. The recipe is on page 182.

General points for making flaked pastries

* Always handle lightly and as little as possible.

* The fat for flaky and puff pastries should be of about the same consistency as the dough with which it is to be combined. This is the reason for working it on a plate beforehand. The fat for rough puff pastry should be firm so that the cubes of fat retain their shape while being mixed into the dry ingredients.

* Remember to 'rest' all flaked pastries, i.e. cover and leave them in a cool place or in the refrigerator for about 15 minutes, both during and after the making and also after shaping. This will prevent the fat from melting and spoiling the flaked texture when the pastry is cooked.

* Always roll out lightly and evenly, without taking the rolling pin over the edges of the pastry. Never stretch the dough during shaping, or the finished dish will tend to be misshapen.

CHOUX PASTRY

To ensure a good result with this special type of pastry, used for making éclairs and profiteroles, there are a few points worth observing:

* Remove the pan from the heat before adding the flour, which must be added all at once. Beat thoroughly.

* After adding the flour, return the pan to the heat and continue beating until the mixture comes away from the sides of the pan and forms a ball in the centre.

*Beating until
the mixture
forms a ball*

* Add the beaten egg gradually to the mixture, taking care to add only just enough to give a piping consistency. When beating by hand with a wooden spoon the arm tends to tire, the beating speed is reduced and the final consistency is often too slack to retain its

shape. In this case, a little less egg should be added. Use size 4 eggs if beating by hand and size 2 eggs when using an electric mixer.

* To make the choux pastry a little easier to handle, chill it in the piping bag in the refrigerator for about 30 minutes before piping.

* The oven door must not be opened during cooking.

* Eclairs and profiteroles should be split open as soon as they are cooked to allow the steam to escape and the inside of the pastry to dry out.

* Dampen baking sheets slightly with water before piping choux pastry on to them. This helps prevent sticking.

The recipe for choux pastry is on page 185.

HOT-WATER CRUST PASTRY

This pastry is used to make savoury raised pies such as veal and ham pie and game pie. It is mixed with boiling water, which makes it pliable enough to mould into a raised pie that will hold its shape as it cools and during the baking. It is a strong pastry, fit to withstand the extra handling that it must receive during the shaping and also the weight of the savoury filling it must hold. Care must be taken when moulding hot-water crust pastry to ensure that there are no cracks through which the meat juices can escape during baking.

Keep the part of the pastry that is not actually being used covered with a cloth or an upturned bowl, to prevent it hardening before use. If you do not wish to raise the pie by hand, you can use a cake tin. For a more elaborate raised pie, you can buy a special metal mould, made in two parts joined by a hinge, so that they can easily be removed when the pie is cooked.

The recipe for hot-water crust pastry is on page 195.

PHYLLO (FILO) AND STRUDEL PASTRY

Phyllo is a pastry of wafer-like thinness from the Middle East, which is used for both savoury and sweet pastries. It is identical to strudel pastry which originated in Europe and is used for the popular Apple Strudel. Phyllo and strudel pastry are fairly difficult and time-consuming to make. Unlike most pastries, they require warm ingredients and, instead of light handling, have to be kneaded and beaten. The dough is kneaded vigorously to enable the gluten in the flour to develop strength so the pastry can be stretched into a very thin, resilient sheet. For the same reason, strong plain flour is used as it yields more gluten which helps to produce an elastic dough. The thin sheet of dough is either spread with a filling and rolled or folded, or it is cut into rectangles and stacked, with a filling in between the layers.

Ready-made phyllo or strudel pastry is available in sheets from continental shops and delicatessens.

The recipe for phyllo or strudel pastry is on page 194.

STEPS TO MAKING PERFECT PASTRY

·

RUBBING IN

This is the method used to incorporate fat into flour when making short-textured pastry, such as shortcrust. Make sure the fat is at room temperature, about 18–21°C (65–70°F), so that it is firm but just spreadable. Cut it into small pieces and add it to the flour, which should be seasoned and sieved if necessary, into a mixing bowl. Rub the fat into the flour as quickly as possible, using the thumbs and fingertips. Keep your hands well above the bowl, allowing the mixture to fall back into the bowl – this introduces air into the mixture and helps keep it cool. Stop rubbing in as soon as the mixture resembles fine breadcrumbs.

If you are using an electric mixer, start rubbing in on the lowest speed and gradually increase. Be careful not to over mix.

KNEADING

Pastry doughs are kneaded in a different way from bread doughs because they need much lighter handling. In fact the more you handle pastry dough, the stickier and less manageable it becomes. Having added sufficient water to a rubbed-in mixture to get it to stick together easily, gather the dough together, leaving the sides of the bowl clean, and place it on a cool, unfloured surface. Draw the outer edges of the dough into the centre with your fingertips. Turn as you knead and continue for a few minutes only until the dough is smooth and free from cracks. If time permits, wrap the dough and chill for 30 minutes before rolling out.

ROLLING OUT

To roll out is to flatten pastry dough to the required thickness, shape and size, using a rolling pin or similar cylindrical utensil.

Dust the working surface and rolling pin – never the pastry – with as little flour as possible. Roll the dough out lightly and evenly in one direction only (away from you), rotating it frequently to keep it an even shape. Short pastries are usually rolled to about 0.3 cm (⅛ inch) thickness, and puff pastries to 0.5 cm (¼ inch) thickness. Lessen the pressure on the rolling pin slightly as you get to the edges of the pastry or they will be thinner than the centre. Leave rolled-out pastry to 'rest' for 5 minutes before using. This helps to stop the pastry from shrinking during cooking.

LINING CASES AND TINS

Flan cases See quantity chart on page 180. Choose a plain or fluted flan ring placed on a baking sheet, a loose-bottomed flan tin, a china fluted flan dish or a sandwich tin.

1 Roll out the pastry thinly to a circle about 5 cm (2 inches) wider than the ring. With a rolling pin, lift the pastry and lower it into the ring, or fold the pastry in half and position it in the ring.

2 Lift the edges carefully and ease the pastry into the flan shape, lightly pressing the pastry against the edges – with a fluted flan ring press your finger into each flute to ensure a good finish. No air should be left between the container and pastry.

3 Turn any surplus pastry outwards over the rim and roll across the top with the rolling pin or use a knife to trim the edges.

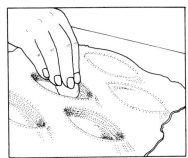

Lining small tins or moulds

Individual tartlet tins or moulds
1 Arrange the tins close together on a baking sheet. Roll out the pastry to a size large enough to cover the whole area of the tins. Lift the pastry on to the rolling pin and lay loosely over the tins.

2 With a small knob of dough, press the pastry into each tin. With a rolling pin, roll across the complete set of tins and lift the surplus pastry away.

3 Prick the bases and sides lightly with a fork. With a sheet of patty tins, cut rounds of thinly rolled pastry slightly larger than the top of the tin and ease one round into each shape.

COVERING A PIE DISH

1 Roll out the pastry to the required thickness and 5 cm (2 inches) wider than the pie dish, using the inverted dish as a guide. Cut a 2.5 cm (1 inch) wide strip from the outer edge and place it on the dampened rim of the dish. Seal the join and brush the whole strip with water.

2 Fill the pie dish generously with filling, so that the surface is slightly rounded – use a pie funnel if insufficient filling is available.

3 Lift the remaining pastry on the rolling pin and lay it over the pie dish. Press the lid lightly on to the dampened pastry-lined rim to seal. Trim off any excess pastry with the cutting edge of a knife held at a slight angle away from the dish.

4 Seal the edges firmly so that they do not open up during cooking (see Knocking Up, page 178). If you wish, scallop the edges, (see page 178) and use trimmings rolled thinly, to make decorative shapes for the top (see page 178). Cut a slit in the centre of the pie crust for the steam to escape.

SEALING THE EDGES

Knocking up After the pastry edges have been trimmed all pies should then be 'knocked up' to seal the edges firmly before decorating. Press your index finger along the rim and, holding a knife horizontally, tap the edge of the pastry sharply with the blunt side of the blade to give a 'flaky' appearance.

Scallop/flute Press a thumb on the rim of the pastry and at the same time draw back the floured blade of a round-bladed or table knife about 1 cm (½ inch) towards the centre. Repeat around the edge of the pie. Traditionally, sweet dishes should have about 0.5 cm (¼ inch) scallops and savoury dishes 2.5 cm (1 inch) scallops.

Crimp Push the thumb or finger of one hand into the rim of the pastry. Use the thumb and first finger of the other hand to gently pinch the pastry pushed up by this action. Continue around the edge of the pie. Crimping is traditionally used to seal Cornish pasties as well as to decorate pie edges.

DECORATIVE SHAPES

To attach pastry decorations, dampen with water and press into place.

Leaves Cut thinly rolled-out pastry trimmings into 2.5 cm (1 inch) wide strips. Cut these diagonally to form diamond shapes and mark the veins of a leaf on each one with the back of a knife blade. Pinch one of the long ends to form a stem.

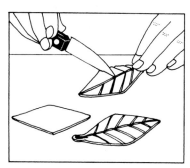

Making pastry leaves

Tassels Cut a strip from the rolled-out pastry trimmings 2.5 cm (1 inch) wide and 10–15 cm

(4–6 inches) long. Use a knife to make 2 cm (¾ inch) slits at short intervals to resemble a fringe. Roll up and stand on the uncut end while you spread out the cut strips.

Making pastry tassels

Lattice work Lattice is probably the best known decoration for open-pie tarts. A lattice can be either simple or interwoven.

Simple lattice

1 Use either a knife or pastry wheel to cut the rolled-out pastry into 1 cm (½ inch) wide strips slightly longer than the tart.

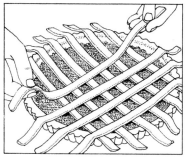

Making a pastry lattice

2 Lay half the strips at intervals across the surface of the dish, an equal distance apart. Place the other half diagonally across the first. Flatten the ends, moisten and press firmly to the pastry rim to seal.

Interwoven lattice

1 Make strips of pastry as in step 1 above.
2 Lay half the strips at intervals across the surface of the dish, an equal distance apart. Flatten the ends of the strips at one side of the dish only, moisten them and press them firmly to the pastry rim to seal.
3 Fold back alternate strips and lay across another strip, at right angles to those of the first layer.

4 Return the folded back strips to their original position, and fold back the *other* alternate strips of the first layer. Lay across a second strip at right angles to the first layer and return the folded back strips to their original position.

5 Continue weaving the strips in this way until all the strips are used up. Make sure that the second layer of strips are all an equal distance apart.

6 Flatten all the ends, moisten them and press firmly to the pastry rim to seal.

BAKING BLIND

This is the term used to describe the cooking of pastry cases without any filling. The pastry shell is lined with foil or greaseproof paper and then, for larger cases, filled with baking beans (dried or ceramic) before cooking. The pastry may be partially prebaked to be cooked for a further period when filled, or completely cooked if the filling requires no further cooking. All short-crust pastries and puff pastries may be baked blind.

Pastry cases which have been baked blind keep for several days in an airtight tin and freeze well, if wrapped in freezer foil and stored in a rigid container.

1 Make the pastry and line the flan case (see page 177). Chill in the refrigerator for 30 minutes, if possible, to rest the pastry.

2 Cut out a piece of foil or greaseproof paper rather larger than the tin. Remove the case from the refrigerator and prick the base thoroughly.

3 Press the paper or foil against the pastry, then fill with a 1 cm (½ inch) layer of beans. For small pastry cases, it is usually sufficient simply to prick the pastry well, with a fork, before baking.

4 For partially prebaked cases, bake in the oven at 200°C (400°F) mark 6 for 10–15 minutes until set. Lift out the paper or foil and beans, and bake for a further 5 minutes until the base is just firm and lightly coloured.

Pastry cases which need complete baking should be returned to the oven for a further 15 minutes or until firm and golden brown.

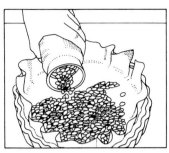

Preparing a flan case for baking blind

QUANTITY GUIDE

·

When a recipe specifies, for example 100 g (4 oz) pastry, this means pastry made using 100 g (4 oz) flour with the other ingredients in proportion. It does not refer to the combined weight of the ingredients.

The pastry amounts given in the chart overleaf are generous to allow a certain flexibility for depths and metric proportions. When experienced in making pastry, you will probably use less than the amounts stated. Leftover trimmings can be used to make decorations, a pastry turnover or a few tartlet cases.

Tin sizes can only be approximate as manufacturers' ranges do vary.

STORING AND FREEZING PASTRY

·

All pastry doughs can be stored in the refrigerator for a day or so before cooking, wrapped in greaseproof paper, cling film or foil, or rolled and shaped ready for filling and cooking at the last minute.

For freezing, wrap unshaped pastry in cling film. To use, thaw at room temperature for 3–4 hours or overnight in the refrigerator. Freeze flan cases cooked or uncooked in foil containers or freezer-proof earthenware or glass dishes. Bake flan cases from frozen, adding about 5 minutes to the normal baking time. Uncooked frozen pastry can be stored for 3–4 months in the freezer and cooked pastry will keep for up to 6 months.

DISH	PASTRY QUANTITY (FLOUR WEIGHT)	SIZE	NUMBER
Shortcrust pastries			
fluted flan rings	100 g (4 oz) lines	15 cm (6 inch)	1
	150 g (5 oz) lines	18 cm (7 inch)	1
	175 g (6 oz) lines	20.5 cm (8 inch)	1
	200 g (7 oz) lines	23 cm (9 inch)	1
	225 g (8 oz) lines	25.5 cm (10 inch)	1
	250 g (9 oz) lines	28 cm (11 inch)	1
tartlets	225 g (8 oz) lines	6 cm (2½ inch)	18
		8 cm (3 inch)	12
pie dish	225 g (8 oz) covers	1 litre (2 pint)	1
	175 g (6 oz) covers	900 ml (1½ pint)	1
pie plate	250 g (9 oz) lines and covers	20.5 cm (8 inch)	1
Pâte sucrée			
flan ring	200 g (7 oz) lines	23 cm (9 inch)	1
tartlets	200 g (7 oz) lines	6 cm (2½ inch)	24
Hot-water crust			
hinged pie mould	450 g (1 lb) lines and covers	1.75 litre (3 pint) raised pie	1
jam jars	450 g (1 lb) lines and covers	350 g (12 oz) raised pies	6
cake tin	350 g (12 oz) lines and covers	15 cm (6 inch) diameter raised pie	1
Rough puff or flaky			
tartlets	225 g (8 oz) lines	12 × 8 cm (3 inch)	1
Puff			
baking tray	225 g (8 oz) makes	8 cm (3 inch) vol-au-vents	10
		9 cm (3½ inch) vol-au-vents	8
		5 cm (2 inch) bouchées	30
		cream horns made from 3 mm (⅛ inch) thick pastry	4–5
oval pie dish	100 g (4 oz) covers	1 litre (2 pint)	1
Choux			
éclairs	65 g (2½ oz) makes	10 cm (4 inch) long	10
		4 cm (1½ inch) long	25
choux buns	65 g (2½ oz) makes	5 cm (2 inch) diameter	10
profiteroles	65 g (2½ oz) makes	3 cm (1¼ inch) diameter	20

THAWING BOUGHT PACKET PASTRY IN A MICROWAVE OVEN

TYPE	QUANTITY	APPROXIMATE TIME ON LOW SETTING	SPECIAL INSTRUCTIONS
Shortcrust and puff pastry	212 g (7½ oz) packet	1 minute	Stand for 20 minutes
	368 g (13 oz) packet	2 minutes	Stand for 20–30 minutes

Maids of Honour (page 183) and Almond Fingers (page 194)

FLAKY PASTRY

This pastry can be used instead of puff pastry in many savoury and sweet dishes where a great rise is not needed. The fat should be of about the same consistency as the dough with which it is to be combined, which is why it is worked on a plate beforehand. This amount is equivalent to one 368 g (13 oz) packet.

———————————— • ————————————

225 g (8 oz) plain flour

pinch of salt

175 g (6 oz) butter or a mixture of butter and lard

a squeeze of lemon juice

1   Mix the flour and salt together in a bowl. Soften the fat by working it with a knife on a plate, then divide it into four equal portions.
2   Add one-quarter of the fat to the flour and rub it in until the mixture resembles fine bread-crumbs.
3   Stirring with a round-bladed knife, add a squeeze of lemon juice and about 120 ml (8 tbsp) chilled water or sufficient to make a soft, elastic dough. Turn the dough on to a lightly floured surface, knead until smooth, then roll out into an oblong three times as long as it is wide.
4   Using a round-bladed knife, dot a second quarter of the fat over the top two-thirds of the pastry in flakes, so that it looks like buttons on a card.
5   Fold the bottom third of the pastry up and the top third down, then turn it so that the folded edges are at the sides.
6   Seal the edges of the pastry by pressing with a rolling pin. Wrap the pastry and leave in the refrigerator to rest for 15 minutes. Re-roll as before and repeat twice more until the remaining fat has been used up.
7   Wrap the pastry loosely and leave to rest in the refrigerator for at least 30 minutes before using.
8   Roll out the pastry on a lightly floured surface to 0.3 cm (⅛ inch) thick and use as required. Leave to rest in the refrigerator for 30 minutes before baking. Brush with beaten egg before baking to give the characteristic glaze.
9   Bake at 200°C (400°F) mark 6, unless otherwise stated.

PUFF PASTRY

The richest of all the pastries, puff requires patience, practice and very light handling. Whenever possible it should be made the day before use. It is not practical to make in a quantity with less than 450 g (1 lb) flour weight. This is equivalent to two 368 g (13 oz) packets.

•

450 g (1 lb) strong plain flour

pinch of salt

450 g (1 lb) butter or block margarine, chilled

15 ml (1 tbsp) lemon juice

1 Mix the flour and salt together in a bowl. Cut off 50 g (2 oz) of butter and flatten the remaining butter with a rolling pin to a slab 2 cm (¾ inch) thick.

2 Cut the 50 g (2 oz) butter into small pieces, add to the flour and rub in. Using a round-bladed knife, stir in the lemon juice and about 300 ml (½ pint) chilled water or sufficient to make a soft, elastic dough.

3 Quickly knead the dough until smooth and shape into a round. Cut through half the depth in the shape of a cross. Open out to form a star.

4 Roll out, keeping the centre four times as thick as the flaps. Place the slab of butter in the centre of the dough and fold the flaps envelope-style.

5 Press gently with a rolling pin and roll out into a rectangle measuring about 40 × 20 cm (16 × 8 inches).

6 Fold the bottom third up and the top third down, keeping the edges straight. Seal the edges.

7 Wrap the pastry in greaseproof paper and leave in the refrigerator to rest for 30 minutes. Put the pastry on a lightly floured working surface with the folded edges to the sides and repeat the rolling, folding and resting sequence five times.

8 Shape the pastry as required, then leave to rest in the refrigerator for 30 minutes before baking. Brush with beaten egg before baking.

9 Bake at 220°C (425°F) mark 7, for about 15 minutes on its own or longer if filled, except where otherwise specified.

ROUGH PUFF PASTRY

Similar in texture to flaky pastry, rough puff can be used instead of flaky, except when even rising and appearance are particularly important. Rough puff is quicker and easier to make than puff or flaky pastry. This quantity is equivalent to one 368 g (13 oz) packet.

•

225 g (8 oz) plain flour

pinch of salt

75 g (3 oz) butter or block margarine, chilled

75 g (3 oz) lard chilled

1 Mix the flour and salt together in a bowl. Cut the butter and lard into 2 cm (¾ inch) cubes. Stir into the flour without breaking up the pieces.

2 Add a squeeze of lemon juice and about 150 ml (¼ pint) chilled water or sufficient to mix to a fairly stiff dough using a round-bladed knife. On a lightly floured surface, roll out into an oblong three times as long as it is wide.

3 Fold the bottom third up and the top third down, then turn the pastry so that the folded edges are at the sides. Seal the ends of the pastry with a rolling pin. Wrap the pastry in grease-proof paper and chill for 15 minutes.

4 Repeat this rolling and folding process three more times, turning the dough so that the folded edge is on the left-hand side each time. Wrap and chill for 30 minutes.

5 Roll out the pastry to 0.3 cm (⅛ inch) thick and use as required. Leave to rest in the refrigerator for 30 minutes before baking. Brush with beaten egg before baking to give the characteristic glaze.

6 Bake at 220°C (425°F) mark 7 unless otherwise specified.

MAIDS OF HONOUR

These originated in Henry VIII's palace at Hampton Court, where they were popular with the Queen's maids of honour, hence the name.

·

MAKES 12

568 ml (1 pint) pasteurized milk
15 ml (1 tbsp) rennet
212 g (7½ oz) packet frozen puff pastry, thawed or ¼ quantity puff or ½ quantity flaky pastry (see pages 182 and 181)
1 egg, beaten
15 g (½ oz) butter or margarine, melted
50 g (2 oz) caster sugar

1 First make a junket: gently heat the milk in a saucepan until tepid. Remove from the heat and stir in the rennet. Leave for 1½–2 hours until set.

2 When set, put the junket into a muslin bag and leave to drain overnight. Next day, discard the whey and refrigerate the curd for several hours or until very firm.

3 Grease 12 6.5 cm (2½ inch) patty tins. On a lightly floured surface, roll out the pastry very thinly and using a 7.5 cm (3 inch) plain cutter, cut out 12 rounds. Line the patty tins with the pastry and prick well.

4 Stir the egg, butter and sugar into the drained curd. Divide the mixture between the pastry cases and bake in the oven at 200°C (400°F) mark 6 for 30 minutes, until well risen and just firm to the touch. Serve warm.

JALOUSIE

A simple puff pastry cake filled with raspberry conserve, perfect for afternoon tea, or to have with coffee.

·

MAKES 8 SLICES

368 g (13 oz) packet frozen puff pastry, thawed or ½ quantity puff or 1 quantity flaky pastry (see pages 182 and 181)
225 g (8 oz) raspberry conserve
1 small egg, beaten with 10 ml (2 level tsp) sifted icing sugar
icing sugar for sifting

1 Roll out the puff pastry on a lightly floured surface to a square a little larger than 30 cm (12 inches). Trim the pastry edges to form an exact 30 cm (12 inch) square. Cut in half. Place on baking sheets and chill for about 10 minutes. Chilling the pastry at this stage will make it much easier to assemble.

2 Spread the raspberry conserve down the centre of one of the pieces of pastry, leaving a 2.5 cm (1 inch) border all round.

3 Remove the second piece of pastry from the baking sheet and fold in half lengthways, then make cuts all along the folded edge to within 2.5 cm (1 inch) of the edges, spacing the cuts about 1 cm (½ inch) apart.

4 Without unfolding the pastry, place it on top of the pastry spread with jam so that the edges line up with the bottom piece of pastry, then carefully unfold the pastry to cover the jam completely. Press all the pastry edges well together to seal. Chill for 30 minutes.

5 Remove the chilled jalousie from the refrigerator, then flake the edge with a small knife and mark into flutes. Brush the top with the beaten egg – do not allow the glaze to run down the sides as it will prevent the pastry from rising.

6 Bake at 230°C (450°F) mark 8 for 20–30 minutes until well risen and golden brown. Leave to cool.

7 Sift with icing sugar then place on a doily-lined tray. To serve, cut into slices across the jalousie.

PROFITEROLES *(opposite)* AND CHERRY PIE *(page 186)*

PROFITEROLES

Choux pastry is the basis for many favourite pastries. Follow these instructions carefully, and read the tips on pages 175–6, for perfect results every time.

·

SERVES 4

FOR THE CHOUX PASTRY

50 g (2 oz) butter or margarine
65 g (2½ oz) plain flour
2 eggs, lightly beaten

FOR THE CHOCOLATE SAUCE AND FILLING

100 g (4 oz) plain chocolate
15 g (½ oz) butter or margarine
30 ml (2 tbsp) golden syrup
2–3 drops vanilla flavouring
150 ml (¼ pint) double cream
sugar, for dredging

1 To make the choux pastry, put the butter in a saucepan with 150 ml (¼ pint) water. Heat until the butter is melted then bring to the boil. Remove from the heat and quickly tip in the flour all at once. Beat vigorously with a wooden spoon until the paste forms a ball in the centre of the pan. Return the pan to the heat and continue beating until smooth.

2 Allow to cool for a minute or two. Beat in the egg a little at a time adding just enough to give a piping consistency. It is important to beat the mixture vigorously at this stage to trap in as much air as possible. Continue beating until the mixture develops an obvious sheen.

3 Using a piping bag fitted with a 1 cm (½ inch) plain nozzle, pipe about 20 small bun shapes on to 2 damp baking sheets. Bake in the oven at 220°C (425°F) mark 7 for about 20–25 minutes until well risen and golden brown. Lower the oven temperature to 180°C (350°F) mark 4. Make a hole in the side of each bun with a skewer or knife and return to the oven for 5 minutes. Cool on a wire rack.

4 For the chocolate sauce, melt the chocolate, butter, 30 ml (2 tbsp) water, the golden syrup and vanilla flavouring in a small saucepan over a very low heat. Stir well until smooth and well blended.

5 Whip the cream until it just holds its shape. Spoon into a piping bag fitted with a medium plain nozzle and use to fill the choux buns. Dust with icing sugar and serve with the chocolate sauce spooned over or served separately.

VARIATIONS

Chocolate Eclairs

1 Make the choux dough as above, then pipe 7.5 cm (3 inch) long strips on damp baking sheets.
2 Bake as above and cool on a wire rack.
3 Fill with cream and dip the tops in **melted chocolate** or glacé icing made with **100 g (4 oz) icing sugar** and **10 ml (2 level tsp) cocoa powder** blended with a little hot water.

Croquembouche (French Wedding Cake)

1 Make a **20.5 cm (8 inch) round pastry flan case** with pâte sucrée (see page 191).
2 Make **three times the quantity of choux pastry** in the above recipe and pipe about ninety 3 cm (1¼ inch) rounds on damp baking sheets. Cook as above and cool on a wire rack.
3 Make **three times the quantity of Crème Pâtissière** in the recipe for Gâteau Saint-Honoré (see page 130) and flavour with a little **kirsch**.
4 Make a caramel with **450 g (1 lb) granulated sugar** and **150 ml (¼ pint) water** (see page 31). Using the caramel to stick the buns together, layer them up on the flan case to make a huge pyramid.
5 Make spun sugar with the remaining caramel: hold two forks together facing each other, dip them in the caramel, then swing them around the croquembouche – the sugar should fall off the forks in long silvery threads which harden immediately. Decorate with **sugared almonds** and **fresh flowers**.

CHERRY PIE

*If you have time, use the pastry trimmings to make a
cherry pattern on top of the pie.*

·

SERVES 4 – 6

FOR THE PASTRY

225 g (8 oz) plain flour

pinch of salt

100 g (4 oz) butter or margarine

FOR THE FILLING

700 g (1½ lb) fresh red or black cherries

100 g (4 oz) caster sugar

30 ml (2 level tbsp) plain flour

5 ml (1 tsp) kirsch (optional)

caster sugar, to dredge

1   To make the pastry, put the flour and salt in
a bowl and rub in the butter until the mixture
resembles fine breadcrumbs. Stir in about 45 ml
(3 tbsp) cold water or sufficient to bind the
mixture to a soft dough.
2   Stone the cherries, but keep them as whole
as possible. Then mix the sugar and flour
together and layer the cherries and sugar
mixture in a 20.5 cm (8 inch) pie plate. Sprinkle
over 15 ml (1 tbsp) water and kirsch, if using.
3   Roll out the pastry on a floured surface to a
shape 5 cm (2 inches) larger than the pie plate.
Dampen the rim of the dish, then cut a 2.5 cm
(1 inch) strip from the outer edge of the pastry
and press on to the rim. Dampen the pastry rim
and cover with the remaining pastry to make a
lid. Press the edges together to seal and crimp.
Use the pastry trimmings, to decorate. Chill for
30 minutes.
4   Make a hole in the centre of the pastry. Bake
in the oven at 200°C (400°F) mark 6 for 25–30
minutes until the pastry is lightly browned and
the fruit is cooked. Sprinkle with caster sugar
and serve warm.

ECCLES CAKES

*If you want to make Eccles cakes for eating next day, do
not sprinkle with caster sugar; store in an airtight tin,
reheat the next day, then sprinkle with sugar.*

·

MAKES 8 – 10

212 g (7½ oz) packet frozen puff pastry, thawed,
or ¼ quantity puff or ½ quantity flaky pastry
(see pages 182 and 181)

25 g (1 oz) butter, softened

25 g (1 oz) dark brown soft sugar

25 g (1 oz) finely chopped mixed peel

50 g (2 oz) currants

caster sugar

1   Roll out the pastry on a lightly floured
surface and cut into 9 cm (3½ inch) rounds.
2   For the filling, mix the butter, sugar, mixed
peel and currants in a bowl.
3   Place 5 ml (1 tsp) of the fruit and butter
mixture in the centre of each pastry round.
Draw up the edges of each pastry round to
enclose the filling and then reshape.
4   Turn each round over and roll lightly until
the currants just show through.
5   Prick the top of each with a fork. Leave to
rest for about 10 minutes in a cool place.
6   Put the Eccles Cakes on a damp baking sheet
and bake in the oven at 230°C (450°F) mark 8
for about 15 minutes until golden. Transfer to a
wire rack to cool for 30 minutes. Sprinkle with
caster sugar while still warm.

BAKED ROLY-POLY
PUDDING

*For a lighter texture or if using wholemeal flour, replace
25 g (1 oz) of the flour with 25 g (1 oz) fresh breadcrumbs.*

·

SERVES 6

175 g (6 oz) self-raising flour

large pinch of salt

75 g (3 oz) shredded suet

60–90 ml (4–6 level tbsp) jam or curd

a little milk

1 Grease a piece of foil 23 × 33 cm (9 × 13 inches).

2 Mix the flour, salt and suet together in a bowl. Using a round-bladed knife, stir in enough chilled water to give a light, elastic dough. Knead very lightly until smooth.

3 Roll out the suetcrust pastry on a lightly floured surface to an oblong about 23 × 25 cm (9 × 11 inches). Spread the jam or curd on the pastry, leaving 0.5 cm (¼ inch) clear along each edge. Brush the edges with milk and roll up the pastry evenly, starting from one short side.

4 Place the roll on the greased foil and wrap the foil around it loosely, to allow room for expansion, but seal the edges well. Bake in the oven at 200°C (400°F) mark 6 for about 45 minutes. Serve immediately, with custard.

BAKEWELL PUDDING

A buttery mixture, flavoured with ground almonds and baked in a light, flaky pastry case, is the basis of this traditional Derbyshire recipe, also known as a tart.

SERVES 6

212 g (7½ oz) frozen packet puff pastry, thawed or ¼ quantity puff or ½ quantity flaky pastry (see pages 182 and 181)

60 ml (4 tbsp) strawberry or raspberry jam

100 g (4 oz) ground almonds

100 g (4 oz) caster sugar

50 g (2 oz) butter

3 eggs, beaten

1.25 ml (¼ tsp) almond flavouring

1 Roll out the pastry on a floured surface and use to line a 900 ml (1½ pint) shallow pie dish.

2 'Knock up' the edge of the pastry (see page 178) with the back of a knife and mark the rim with the prongs of a fork. Spread the jam over the base. Chill while making the filling.

3 To make the filling, beat the almonds with the sugar, butter, eggs and almond flavouring.

4 Pour the filling over the jam and spread it evenly. Bake in the oven at 200°C (400°F) mark 6 for 30 minutes or until the filling is set. Serve warm or cold, with cream or custard.

PANADE

A speciality of the boulangeries of France, Panade is an unusual fruit tart made of grated apples and pears cooked in orange juice then enclosed in a cinnamon-scented crust.

SERVES 6–8

FOR THE PASTRY

100 g (4 oz) butter or margarine

225 g (8 oz) plain flour

large pinch ground cinnamon

FOR THE FILLING

50 g (2 oz) butter

700 g (1½ lb) sweet eating apples, peeled, cored and grated

700 g (1½ lb) ripe pears, peeled, cored and grated

finely grated rind and juice of 1 large orange

beaten egg and caster sugar to glaze

1 Rub the butter into the flour and cinnamon until the mixture resembles fine breadcrumbs. Add about 90 ml (6 tbsp) water or enough to bind to a soft paste. Wrap and chill for 10 minutes.

2 On a lightly floured surface, roll the dough out thinly and use to line a 24 cm (9½ inch) loose-based fluted flan tin. Reroll the excess pastry and cut into 1 cm (½ inch) wide strips. Chill the pastry strips until required.

3 Bake the flan blind at 200°C (400°F) mark 6 for about 20 minutes or until light brown.

4 Meanwhile make the filling. Melt the butter in a large non-stick frying pan. Stir in the apples and pears, the orange rind and 45 ml (3 tbsp) of the orange juice.

5 Cook over a high heat, stirring constantly, until all excess moisture has evaporated and the mixture is quite dry. Spoon into the warm flan case.

6 Quickly lattice the pastry strips over the fruit mixture (see pages 178–9). Brush with beaten egg and dust with caster sugar. Bake in the oven at 200°C (400°F) mark 6 for about 20 minutes or until golden brown and crisp. Serve warm.

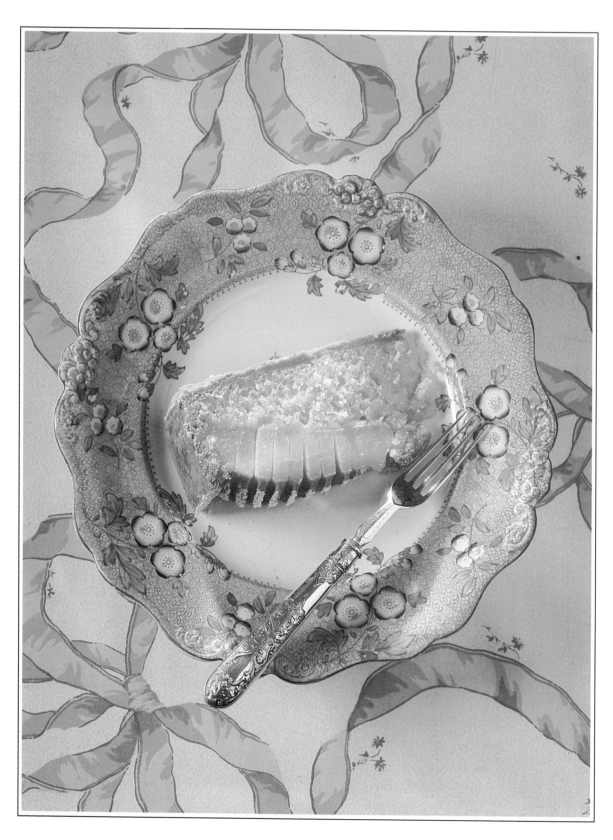

RICH PEAR SPONGE FLAN

Make sure you use ripe even-sized pears or the appearance of the finished flan will be spoilt.

•

SERVES 12

FOR THE PASTRY

275 g (10 oz) plain flour

pinch of salt

150 g (5 oz) butter or margarine

2 egg yolks

FOR THE FILLING AND DECORATION

150 g (5 oz) butter or margarine

150 g (5 oz) caster sugar

almond flavouring

3 eggs

100 g (4 oz) self-raising flour

75 g (3 oz) cornflour

5 ml (1 level tsp) baking powder

75 g (3 oz) ground almonds

30 ml (2 tbsp) milk

3 small ripe, even-sized pears

icing sugar, to dredge

1   Grease a 24 cm (9½ inch) round spring-form tin.

2   To make the pastry, put the flour and salt in a bowl and rub in the butter until the mixture resembles fine breadcrumbs. Add the egg yolks and 30–45 ml (2–3 tbsp) of water to bind the mixture together. Knead lightly then roll out and use to line the tin. Chill in the refrigerator while making the filling.

3   To make the filling, cream the butter and sugar together until pale and fluffy. Beat in a few drops of almond flavouring, then add the eggs, one at a time. Fold in the flours, baking powder and ground almonds. Fold in the milk.

4   Turn the mixture into the flan case and level the surface. Peel and core the pears and cut in

RICH PEAR SPONGE FLAN (above)

half. Make a series of parallel cuts across the width of the pear, but do not cut right through. Handling the pear halves carefully, arrange them, rounded sides up, on top of the filling.

5   Bake in the oven at 190°C (375°F) mark 5 for 1¼ hours or until a fine skewer inserted in the centre comes out clean. Cool in the tin for 15 minutes then carefully remove the sides of the tin. Serve warm or cold, dredged with icing sugar.

PALMIERS

These crisp heart-shaped biscuits can be served sandwiched together with cream.

•

MAKES 12

368 g (13 oz) packet frozen puff pastry, thawed or ½ quantity flaky pastry (see pages 182 and 181)

caster sugar, for dredging

150 ml (¼ pint) double cream

75 ml (3 fl oz) single cream

1   Roll out the pastry on a lightly floured surface to a rectangle measuring 30 × 25 cm (12 × 10 inches).

2   Dredge with caster sugar. Fold the long sides of the puff pastry halfway towards the centre.

3   Dredge with more caster sugar and fold again, taking the sides right to the centre.

4   Dredge with sugar again and fold in half lengthways, hiding the first folds and pressing lightly.

5   Cut across the pastry length into 24 equal-sized slices. Dampen a baking sheet and place the palmiers on it, cut-side down. Flatten them slightly with a palette knife or the palm of your hand.

6   Bake in the oven at 220°C (425°F) mark 7 for 8 minutes until golden brown. Turn each over and bake for a further 4 minutes. Transfer to a wire rack and cool for about 20 minutes.

7   Whip the creams together with a little caster sugar, until just standing in soft peaks. Sandwich the palmiers together with the cream before serving. Sprinkle with caster sugar.

GLAZED FRUIT TARTS

Strawberry tarts are always popular, but if preferred, these tarts can be made with a mixture of fruits of your choice instead.

•

MAKES 8

FOR THE PÂTE SUCRÉE

100 g (4 oz) plain flour

pinch of salt

50 g (2 oz) caster sugar

50 g (2 oz) butter, at room temperature

2 egg yolks

FOR THE FILLING AND GLAZE

150 ml (¼ pint) double cream

50 ml (2 fl oz) single cream

225 g (8 oz) fresh strawberries

60 ml (4 level tbsp) redcurrant jelly, to glaze

1   To make the pâte sucrée, sift the flour and salt together on to a clean surface. Make a well in the centre of the mixture and add the sugar, butter and egg yolks.

2   Using the fingertips of one hand, pinch and work the sugar, butter and egg yolks together until well blended. Gradually work in all the flour, adding a little water if necessary to bind it together.

3   Knead lightly until smooth, then wrap and leave to rest in the refrigerator for about 1 hour.

4   Roll out the pâte sucrée on a lightly floured working surface and use to line eight 9 cm (3½ inch) shallow patty tins. Bake blind in the oven at 190°C (375°F) mark 5 for 15–20 minutes until pale golden. Turn out on to a wire rack and leave to cool.

5   Whip the creams together until just standing in soft peaks. Spread a layer of cream over the tart bases. Using a sharp knife, slice the strawberries. Arrange on top of the cream in an overlapping circle on each tart.

6   Melt the redcurrant jelly over a very low heat, adding a little water if necessary. Brush over the strawberries to glaze.

MILLE FEUILLES

The name of this French pastry literally means 'thousand leaves' and that's what it should be: layers of light crisp pastry sandwiched with cream and jam.

•

MAKES 6

212 g (7½ oz) packet frozen puff pastry, thawed or ¼ quantity puff or ½ quantity flaky pastry (see pages 182 and 181)

100 g (4 oz) raspberry jam

300 ml (½ pint) double cream, whipped

FOR THE GLACÉ ICING

175 g (6 oz) icing sugar

red food colouring

1   Roll out the pastry on a lightly floured surface into a rectangle measuring 25 × 23 cm (10 × 9 inches) and place on a damp baking sheet. Prick all over with a fork.

2   Bake in the oven at 220°C (425°F) mark 7 for 10 minutes, until well risen and golden brown. Transfer to a wire rack and leave for 30 minutes to cool.

3   When cold, trim the pastry edges, cut in half lengthways and cut each half across into six slices. Spread half with raspberry jam, then cover with the cream.

4   Spread jam on the bases of the remaining pastry pieces and place on top of the first layers.

5   Sift the icing sugar into a basin. Gradually add about 15–30 ml (1–2 tbsp) warm water to make a smooth, thick icing.

6   Mix 15 ml (1 tbsp) icing with a few drops of red colouring. Set aside. Spread the remaining white icing over the pastries.

7   Pour the pink icing into a greaseproof paper piping bag. Cut off the tip and carefully pipe fine pink lines 1 cm (½ inch) apart on top of the white icing, across each pastry.

8   Draw a skewer down the length of the mille feuilles at 1 cm (½ inch) intervals to make a feathered pattern. Leave to set.

LEMON MERINGUE PIE

If you prefer a more cooked meringue, bake in the oven at 150°C (300°F) mark 2 for about 35 minutes. To make Lime Meringue Pie, substitute the finely grated rind and juice of 5 limes for the lemons. Decorate the top of the meringue with shredded lime rind.

·

S E R V E S   6 – 8

FOR THE PÂTE SUCRÉE

150 g (5 oz) plain flour
pinch of salt
25 g (1 oz) icing sugar
75 g (3 oz) butter, cubed
2 egg yolks

FOR THE FILLING

pared rind and juice of 4 large lemons
65 g (2½ oz) cornflour
50–75 g (2–3 oz) caster sugar
3 egg yolks

FOR THE MERINGUE

3 egg whites
175 g (6 oz) caster sugar

1   Sift the flour, salt and icing sugar into a bowl. Rub in the butter until the mixture resembles fine breadcrumbs. Add the egg yolks and mix with a round-bladed knife to form a dough. Turn on to a lightly floured surface and knead for a few seconds until smooth. Chill for 30 minutes.

2   Roll out the pâte sucrée on a lightly floured surface to a round 2.5 cm (1 inch) larger than a 23 cm (9 inch) fluted flan tin. Line the dish with the pastry, pressing it well into the flutes.

3   Trim the edge, then prick the pastry well, all over, with a fork. Chill for 30 minutes, then bake blind at 220°C (425°F) mark 7 for 25–30 minutes, until cooked and lightly browned. Allow to cool. Leave the oven on.

4   Meanwhile, prepare the filling, put the lemon rind in a saucepan with 600 ml (1 pint) water, bring to the boil, then remove from the heat, cover, and leave to stand for at least 30 minutes.

5   Remove all of the lemon rind from the pan, then stir in the lemon juice. Blend the cornflour with a little of the lemon liquid to form a smooth paste, pour it into the pan and stir well. Bring the lemon mixture to the boil, stirring continuously. Reduce the heat and continue cooking until every trace of raw cornflour disappears, and the mixture has thickened.

6   Stir in the sugar to taste, adding a little more if liked, then beat in the egg yolks. Pour the lemon filling into the pastry case.

7   To make the meringue, whisk the egg whites until stiff, but not dry, then gradually whisk in the sugar, adding a little at a time and whisking well between each addition, until the meringue is very stiff and shiny. Put the meringue into a large piping bag fitted with a large star nozzle, then pipe it attractively on top of the lemon filling. Alternatively, spoon the meringue on to the filling and shape it into swirls with a palette knife.

8   Bake for 5–10 minutes until the meringue is very lightly browned. Remove the pie from the oven and allow to cool, then refrigerate until quite cold.

HOT CHOCOLATE CHEESECAKE

This cheesecake has a rich, irresistible flavour. Unusually for a cheesecake, it is served straight from the oven; however, should there be any left it does taste good cold as well.

•

SERVES 10–12

FOR THE CHOCOLATE PASTRY

150 g (5 oz) plain white flour

30 ml (2 level tbsp) cocoa powder

75 g (3 oz) butter or margarine

30 ml (2 level tbsp) caster sugar

25 g (1 oz) ground hazelnuts

1 egg yolk

FOR THE FILLING

2 eggs, separated

75 g (3 oz) caster sugar

350 g (12 oz) curd cheese

40 g (1½ oz) ground hazelnuts

150 ml (¼ pint) double cream

25 g (1 oz) cocoa powder

10 ml (2 tsp) dark rum

icing sugar, for dredging

1 Grease a 20.5 cm (8 inch) round loose-bottomed cake tin.
2 To make the pastry, put the flour in a bowl and rub in the butter until the mixture resembles fine breadcrumbs. Stir in the cocoa powder, sugar and hazelnuts. Add the egg yolk and enough water to give a soft dough.
3 Roll out the pastry and use to line the tin. Chill while making the filling.
4 Whisk the egg yolks and sugar together until thick enough to leave a trail on the surface when the whisk is lifted. Whisk in the cheese, nuts, cream, cocoa powder and rum until evenly blended.
5 Whisk the egg whites until stiff, then fold into the cheese mixture. Pour into the pastry case and fold the edges of the pastry over the filling.

6 Bake in the oven at 170°C (325°F) mark 3 for 1½ hours until risen and just firm to the touch. Remove carefully from the tin and sift icing sugar over the top to coat lightly. Serve while still hot.

BAKED LEMON CHEESECAKE

Lemon flavouring and sultanas are the traditional ingredients of a European baked cheesecake.

•

SERVES 10

FOR THE PASTRY

175 g (6 oz) plain flour

75 g (3 oz) butter or margarine

10 ml (2 level tsp) caster sugar

juice of 1 lemon

FOR THE FILLING

550 g (1¼ lb) curd cheese

150 ml (¼ pint) double cream

75 g (3 oz) caster sugar

45 ml (3 level tbsp) cornflour

finely grated rind and juice of 2 lemons

1 egg

100 g (4 oz) sultanas

1 Grease a 20.5 cm (8 inch) round loose-bottomed cake tin.
2 To make the pastry, put the flour in a bowl and rub in the butter until the mixture resembles fine breadcrumbs. Stir in the sugar and enough lemon juice to bind to a smooth dough.
3 Roll out the pastry on a lightly floured surface and use to line the base and extend 2.5 cm (1 inch) up the sides of the tin. Chill while making the filling.
4 To make the filling, put all of the ingredients except the sultanas in a blender or food processor and purée until smooth. Stir in the sultanas and spoon into the pastry case.
5 Bake in the oven at 200°C (400°F) mark 6 for 1 hour 20 minutes, until the filling is just set. Leave to cool in the tin.

HOT CHOCOLATE CHEESECAKE (opposite)

APPLE STRUDEL

Strudel dough is exceptionally strong. It is not difficult to make as long as the instructions are followed carefully. The 15 minutes of kneading, in step 2, is vitally important to develop the gluten in the flour and so make the dough elastic and strong enough to be rolled extremely thinly.

•

SERVES 6

FOR THE STRUDEL PASTRY

225 g (8 oz) strong flour

2.5 ml (½ level tsp) salt

1 egg, lightly beaten

30 ml (2 tbsp) vegetable oil

FOR THE FILLING

900 g (2 lb) cooking apples, peeled, cored and roughly chopped

finely grated rind and juice of 1 lemon

50 g (2 oz) sultanas

50 g (2 oz) chopped almonds

75 g (3 oz) caster sugar

5 ml (1 level tsp) ground cinnamon

40 g (1½ oz) butter, melted

100 g (4 oz) ground almonds

icing sugar, for dredging

1 To make the strudel pastry, put the flour and salt into a large mixing bowl and make a well in the centre. Pour in the egg and oil. Gradually add 60 ml (4 tbsp) lukewarm water, stirring with a fork to make a soft, sticky dough.

2 Work the dough in the bowl until it leaves the sides clean, then turn it out on to a lightly floured surface and knead for 15 minutes.

3 Form into a ball, place on a cloth and cover with a warmed bowl. Leave the dough to rest in a warm place for about 1 hour.

4 Warm a rolling pin. Spread a clean cotton cloth on a large surface and sprinkle lightly with flour. Place the dough on the cloth and roll out into a rectangle about 0.3 cm (⅛ inch) thick, lifting and turning it to prevent it sticking to the cloth.

5 Gently stretch the dough, working from the centre to the outside and using the backs of the hands until it is paper thin. Trim the edges to form a rectangle about 68 × 51 cm (27 × 20 inches). Leave the strudel dough on the cloth to dry and rest at room temperature for about 15 minutes before filling and rolling.

6 Meanwhile, make the filling, mix together the apples, lemon rind and juice, sultanas, chopped almonds, sugar and cinnamon.

7 Position the dough with one of the long sides towards you, brush with half the melted butter and sprinkle with the ground almonds. Spread the apple mixture over the dough, leaving a 5 cm (2 inch) border all round the edge.

8 Fold the pastry edges over the apple mixture, towards the centre. Lift the corners of the cloth nearest to you over the pastry, causing the strudel to roll up, but stop after each turn in order to pat it into shape and to keep the roll even.

9 Form the roll into a horseshoe shape, brush it with the rest of the melted butter and slide it on to a buttered baking sheet. Bake in the oven at 190°C (375°F) mark 5 for about 40 minutes or until golden brown. Dredge thickly with icing sugar. Serve warm.

ALMOND FINGERS

These are far superior to the shop-bought version.

•

MAKES 8 – 12

FOR THE PASTRY

100 g (4 oz) plain flour

pinch of salt

50 g (2 oz) butter or block margarine

5 ml (1 level tsp) caster sugar

1 egg yolk

FOR THE FILLING

45 ml (3 level tbsp) raspberry jam

1 egg white

45 ml (3 level tbsp) ground almonds

50 g (2 oz) caster sugar

few drops almond flavouring

45 ml (3 level tbsp) flaked almonds

1   Lightly grease a shallow 18 cm (7 inch) square tin.

2   To make the pastry, sift the flour and salt and rub in the butter until the mixture resembles fine breadcrumbs. Stir in the sugar and add the egg yolk and enough water to mix to a firm dough.

3   Knead lightly on a floured surface and roll out to an 18 cm (7 inch) square; use to line the base of the tin. Spread the pastry with the jam, almost to the edges.

4   Whisk the egg white until stiff. Fold in the ground almonds, sugar and flavouring. Spread the mixture over the jam.

5   Sprinkle with flaked almonds and bake in the oven at 180°C (350°F) mark 4 for about 35 minutes until crisp and golden. Cool in the tin, then cut into 8–12 fingers and remove with a palette knife.

RAISED PORK PIE

Raised Pork Pie is a classic pie for picnics and buffets. Serve with a selection of salads, pickles and relishes. Fruity flavours such as orange, apple, lemon and lime help counteract the richness of the meat and pastry, so try to include these in your choice of salads.

·

S E R V E S   8

FOR THE FILLING

3–4 small veal bones

2 onions, skinned

1 bay leaf

6 peppercorns

900 g (2 lb) boneless leg or shoulder of pork

1.25 ml (¼ level tsp) cayenne pepper

1.25 ml (¼ level tsp) ground mace

1.25 ml (¼ level tsp) ground ginger

1.25 ml (¼ level tsp) ground sage

1.25 ml (¼ level tsp) dried marjoram

15 ml (1 level tbsp) salt

freshly ground black pepper

FOR THE HOT-WATER CRUST PASTRY

450 g (1 lb) plain flour

10 ml (2 level tsp) salt

100 g (4 oz) lard, or lard and butter

beaten egg, to glaze

1   Grease a 20.5 cm (8 inch) round spring-form cake tin and line with greaseproof paper.

2   To make the filling, put the veal bones, onions, bay leaf and peppercorns in a saucepan and add water to cover. Simmer for 20 minutes, then bring to the boil and boil rapidly until the liquid is reduced to 150 ml (¼ pint). Strain the liquid and leave to cool.

3   Meanwhile, cut the pork into cubes. Put in a bowl with the spices and herbs, salt, and pepper to taste. Mix well.

4   For the hot-water crust pastry, mix the flour and salt together in a bowl. Make a well in the centre. In a small saucepan, melt the lard in 250 ml (9 fl oz) water, then bring to the boil and pour into the well. Working quickly, beat with a wooden spoon to form a fairly soft dough. Using one hand, pinch the dough lightly together and knead until smooth and silky.

5   Roll out two-thirds of the pastry on a lightly floured surface and mould into the prepared tin. Cover and chill for 30 minutes. Cover the remaining pastry with a damp cloth and leave in a warm place.

6   Spoon the meat mixture and 60 ml (4 tbsp) of the cold stock into the pastry case.

7   Roll out the reserved pastry, for the lid. Use to cover the pie and seal the edge (see page 178). Decorate with the pastry trimmings. Make a hole in the centre and brush with beaten egg to glaze.

8   Bake in the oven at 220°C (425°F) mark 7 for 30 minutes. Cover loosely with foil, reduce the oven temperature to 180°C (350°F) mark 4 and bake for a further 2½ hours. Leave the pie to cool in the tin for 2 hours, then chill overnight.

9   Warm the remaining stock (which will have jellified) to liquefy and pour into the centre of the pie, through the hole. Chill for about 1 hour until set before serving.

STEAK AND MUSHROOM PIE (below)

STEAK AND MUSHROOM PIE

The meat can be cooked the day before the pie is required.

•

SERVES 4

700 g (1½ lb) stewing steak, cut into small pieces

30 ml (2 level tbsp) seasoned flour

1 medium onion, skinned and sliced

450 ml (¾ pint) beef stock

100 g (4 oz) button mushrooms

212 g (7½ oz) packet frozen puff pastry, thawed or ¼ quantity puff or ½ quantity flaky pastry (see pages 182 and 181)

beaten egg, to glaze

1 Coat the meat with the seasoned flour. Put in a large saucepan with the onion and stock.
2 Bring to the boil, reduce the heat and simmer for 1½–2 hours, until the meat is tender. Season to taste. Alternatively, cook for 2 hours in a covered casserole in the oven at 170°C (325°F) mark 3. Leave until cold. Then transfer to a 1.1 litre (2 pint) pie dish with enough of the gravy to half fill it.
3 Roll out the pastry 2.5 cm (1 inch) larger than the top of the dish. Cut off a 1 cm (½ inch) strip from round the edge of the pastry and put this strip round the dampened rim of the dish. Dampen the edges of the pastry with water and cover with the pastry lid. Trim and knock up the edges (see page 178). Brush the top with egg.
4 Bake in the oven at 220°C (425°F) mark 7 for 20 minutes. Reduce the heat to 180°C (350°F) mark 4 and cook for about a further 20 minutes. Reheat the remaining gravy to serve.

Spicy Vegetable Pie (overleaf)

SPICY VEGETABLE PIE

*This wholesome vegetable pie is very filling so it only
needs a green salad as an accompaniment.*

•

S E R V E S   4

FOR THE FILLING

4 carrots, thinly sliced

4 leeks, washed, trimmed and thickly sliced

6 courgettes, washed, trimmed and thinly sliced

salt

100 g (4 oz) butter or margarine

1 onion, skinned and sliced

10 ml (2 level tsp) ground cumin

50 g (2 oz) wholemeal flour

450 ml (¾ pint) milk plus 30 ml (2 tbsp)

100 g (4 oz) Cheddar cheese, grated

1.25 ml (¼ level tsp) ground mace

salt and freshly ground pepper

*45 ml (3 level tbsp) chopped fresh coriander or
parsley*

FOR THE PASTRY

100 g (4 oz) wholemeal flour

2.5 ml (½ level tsp) baking powder

salt

50 g (2 oz) butter or margarine

beaten egg, to glaze

*10 ml (2 level tsp) freshly grated Parmesan
cheese*

pinch of cayenne or paprika

1 To make the vegetable filling, blanch the
carrots, leeks and courgettes in boiling salted
water for 1 minute only. Drain well.
2 Melt 40 g (1½ oz) of the butter in a heavy-
based pan, add the onion and cumin and fry
gently for 5 minutes until soft. Add the carrots,
leeks and courgettes and fry for a further
5 minutes, stirring to coat in the onion mixture.
Remove from the heat and set aside.
3 Melt the remaining 65 g (2½ oz) butter in a
separate pan, sprinkle in the flour and cook for
1–2 minutes, stirring, until lightly coloured.
Remove from the heat and whisk in the milk.

Return to the heat and simmer for 5 minutes
until thick and smooth.
4 Stir in the Cheddar cheese, mace and salt
and pepper to taste. Fold into the vegetables
with the chopped coriander then turn into a
900 ml (1½ pint) ovenproof pie dish. Leave for
2 hours until cold.
5 To make the pastry, sift the flour, baking
powder and a pinch of salt into a bowl. Rub in
the butter until the mixture resembles fine
breadcrumbs, then add just enough water to
mix to a firm dough.
6 Gather the dough into a ball and knead
lightly. Wrap and chill for 30 minutes.
7 Remove the dough from the refrigerator and
roll out on a floured surface. Cut out a thin strip
long enough to go around the rim of the pie
dish. Moisten the rim with water and place the
strip on the rim.
8 Roll out the remaining dough for a lid,
moisten the strip of dough, then place the lid on
top and press to seal. Knock up and flute the
edge (see page 178). Decorate the top with any
trimmings.
9 Brush the pie with beaten egg, dust with
Parmesan and cayenne. Bake in the oven at
190°C (375°F) mark 5 for 20–25 minutes.

CHEESE D'ARTOIS

*D'Artois or dartois is a French pastry dish, made with
either puff pastry as here, or with flaky pastry.*

•

M A K E S   3 0 – 4 0

150 g (5 oz) Gruyère cheese, grated

25 g (1 oz) walnut pieces, coarsely chopped

freshly ground pepper

1 egg, beaten

*368 g (13 oz) packet frozen puff pastry, thawed
or ½ quantity puff or 1 quantity flaky pastry
(see pages 182 and 181)*

1 In a bowl, mix together the cheese, nuts and
pepper to taste. Bind with the egg, reserving a
little egg to glaze the pastry.
2 Roll out the pastry to a 40.5 × 38 cm (16 ×
15 inch) rectangle. Using a pastry wheel cut the

pastry into 10 strips, each measuring 20.5 × 7.5 cm (8 × 3 inches) long.

3   Lay 5 strips on a damp baking sheet, divide the filling between them and spread it out evenly, almost to the edges of each strip.

4   Cover with the remaining 5 strips of pastry and lightly press the edges to seal. Cover and chill in the refrigerator for 30 minutes.

5   Mark each strip into 6–8 fingers and brush with the reserved egg. Bake in the oven at 200°C (400°F) mark 6 for about 15 minutes until risen and golden brown. Cut through the pastry into fingers and serve immediately.

FETA CHEESE PUFFS

These tasty cheese puffs are ideal for picnics.

MAKES 8

225 g (8 oz) Feta cheese

150 g (5 oz) thick set natural yogurt

30 ml (2 level tbsp) chopped fresh basil or 5 ml (1 level tsp) dried

freshly ground black pepper

368 g (13 oz) packet puff pastry or ½ quantity puff or 1 quantity flaky pastry (see pages 182 and 181)

beaten egg, to glaze

whole basil leaves to garnish

1   Crumble the cheese and mix with the yogurt, basil and lots of black pepper. Don't add salt as the cheese is salty enough.

2   Roll out the pastry thinly and cut out sixteen 12.5 cm (5 inch) rounds. Fold and re-roll the pastry as necessary.

3   Place half the rounds on two baking sheets. Spoon the cheese mixture into the centre of each one.

4   Brush the pastry edges with beaten egg. Cover with the remaining pastry rounds, knocking the pastry edges together (see page 178) to seal. Make a small slit in the top of each and brush with beaten egg.

5   Bake in the oven at 220°C (425°F) mark 7 for about 15 minutes, or until well browned and crisp. Serve warm garnished with basil leaves.

CHEESE TWISTS

Make a selection of twists, medallions and straws to serve with drinks.

MAKES ABOUT 70

65 g (2½ oz) butter, softened

40 g (1½ oz) full-fat soft cheese

1 egg yolk

175 g (6 oz) plain flour

salt

cayenne

30 ml (2 tbsp) freshly grated Parmesan cheese

1   In a bowl, beat the butter with the soft cheese and egg yolk. Sift in the flour with a pinch each of salt and cayenne, then stir until evenly mixed. Stir in 10 ml (2 tsp) water to form a dough. Knead lightly until smooth then wrap and chill for 30 minutes.

2   Roll out the pastry thinly and cut into narrow strips measuring about 7.5 cm × 5 mm (3 × ¼ inch). Twist the strips twice and place on damp baking sheets, pressing the ends down well to prevent the strips unwinding. Sprinkle with the cheese.

3   Bake in the oven at 180°C (350°F) mark 4 for about 15 minutes. Transfer to wire racks and leave to cool for about 15 minutes. Store in an airtight container for up to 2 weeks.

VARIATIONS

Medallions

1   Prepare the pastry as above, roll out and cut into 2.5 cm (1 inch) rounds. Sprinkle with grated Parmesan cheese and bake as above. Cool on wire racks.

2   Either sandwich together or top the rounds with softened pâté, fish paste or cream cheese; garnish with slices of olives, radish or gherkin.

Blue Cheese Straws

Rub the butter into the flour with the seasonings. Grate **75 g (3 oz) blue cheese** into the mixture, add the egg yolk and **2.5 ml (½ tsp) Dijon mustard**. Mix to form a soft dough. Wrap and chill for 30 minutes and bake as above.

BISCUITS AND COOKIES

Homemade biscuits beat bought ones any day and they are so simple to make it is a pity to pass them by.

Most biscuits fall into one of 5 categories. The traditional mixture makes a dough that is rolled out, then cut into shapes with biscuit cutters. Dropped and piped biscuits are a little more difficult to handle as the mixture is softer. As their names suggest, they are dropped from a spoon or piped on to baking sheets. They are inclined to spread so leave lots of space between each one. Bar cookies are especially easy and quick to make; all the ingredients are mixed together, poured into a shallow tin, then cut into bars after baking. Refrigerator biscuits are made of a dough which is shaped into a neat roll, wrapped and stored in the refrigerator or freezer. When you feel like baking some biscuits, simply cut off the number required, thaw slightly (if frozen), then bake as usual. The dough will keep quite happily in the refrigerator for 2 weeks and in the freezer for 3 months.

Left to right: OATMEAL COOKIES *(page 206),* GINGERNUTS *(page 214),* CHOCOLATE SHORTIES *(page 210),* CHOCOLATE BOURBONS *(page 208)*

GENERAL POINTS FOR BISCUIT MAKING

·

MIXING AND ROLLING THE DOUGH

* Weigh the ingredients accurately.
* Plain flour is generally used, but for a 'shorter' result, substitute with a little corn-flour or rice flour.
* Caster sugar generally gives much better results than granulated sugar as the coarse crystals of granulated sugar give a speckled result.
* Dark brown soft sugar is preferable to demerara sugar for the same reason as above. Brown sugars give a richer colour and flavour than white.
* Golden syrup and black treacle are often used in place of some or all of the sugar. The easiest way to measure syrup or treacle is to weigh the jar without its lid, deduct the amount needed in the recipe, then spoon out from the jar or tin until the scales register the calculated amount.
* Butter gives the richest flavour and colour, but block margarine can also be used. Soft tub margarine is not recommended for biscuit making. For best results, always use fat at room temperature.
* Use damp hands when shaping ball-type biscuits as it stops the mixture sticking.
* If you find it difficult to roll out the dough thinly, roll it between sheets of non-stick paper.
* In a hot kitchen, handle rolled-out doughs a little at a time, leaving the rest in the re-frigerator until you are ready to use it.

BAKING

* Have all biscuits even in size and rolled to the same thickness for overall browning.
* Use a flat baking sheet with hardly any sides. High sides prevent proper browning.
* If cooking two sheets of biscuits at a time, swap their position in the oven halfway through cooking.
* Check the biscuits just before the minimum baking time is up.
* To cool, transfer them with a wide flexible spatula to wire racks. To remove the biscuits from the baking sheet, press down the spatula on the baking sheet and ease it under the biscuits.
* Some biscuits – especially those with syrup or honey as an ingredient – are still soft im-mediately after baking, so leave them for a few minutes before lifting them off the sheet.
* Do not overlap the biscuits while cooling.

STORING

* Line the bottom of an airtight container with greaseproof paper or non-stick paper and place a sheet between each two layers of biscuits or between each single layer of soft ones.
* Store different types of biscuit in separate containers.
* Bar biscuits can be kept in the baking tin and covered tightly with foil to save space.
* Most homemade varieties will keep for up to two weeks. If plain biscuits lose their crispness, return them to a baking sheet and freshen in the oven at 170°C (325°F) mark 3 for 5 minutes without overbrowning.
* Biscuits and cookies keep well in the freezer for several months. Pack fragile ones in rigid boxes but just wrap others in foil or freezer film. Thaw in a single layer.
* Do not store biscuits with cakes as they lose their crispness and can take up strong flavours.

AMARETTI BISCUITS

These classic Italian biscuits are delicious served with coffee or with mousses, sorbets and ice creams, or they may be crushed and used to decorate trifles.

·

MAKES ABOUT 24

100 g (4 oz) ground almonds

15 g (½ oz) ground rice

225 g (8 oz) caster sugar

2 egg whites

2.5 ml (½ tsp) almond flavouring

about 24 split almonds

1 Line two baking sheets with rice paper.
2 Mix together the ground almonds, ground rice and sugar. Add the egg whites and almond flavouring and beat together until smooth.
3 Put the mixture into a piping bag fitted with a 1 cm (½ inch) plain nozzle. Pipe small rounds about 2.5 cm (1 inch) in diameter on to the paper, leaving plenty of room for spreading. Top each biscuit with a split almond.
4 Bake in the oven at 180°C (350°F) mark 4 for about 20 minutes or until pale golden brown. Cool on a wire rack. Remove the rice paper from around each Amaretti before serving.

ALMOND CRISPS

These crispy biscuits are delicious served with ice cream and hot chocolate sauce.

·

MAKES ABOUT 24

125 g (4 oz) butter or margarine

75 g (3 oz) caster sugar

1 egg yolk

few drops of almond flavouring

150 g (5 oz) self-raising flour

75 g (3 oz) chopped almonds

1 Cream together the butter and sugar until light and fluffy. Beat in the egg yolk and almond flavouring and finally the flour, to give a smooth dough.

2 Divide the dough into 24 then roll each piece into a ball, then roll in the chopped almonds. Place well apart on the baking sheets and bake at 190°C (375°F) mark 5, for 15–20 minutes. Cool on a wire rack.

BROWN SUGAR RINGS

The biscuit mixture is chilled twice before cooking. To save time pop the mixture into the freezer (instead of the refrigerator) for about 5 minutes or until firm to the touch.

·

MAKES ABOUT 20

175 g (6 oz) plain wholemeal flour

1.25 ml (¼ level tsp) bicarbonate of soda

1.25 ml (¼ level tsp) salt

50 g (2 oz) light brown soft sugar

75 g (3 oz) butter or block margarine, cut into pieces

125 g (4 oz) currants

50 g (2 oz) oatflakes

1 egg, beaten

1 Grease two baking sheets. Mix the flour, bicarbonate of soda, salt and sugar in a bowl. Rub in the fat until the mixture resembles fine breadcrumbs.
2 Stir in the currants and oatflakes, then stir in the beaten egg and about 15 ml (1 tbsp) water to bind the mixture together. Knead in the bowl until smooth. Cover and chill for 20 minutes.
3 On a lightly floured surface, roll out the dough until about 5 mm (¼ inch) thick. Cut into 6.5 cm (2½ inch) rounds using a fluted cutter and remove centres with a 2.5 cm (1 inch) cutter.
4 Carefully transfer the rings to the prepared baking sheets. Re-roll trimmings as necessary. Chill for at least 20 minutes.
5 Bake in the oven at 190°C (375°F) mark 5 for about 15 minutes until golden brown and firm to the touch. Transfer to a wire rack to cool.

GINGERBREAD PEOPLE

The finished Gingerbread People can be decorated with glacé icing to give them each a personality of their own.

•

MAKES ABOUT 12

350 g (12 oz) plain flour
5 ml (1 level tsp) bicarbonate of soda
10 ml (2 level tsp) ground ginger
100 g (4 oz) butter or margarine
175 g (6 oz) light brown soft sugar
60 ml (4 level tbsp) golden syrup
1 egg
currants, to decorate

1 Sift the flour, bicarbonate of soda and ginger into a bowl. Rub in the butter until the mixture resembles fine breadcrumbs. Stir in the sugar. Beat the syrup into the egg and stir into the flour mixture.

2 Mix to form a dough and knead until smooth.

3 Divide into two and roll out on a lightly floured surface to about 0.5 cm (¼ inch) thick. Using gingerbread cutters, cut out figures and place them on three greased baking sheets. Decorate with currants to represent eyes and buttons.

4 Bake in the oven at 190°C (375°F) mark 5 for 12–15 minutes, until golden brown. Cool slightly, then transfer to a wire rack to cool.

GINGERBREAD PEOPLE *(above)*

VIENNESE FINGERS

To make chocolate Viennese Fingers simply replace 15 g (½ oz) of the flour with cocoa powder.

·

M A K E S   A B O U T   2 0

125 g (4 oz) butter or margarine

25 g (1 oz) icing sugar

125 g (4 oz) plain flour

1.25 ml (¼ level tsp) baking powder

few drops of vanilla flavouring

50 g (2 oz) plain chocolate

icing sugar, for dredging

1 Beat the butter until smooth, then beat in the icing sugar until pale and fluffy.

2 Sift in the flour and baking powder. Beat well, adding the vanilla flavouring.

3 Put into a piping bag fitted with a medium star nozzle. Pipe out finger shapes, about 7.5 cm (3 inches) long, on to two greased baking sheets, spacing them well apart.

4 Bake in the oven at 190°C (375°F) mark 5 for 15–20 minutes until pale golden brown. Cool on a wire rack.

5 Break up the chocolate and place in a bowl over a pan of simmering water. Heat gently until the chocolate melts. Dip the ends of each Viennese Finger in the melted chocolate. Leave to set on the wire rack. Dredge with icing sugar.

VIENNESE FINGERS (*above*)

CHOCOLATE CHIP COOKIES

Buy ready-made chocolate chips or polka dots, or make your own by roughly chopping a bar of chocolate.

·

MAKES ABOUT 20

75 g (3 oz) butter or margarine

75 g (3 oz) caster sugar

75 g (3 oz) light brown soft sugar

few drops of vanilla flavouring

1 egg

175 g (6 oz) self-raising flour

pinch of salt

50 g (2 oz) walnut pieces, chopped

50–100 g (2–4 oz) chocolate chips

1   Cream together the butter, sugars and vanilla flavouring until pale and fluffy, then gradually beat in the egg.

2   Sift in the flour and salt, then fold in with the nuts and chocolate chips.

3   Drop spoonfuls of the mixture on to two greased baking sheets and bake in the oven at 180°C (350°F) mark 4 for 12–15 minutes.

4   Cool on the baking sheets for 1 minute, then transfer to a wire rack to cool completely.

CHOCOLATE SHORTIES

Sprinkling the grated chocolate on to the biscuits as soon as they come out of the oven ensures that it sticks.

·

MAKES ABOUT 36

200 g (7 oz) self-raising flour

150 g (5 oz) caster sugar

1.25 ml (¼ level tsp) ground nutmeg

150 g (5 oz) butter or margarine

100 g (4 oz) ground almonds

50 g (2 oz) plain chocolate, coarsely grated

1 egg, beaten

1   Grease three baking sheets. Sift the flour, sugar and nutmeg into a bowl. Rub the butter into the flour mixture until the mixture resembles fine breadcrumbs. Stir in the ground almonds and 25 g (1 oz) of the grated chocolate. Add the egg and mix together to form a dough.

2   Divide the mixture into 2 and roll each piece on a sheet of greaseproof or non-stick paper into a 30.5 cm (12 inch) long, thin sausage shape.

3   Chill in the ice cube compartment of the refrigerator for about 30 minutes until firm.

4   Cut each roll at an angle, into about 18 slices. Place well apart on three greased baking sheets. Bake in the oven at 190°C (375°F) mark 5 for 15–20 minutes. Sprinkle with the remaining grated chocolate then transfer to wire racks.

CHERRY GARLANDS

These crisp, melt-in-the-mouth biscuits look very pretty if piped in rings and decorated with cherries and angelica.

·

MAKES 24

225 g (8 oz) butter or margarine

50 g (2 oz) icing sugar

200 g (7 oz) plain flour

150 g (5 oz) cornflour

vanilla flavouring

50 g (2 oz) glacé cherries, very finely chopped

quartered cherries and angelica, to decorate

icing sugar, for dredging

1   Cream the butter and sugar together until pale and fluffy, then beat in the flours, a few drops of vanilla flavouring and the chopped cherries. Continue beating until very soft.

2   Spoon half of the mixture into a piping bag fitted with a 1 cm (½ inch) star nozzle. Pipe 5 cm (2 inch) rings on to the baking sheets allowing room for spreading. Decorate with a quartered cherry and pieces of angelica. Repeat with the remaining mixture.

3   Bake in the oven at 190°C (375°F) mark 5 for about 20 minutes until pale golden.

4   Allow to firm up slightly on the baking sheets for about 30 seconds before sliding on to a wire rack to cool. Dredge with icing sugar.

CHOCOLATE NUT SNAPS

Short biscuit doughs are often difficult to roll without breaking. Chilling helps, but you could also try rolling the dough between sheets of cling film. This not only holds the dough together, but eliminates the need for extra flour on the board, which can harden the surface of the baked biscuits. After rolling, remove the top sheet of film to cut the biscuits, then lift each one on the bottom piece of cling film to transfer it to the baking sheet.

•

MAKES 24

1 egg, separated
100 g (4 oz) caster sugar
150 g (5 oz) plain chocolate
125 g (4 oz) hazelnuts, finely chopped
40 g (1½ oz) plain flour

1   Grease two baking sheets. Whisk the egg white until stiff. Fold in the caster sugar.
2   Coarsely grate 75 g (3 oz) plain chocolate into the mixture and stir in with the hazelnuts, flour and egg yolk.
3   Turn out on a well-floured surface and knead lightly. Cover and refrigerate for about 30 minutes.
4   Roll the dough out to 5 mm (¼ inch) thickness. Using a 5 cm (2 inch) plain cutter, cut out 24 shapes. Knead lightly and place on 2 greased baking sheets. Cover and refrigerate the biscuits again for 30 minutes.
5   Bake in the oven at 190°C (375°F) mark 5 for about 20 minutes until crisp. Immediately ease off the baking sheet on to a wire rack to cool for 30 minutes.
6   Break the remaining chocolate into a heat-proof bowl and place over a pan of simmering water. Stir until the chocolate is melted, then remove from the heat.
7   Cut the tip off a paper icing bag and spoon in the melted chocolate. Pipe lines of chocolate across the biscuits. Leave to set.

CHOCOLATE DATE BARS

This moist mixture of chocolate and dates is very rich, so cut it into small bars.

•

MAKES 12

175 g (6 oz) stoned dates, chopped
10 ml (2 level tsp) plain flour
100 g (4 oz) plain chocolate
100 g (4 oz) self-raising flour
150 g (5 oz) rolled oats
100 g (4 oz) light brown soft sugar
175 g (6 oz) butter or margarine

1   Grease a shallow 18 cm (7 inch) square tin and line the base with greaseproof paper.
2   Put the dates, flour, chocolate and 150 ml (¼ pint) water in a small saucepan and cook gently for 5 minutes until the chocolate has melted and the mixture thickened slightly. Leave to cool.
3   Meanwhile, mix together the self-raising flour, oats and sugar and rub in the butter. Spread half of the mixture over the base of the prepared tin, pressing down well. Cover with the cooled date and chocolate mixture, then the remainder of the oat mixture. Press down with a round-bladed knife.
4   Bake in the oven at 190°C (375°F) mark 5 for about 25 minutes, until golden brown. Cool in the tin for 15 minutes then mark into 12 fingers. Cool completely in the tin.

SESAME CRACKERS

Keep a batch of these easy-to-make biscuits on hand for a high protein snack or lunch box filler.

•

MAKES 20

100 g (4 oz) plain wholemeal flour
100 g (4 oz) plain flour
2.5 ml (½ level tsp) baking powder
2.5 ml (½ level tsp) bicarbonate of soda
45 ml (3 level tbsp) sesame seeds
15 ml (1 level tbsp) light brown soft sugar
45 ml (3 tbsp) sunflower oil
50 g (2 oz) butter or margarine

1 Sift together the flours, baking powder and bicarbonate of soda, adding any bran left in the sieve. Stir in the sesame seeds and sugar. Add the oil, butter and water to make a smooth dough.
2 Roll out on a lightly floured surface until 0.5 cm (¼ inch) thick. Cut out the biscuits with a 7.5 cm (3 inch) cutter. Place on a lightly greased baking sheet.
3 Bake in the oven at 200°C (400°F) mark 6 for 15 minutes or until firm and slightly risen. Cool on the baking sheet for 1 minute before transferring to a wire rack to cool.

RYE CRISPBREADS

Flavour the crispbreads with other seeds such as fennel, sesame or cumin, if you prefer.

•

MAKES 16

225 g (8 oz) rye flour
5 ml (1 level tsp) mustard powder
2.5 ml (½ level tsp) caraway seeds
2.5 ml (½ level tsp) paprika
salt and pepper
50 g (2 oz) butter or margarine
105 ml (7 tbsp) milk

1 Put the flour, mustard, caraway seeds, paprika and seasoning in a bowl. Rub in the butter until the mixture resembles fine breadcrumbs. Add the milk and mix to a firm dough.
2 Roll out the dough on a lightly floured surface to a 30 × 40 cm (12 × 16 inch) rectangle. Cut into 7 × 10 cm (3 × 4 inch) rectangles and place on 2 lightly greased large baking sheets. Prick each piece several times with a fork.
3 Bake at 200°C (400°F) mark 6 for 10–15 minutes or until golden brown. Cool slightly on the baking sheets, then transfer to wire racks.

SAVOURY BISCUITS

Serve these bite-sized biscuits with drinks.

•

MAKES ABOUT 40

175 g (6 oz) plain flour
salt and paprika pepper
75 g (3 oz) butter or margarine
50 g (2 oz) mature Cheddar cheese, finely grated
2.5 ml (½ level tsp) Dijon mustard
1 egg yolk
milk for glazing
Cheddar cheese, Parmesan cheese, paprika pepper or ground almonds for decoration

1 Mix together the flour, salt and a pinch of paprika pepper in a bowl. Rub in the butter until the mixture resembles fine breadcrumbs.
2 Stir in the cheese, mustard, egg yolk and about 25 ml (5 tsp) water. Bind to a soft dough.
3 Knead lightly then roll out to a scant 5 mm (¼ inch) thickness on a lightly floured surface. Cut into shapes, such as diamonds, triangles or squares with a sharp knife or cutters or cut into rounds with a small plain cutter.
4 Place the biscuits on baking sheets and brush with a little milk. Sprinkle over a little grated Cheddar or Parmesan cheese, paprika or ground almonds. Chill for 15 minutes.
5 Bake in the oven at 200°C (400°F) mark 6 for 9 minutes until golden. Cool on a wire rack.

Clockwise from top: SESAME CRACKERS, SAVOURY BISCUITS AND RYE CRISPBREADS (opposite)

SPICE BISCUITS

These biscuits can be cut into any shape you wish.

MAKES ABOUT 36

100 g (4 oz) butter or margarine
200 g (7 oz) caster sugar
1 egg, beaten
10 ml (2 tsp) milk
225 g (8 oz) plain flour
5 ml (1 level tsp) bicarbonate of soda
5 ml (1 level tsp) ground cinnamon
1.25 ml (¼ level tsp) ground nutmeg
pinch of ground cloves
75 g (3 oz) currants

1 Cream the butter with 175 g (6 oz) of the sugar until light and fluffy and then beat in the egg and milk.
2 Stir in the remaining ingredients and mix well until smooth. Cover and chill for 30 minutes or until the mixture is firm enough to handle.
3 On a lightly floured surface roll out the dough as thinly as possible. Sprinkle evenly with the remaining sugar and cut into star or diamond shapes about 5 cm (2 inches) in length.
4 Place on 3 greased baking sheets. Bake at 190°C (375°F) mark 5 for 8 minutes or until lightly browned. Cool on a wire rack.

MELTING MOMENTS

These delicious short biscuits really do live up to their name.

MAKES 24

100 g (4 oz) butter or margarine
75 g (3 oz) caster sugar
1 egg yolk
few drops of vanilla flavouring
150 g (5 oz) self-raising flour
25 g (1 oz) crushed cornflakes

1 Cream the butter and sugar together until pale and fluffy, then beat in the egg yolk. Add the vanilla flavouring, stir in the flour to give a smooth dough and divide the mixture into 24 pieces.
2 Roll each piece into a ball and then coat in the crushed cornflakes.
3 Place on two greased baking sheets and bake in the oven at 190°C (375°F) mark 5 for 15–20 minutes.
4 Cool on the baking sheets for a few moments before lifting on to a wire rack to cool completely.

VARIATION
Instead of rolling the biscuits in cornflakes, use **50 g (2 oz) rolled oats** and press **half a glacé cherry** into the centre of each biscuit before baking.

GINGERNUTS

Once cooked, the Gingernuts should have the traditional cracked tops.

MAKES ABOUT 16

100 g (4 oz) self-raising flour
2.5 ml (½ level tsp) bicarbonate of soda
5–10 ml (1–2 level tsp) ground ginger
5 ml (1 level tsp) ground cinnamon
10 ml (2 level tsp) caster sugar
50 g (2 oz) butter or margarine
75 g (3 oz) golden syrup

1 Sift together the flour, bicarbonate of soda, ginger, cinnamon and sugar.
2 Heat the butter and the syrup together until the butter melts. Stir into the dry ingredients and mix well.
3 With lightly floured hands, roll the dough into small balls, place well apart on 2 greased baking sheets and flatten slightly.
4 Bake in the oven at 190°C (375°F) mark 5, for about 15 minutes. Cool for a few minutes before lifting carefully from the baking sheet on to a wire rack to cool completely.

APRICOT OAT CRUNCHIES

These delicious chewy teatime bars will keep well for several days if tightly wrapped in kitchen foil and kept in an airtight tin.

•

MAKES 12

75 g (3 oz) self-raising wholemeal flour
75 g (3 oz) rolled porridge oats
75 g (3 oz) demerara sugar
100 g (4 oz) butter or margarine
100 g (4 oz) no-soak dried apricots, chopped

1 Lightly grease a shallow tin measuring 28 × 18 × 3.5 cm (11 × 7 × 1½ inches).
2 Mix together the flour, oats and sugar in a bowl. Rub in the butter until the mixture resembles breadcrumbs.
3 Spread half of the mixture over the base of the prepared tin, pressing it down evenly.
4 Drain and chop the apricots. Spread them over the oat mixture in the tin.
5 Sprinkle over the remaining crumb mixture and press down well. Bake in the oven at 180°C (350°F) mark 4 for 25 minutes until golden brown. Leave in the tin for about 1 hour until cold. Cut into bars to serve.

BUTTER BISCUITS

Make these biscuits, with their delicious Cognac-flavoured icing, for a special coffee morning. They keep well in an airtight tin if left un-iced. Once iced they will keep for only a couple of days.

•

MAKES 15–20

225 g (8 oz) plain flour
pinch of salt
1.25 ml (¼ level tsp) baking powder
7.5 ml (1½ level tsp) ground cardamom
175 g (6 oz) unsalted butter, diced
75 g (3 oz) icing sugar
2.5 ml (½ tsp) vanilla flavouring

FOR THE GLACÉ ICING WITH COGNAC

50 g (2 oz) icing sugar
10–15 ml (2–3 tsp) Cognac

1 Sift the flour, salt, baking powder and cardamom into a bowl. Rub in the butter until the mixture resembles breadcrumbs. Sift the icing sugar over, then gently stir in. Sprinkle the vanilla flavouring over, then press the ingredients together to make a smooth dough. Cover and chill for at least 3 hours.
2 Roll out the dough on a lightly floured surface, using a lightly floured rolling pin, to about 5 mm (¼ inch) thick. Cut into rounds with a floured 6.5 cm (2¼ inch) fluted cutter. Transfer to baking sheets, leaving about 1 cm (½ inch) space around each.
3 Bake at 190°C (375°F) mark 5 for about 12 minutes, until lightly golden. Leave to set on the baking sheets for a few minutes, then transfer to a wire rack to cool.
4 To make the icing, sift the icing sugar and mix to a smooth consistency with about 15 ml (1 tbsp) cold water and the Cognac. Spread a thin layer of glacé icing over the tops of half of the biscuits. Leave to set.

SHORTBREAD

Traditional Scottish shortbread moulds are made with a thistle design in the centre. These can be bought at specialist kitchen shops, but they are not essential; an ordinary sandwich cake tin will do the job just as well. Be sure to use a good-quality butter when making shortbread. The flavour of shortbread relies heavily on the butter in the mixture, and margarine makes a poor substitute.

·

MAKES 8 PIECES

150 g (5 oz) plain flour
45 ml (3 level tbsp) rice flour
50 g (2 oz) caster sugar
100 g (4 oz) butter
caster sugar, for dredging

1 Sift the flours into a bowl and add the sugar. Work in the butter with your fingertips – keep it in one piece and gradually work in the dry ingredients. Knead well.

2 Pack into a floured shortbread mould, then turn out on to a baking sheet. Alternatively, pack into an 18 cm (7 inch) sandwich tin, prick well with a fork and pinch up the edges decoratively with finger and thumb.

3 Bake in the oven at 170°C (325°F) mark 3 for about 45 minutes, until firm and pale golden brown. Mark into 8 triangles while still hot. If using a sandwich tin, cool slightly before turning out on to a wire rack.

4 When cool, dredge with sugar. Serve cut into wedges.

SHORTBREAD (*above*)

BRANDY SNAPS

If the cooked biscuits cool and become too brittle to roll, return them to the oven for a minute or two to soften.

•

M A K E S   1 0

50 g (2 oz) butter or margarine

50 g (2 oz) caster sugar

50 g (2 oz) golden syrup

50 g (2 oz) plain flour

2.5 ml (½ level tsp) ground ginger

5 ml (1 tsp) brandy (optional)

finely grated rind of ½ lemon

whipped cream, to serve

BRANDY SNAPS (above)

1   Grease the handles of several wooden spoons and line two or three baking sheets with non-stick paper.

2   Melt the butter with the sugar and syrup in a small saucepan over a low heat. Remove from the heat and stir in the sifted flour and ginger, brandy and lemon rind.

3   Drop small spoonfuls of the mixture about 10 cm (4 inches) apart on to the baking sheets.

4   Bake in rotation in the oven at 180°C (350°F) mark 4, for 7–10 minutes, until bubbly and golden.

5   Allow to cool for 1–2 minutes, then loosen with a palette knife and roll them round the spoon handles. Leave until set, then twist gently to remove.

6   Fill the brandy snaps with whipped cream just before serving.

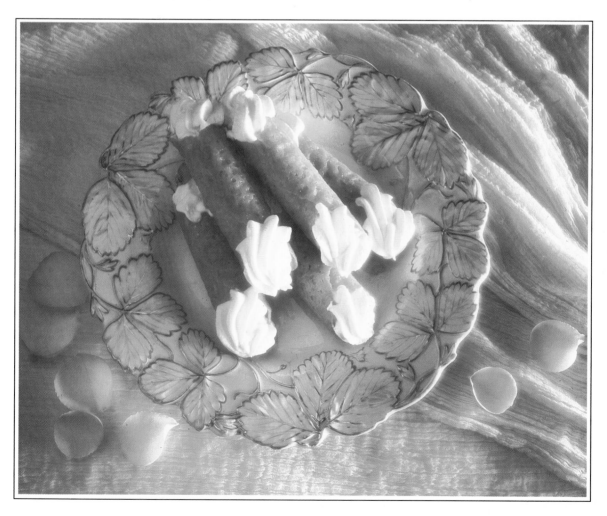

SUNFLOWER FLAPJACKS

We used the jumbo oats available from health food stores, porridge oats give a softer texture.

•

MAKES ABOUT 12

275 g (10 oz) rolled jumbo oats

125 g (4 oz) sunflower seeds

125 g (4 oz) butter or margarine

75 ml (5 tbsp) golden syrup

1 Put the oats and sunflower seeds into a bowl and make a well in the centre. Heat the margarine and syrup until evenly blended then pour into the well.
2 Stir the mixture until evenly coated then spoon into a 270 × 175 × 35 mm (10¾ × 7 × 1⅜ inch) shallow cake tin. Press down well with the back of a spoon.
3 Bake in the oven at 180°C (350°F) mark 4 for about 35 minutes or until golden brown and just firm to the touch.
4 Allow to cool completely in the tin then cut into small triangles.

COCONUT MACAROONS

The cooked macaroons should be golden brown and crisp on the outside, but soft in the middle.

•

MAKES 18

2 egg whites

100 g (4 oz) icing sugar, sifted

100 g (4 oz) ground almonds

few drops of almond flavouring

100 g (4 oz) desiccated coconut

1 Line two baking sheets with non-stick paper or rice paper.
2 Whisk the egg whites until stiff but not dry. Lightly fold in the sugar.
3 Gently stir in the almonds, almond flavouring and desiccated coconut until the mixture forms a sticky dough.
4 Spoon walnut-sized pieces of mixture on to the baking sheets.
5 Bake in the oven at 150°C (300°F) mark 2 for about 25 minutes. Cool on a wire rack.

LEMON AND LIME COOKIES

These cookies are simplicity itself to make, almost like craggy, flat rock cakes. If you have a food processor, steps 1 and 2 can be made in moments, by working all the ingredients together in one go.

•

MAKES ABOUT 24

100 g (4 oz) butter or margarine

100 g (4 oz) caster sugar

1 egg yolk

50 g (2 oz) full-fat soft cheese

175 g (6 oz) plain flour

finely grated rind of 1 small lemon

15 ml (1 tbsp) lemon juice

20 ml (4 tsp) lime marmalade

1 Put the butter and caster sugar in a bowl and beat together until light and fluffy.
2 Beat in the egg yolk, cheese, flour, lemon rind and juice, until a soft mixture is formed.
3 Place small spoonfuls of the mixture on to greased baking sheets, allowing room for spreading.
4 Bake in the oven at 190°C (375°F) mark 5 for about 17 minutes or until light brown. Transfer to a wire rack to cool.
5 Melt the marmalade in a small saucepan and brush over the cookies, to glaze. Leave to set.

LANGUES DE CHAT

The mixture makes a lot of biscuits but they're light and delicate and if any are left over will store well for several days. Do allow the biscuits plenty of room to spread while baking or the mixture will run together forming one enormous biscuit.

•

MAKES ABOUT 48

75 g (3 oz) butter or margarine

75 g (3 oz) caster sugar

1 large egg

50 g (2 oz) plain flour

25 g (1 oz) ground almonds

1 Line 3 or 4 baking sheets with greaseproof paper.
2 Place all of the ingredients in a mixing bowl and whisk together until evenly blended. Spoon into a piping bag fitted with a 5 mm–1 cm (¼–½ inch) plain nozzle. Pipe the thin 5 cm (2 inch) lengths on the baking sheets, allowing plenty of room for spreading.
3 Bake at 200°C (400°F) mark 6 for 6–7 minutes or until tinged with colour. Using a palette knife immediately ease the biscuits off the paper and cool on wire racks.

PEANUT COOKIES

Choose a peanut butter with no added sugar, available mainly through health food stores.

•

MAKES ABOUT 20

50 g (2 oz) butter or margarine

75 g (3 oz) crunchy peanut butter

50 g (2 oz) light brown soft sugar

1 egg

150 g (5 oz) plain wholemeal flour

2.5 ml (½ level tsp) baking powder

50 g (2 oz) unsalted peanuts

1 Beat together the butter, peanut butter, sugar and egg until evenly blended. Stir in the flour and baking powder.

2 Roll the mixture into walnut-sized balls and place well apart on baking sheets. Flatten lightly with a fork. Chill for about 15 minutes.
3 Roughly chop the peanuts and sprinkle over the biscuits.
4 Bake at 190°C (375°F) mark 5 for about 12 minutes or until pale golden brown.
5 Allow to cool for about 5 minutes to firm up slightly then transfer to a wire rack to cool completely.

CHERRY AND WALNUT BISCUITS

Replace the walnuts with pecan nuts or chopped almonds, if you prefer.

•

MAKES ABOUT 24

225 g (8 oz) plain flour

pinch of salt

75 g (3 oz) butter or margarine

100 g (4 oz) caster sugar

finely grated rind of ½ lemon

1 egg, separated

45–60 ml (3–4 tbsp) milk

100 g (4 oz) walnut pieces, finely chopped

12 glacé cherries, halved

1 Sift the flour with the salt, rub in the butter until the mixture resembles fine breadcrumbs, then stir in the sugar, lemon rind, egg yolk and milk to give a fairly firm dough.
2 Form the dough into about 24 small balls, dip these in the slightly whisked egg white and roll them in the chopped walnuts.
3 Place the biscuits on the baking sheets and top each with a cherry half.
4 Bake in the oven at 180°C (350°F) mark 4 for 20–25 minutes, until firm and lightly browned. Cool on a wire rack.

INDEX